P9-EFH-822

A Concise History of Byzantium

A CONCISE HISTORY OF BYZANTIUM

WARREN TREADGOLD

palgrave

© Warren Treadgold 2001

All rights reserved. No reproduction, copy or transmission of
this publication may be made without written permission.

No paragraph of this publication may be reproduced, copied or
transmitted save with written permission or in accordance with
the provisions of the Copyright, Designs and Patents Act 1988,
or under the terms of any licence permitting limited copying
issued by the Copyright Licensing Agency, 90 Tottenham Court
Road, London W1T 4LP.

Any person who does any unauthorised act in relation to this
publication may be liable to criminal prosecution and civil
claims for damages.

The author has asserted his right to be identified
as the author of this work in accordance with the
Copyright, Designs and Patents Act 1988.

First published 2001 by
PALGRAVE
Houndmills, Basingstoke, Hampshire RG21 6XS and
175 Fifth Avenue, New York, N. Y. 10010
Companies and representatives throughout the world

PALGRAVE is the new global academic imprint of St. Martin's Press LLC
Scholarly and Reference Division and Palgrave Publishers Ltd (formerly
Macmillan Press Ltd).

ISBN–10:0–333–71829–1 hardcover
ISBN–13:978–0–333–71829–2 hardcover
ISBN–13:978–0–333–71830–8 paperback
ISBN–10:0–333–71830–5 paperback

This book is printed on paper suitable for recycling and
made from fully managed and sustained forest sources.

A catalogue record for this book is available
from the British Library.

Library of Congress Catalog Card No: 00–034495

12   11   10   9   8   7   6   5
11   10   09   08   07   06   05

*For my mother
Alva Granquist Treadgold
as a small payment on a large debt*

CONTENTS

LIST OF MAPS AND TABLES

Maps

Table

LIST OF FIGURES

PREFACE

This book draws upon the same research as my longer *History of the Byzantine State and Society*, supplemented by my reading and reflection over the past five and a half years. During that time my basic views on Byzantine history have remained much the same, and I have discovered no major errors or inadvertent omissions in the earlier history (or in its shorter companion volume, *Byzantium and Its Army*). Nonetheless, this is a new book, with some new points, rather different emphasis, and the complete rewriting needed to shorten the story while keeping it readable. Since anyone who wants more detail or fuller references can turn to the longer book, I have felt freer than I did there to leave out noteworthy but distracting developments, and views that differ from my own. While I have tried to make both books accessible to general readers as well as to scholars, naturally this one is meant for those with less time or a less specialized interest in Byzantium.

Apart from the introduction and conclusion, each of this book's chapters begins with a narrative account and ends with two descriptive sections on society and culture. Given the fashions of modern academic writing, some scholars might have liked this book better if I had left out all the narrative and simply reprinted the third of my longer book that covers social and cultural history. But the result, even with some added explanations, would have been difficult for readers unfamiliar with Byzantium to follow, and still could not have been a comprehensive treatment of Byzantine civilization, which would require a fully topical organization like that of Cyril Mango's *Byzantium: The Empire of New Rome*. Of course, readers with no interest in narrative, like those interested only in narrative or interested only in one period, can read only the parts of either book that interest them.

On the other hand, such preferences can be more than a matter of taste, because the Byzantine state and Byzantine society constantly interacted. For example, the demographic, economic, and cultural crisis of the sixth century led to the political, military, and religious upheavals of the seventh and eighth centuries, which in turn led to the social, economic, and cultural revival of the ninth century. Some of the best work done in Byzantine history in the last fifty years has demonstrated such connections. Yet they are barely discernible in previous surveys, including George Ostrogorsky's *History of the Byzantine State*, first composed in 1938 and largely based on scholarship from before 1914, or the popularizations of John Julius Norwich, largely based on the eighteenth-century work of Edward Gibbon. I shall be delighted if this book can persuade some narrative history buffs of the value of social and cultural history, or a few social and cultural historians of the value of historical narrative.

St Louis   W. T.

1

INTRODUCTION

The Problem of Decline

In AD 285 the emperor Diocletian divided the Roman Empire into two parts. The eastern part, the subject of this book, became known as the Eastern Roman Empire or, after the last of the western empire disappeared in 480, simply as the Roman Empire. Only after the former eastern empire also fell in 1453 did some scholars feel a need for a name without Rome in it for an empire that had not included Rome. Although the capital of the East had usually been at Constantinople, the term "Constantinopolitan Empire" was ungainly. The renamers settled on "Byzantine Empire" or "Byzantium," Byzantium having been the name of the small town refounded as Constantinople in 324. For better or worse, this name has stuck, though historians disagree about the right date to begin using it. This book begins with 285, when the Eastern Roman Empire began its separate existence, but the town of Byzantium had no special importance as yet. I avoid calling the empire "Byzantine" until the fifth century, when Constantinople truly became its political and cultural capital and the western empire fell away.

Under any name, the Eastern Roman Empire has a long-standing reputation for decadence. This is partly the doing of Edward Gibbon, who (without calling it Byzantium) made it the subject of his magnificent *Decline and Fall of the Roman Empire*. Ever since a Calvinist minister hired by his father talked him out of his youthful conversion to Roman Catholicism, Gibbon was disillusioned with Christianity, and looked down on Byzantium as a Christian society. He knew that the Western Roman Empire had fallen soon after becoming mostly Christian, and that even if the eastern empire had lasted a millennium more, it too had

1

fallen in the end. Besides, to someone with a Classical education like Gibbon's, Byzantium looked like a degenerate mongrel of Greece and Rome, which had lost the city of Rome and spoke bad Greek. Moreover, the whole medieval period, when Byzantium existed, was in his opinion a dark and barbaric age.

Neither Gibbon nor others ever developed such prejudices into a rigorous argument. While a fraction of Byzantine history was a relatively dark age, Byzantine culture was always well in advance of that of contemporary Western Europe. Although the Greek language evolved over time, as it had since Homer and as every language does, the best Byzantine scholars were excellent Hellenists who could read and write ancient Greek perfectly well. Whatever we think of Christianity, it was no less intellectually respectable than the combination of the Olympian gods and mystical Neoplatonism that it replaced. The eastern empire, separated from Rome in the first place by an administrative decision rather than a military defeat, later conquered Rome and held the city for some two centuries. Finally, that Byzantium fell in the end seems less striking than that it lasted for well over a thousand years.

Recently, without really rehabilitating Byzantium, many ancient and medieval historians have abandoned the words "decline" and "dark age" as overly negative, preferring the words "transformation" or "discontinuity." They are reluctant to speak of decline even when plagues killed millions of people, enemy raids wrecked scores of cities, trade collapsed, and literacy rates fell. Most of the same historians have however no hesitation in decrying disease, war, poverty, and illiteracy in their own times. Why these things should have been any less bad for the Byzantines seems inexplicable, unless the Byzantines were inferior people who deserved what happened to them. Distaste for the Byzantines also seems to lie behind objections to using the Byzantine word "barbarian" for German and other northern invaders, though the word simply meant "foreigner." Yet the Germans were undeniably less literate and urbanized than the Byzantines, and no objector seems to care much about the feelings of modern Germans.

The Byzantines did have some opinions that may seem benighted today. Their attitude toward sexuality, for example, was rather like that of contemporary Americans toward smoking or overeating: almost unrelieved disapproval in principle, combined with frequent indulgence in practice. Since the Byzantines thought that the only real good in sexual relations was procreation, they naturally condemned abortion and homosexual acts. They would have regarded the idea that people's interests were determined by gender, ethnic group, or social class as perverse and absurd. The loyalties that the Byzantines considered worth fighting for were to religious doctrines, political leaders, and sometimes athletic teams. Almost without exception, Byzantine rebels wanted not to divide or to overthrow the empire but only to impose their own opinions or leaders on all of it. Practically all Byzantines were loyal to their own ideas of their empire and the Christian religion. To study them we need not share their views, but we should resist the temptation to reinterpret them in modern terms.

In any case, whether we like Byzantines, Christians, or empires should have nothing to do with our judgement of whether, when, or how much they declined, except perhaps in a moral sense. Admittedly decline, in Byzantium as elsewhere, is a complex and problematic concept. It can be of different sorts: advance for the Arabs could mean decline for the Byzantines; within Byzantium, political and military decline could coexist with economic and cultural advance; and one part of the empire could be declining while another was thriving. Of course, every society has its problems, but not all problems imply any decline at all.

Today, with enormous amounts of accurate data about our own society, not all of us agree about whether we ourselves are in decline, or if we are, what sort of decline we might be in. Even if we did agree, we might turn out to be wrong; even contemporaries can easily overlook or misunderstand what is happening around them. Because our available evidence for Byzantine history is often scanty, we may often be unsure whether what was happening there should be called decline, growth, or stability. If anything, however, such practical and conceptual complexities are reasons for doubting that Byzantium was continuously declining during its whole long history.

In ancient and medieval times, probably the best index of social and economic development was urbanization. Scarcely anyone who lived in a city, but almost everyone who did not, farmed, herded, or fished for a living. Any society with few and small cities had a population overwhelmingly composed of subsistence farmers, and little time or money to spare for government, trade, education, art, or literature. The larger the urban population, the more people were likely to be engaged in those typically urban pursuits, which constitute civilization in its root meaning–the activities that take place in a city.

The growth or shrinkage of cities therefore tends to indicate cultural advance or decline. Although minor fluctuations may not matter much as long as a certain level of urbanization is maintained, a shrinkage of cities to mere villages probably means a drastic decline in the quality and quantity of government, trade, education, and higher culture. Such a collapse occurred in Western Europe in the sixth through eighth centuries, and many have argued that something nearly comparable happened to Byzantium around the same time. While some have exaggerated the dark age in Byzantium and minimized that in the West, the archeological and literary evidence seems to show that both dark ages occurred, and that the Byzantine one was much less severe, as measured both by urban shrinkage and by cultural decline. However, though the trends appear clear from such things as the contraction of urban sites and the scarcity of surviving manuscripts, we lack reliable statistics for city populations or indisputable indicators of cultural vitality.

On the level of the state, an obvious way of testing for advance or decline is to look for decreases or increases in the state's territory. Major and sustained territorial losses are likely to be either a result or a cause of some sort of weakness, and major and sustained territorial gains are likely to reveal or to result in some sort of strength. There is also the advantage that we can make a reliable calculation of the approximate size of the Byzantine empire at various dates, while calculations of other possible indexes of the empire's decline, such as its population or state revenues at different dates, are more difficult and less reliable, and something like the Byzantine gross domestic product is probably beyond useful calculation. In Figure 1 one can quibble about little more than my exclusion of the uninhabited Egyptian and Syrian deserts that most maps conventionally attribute to the empire.

The graph shows that Gibbon had a point: especially when we include the Western Roman Empire, as he did, the millennial trend was down. Yet there were important exceptions, some covering hundreds of years. As the West was declining and falling, Byzantium suffered comparatively minor and temporary losses. Then, between 450 and 550, it nearly doubled its territory. Although for the next two centuries something obviously went very wrong, from 750 to 1050 Byzantium more than doubled in size, and by the latter date it was actually larger than it had been 600 years earlier. After 1050 another disaster struck, but Byzantium quickly recovered, and by 1150 was larger than it had been 400 years before. In 1204 an even worse disaster shattered the empire, but even so by 1280 the Byzantine successor states held as much land as the empire of 200 years earlier. Only then did a final decline begin.

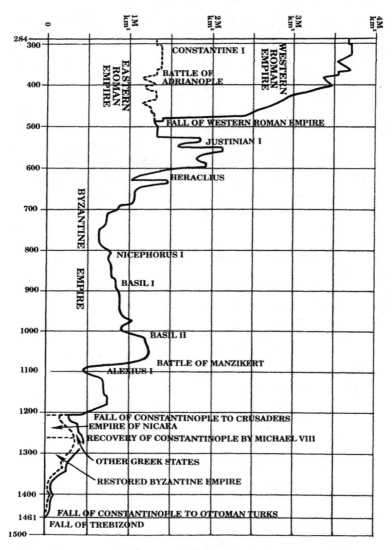

Figure 1   The territorial extent of the Byzantine Empire, 285–1461

As measured by territorial extent, the overall pattern is one of strong resistance to decline, which often became an advance.

Some other measures, though harder to plot on a graph, would show a broadly similar pattern, and if anything a more positive one. For example, it now seems clear that Byzantine economic expansion continued from about 750 right up to 1204, and probably later. Byzantine culture, as measured by its scholarly and artistic achievements, showed great vigor to the very end – and somewhat beyond, if we count Greek scholars and artists who went to renaissance Italy. Even during the worst of the crises of the 600s and 700s, the efficiency of the Byzantine bureaucracy and army apparently began to improve, and in most ways Byzantine society became more cohesive. Such factors evidently helped the empire to recover from political, economic, and cultural decline.

My principal aim in this book is to describe such political, social, economic, and cultural changes, and to try as far as possible to explain them. In looking for causes, I have no exclusive preference either for impersonal forces or for decisions made by identifiable people, both of which were important. Byzantium was a monarchy, ruled by a theoretically absolute emperor and other influential officials in the army, Church, and civil service. These rulers could and did make dramatic and lasting innovations. On the other hand, they also had to deal with developments well beyond their full control, such as the spread of Christianity; outbreaks of the plague; and invasions by the Germans, Persians, Arabs, Bulgars, and Turks. What determined the course of Byzantine history was a combination of the forces faced by the Byzantines and the Byzantines' reactions to them.

The Roman Background

Our story begins with the Roman Empire of the third century, which had problems that seemed to presage not merely decline but fall. Gibbon believed that the trouble had begun in 180 with the death of the emperor Marcus Aurelius, which ended a long period of peace, prosperity, and good government. Yet the real beginning seems to have come as early as 165, when a devastating epidemic had arrived from the east, probably the first appearance of smallpox in the Mediterranean. Such diseases caused much higher mortality in the densely populated empire than among the sparser populations of Germans and other barbarians on the northern frontier, who launched a major invasion of the empire in 166. Marcus was still able to defeat the barbarians, but with difficulty.

Marcus's son Commodus, who showed distinct signs of mental derangement, was assassinated in 192. This set off a brief rash of military revolts, one of which brought the harsh but capable general Septimius Severus to the throne. Though Severus restored order, at his death in 211 he left the empire to an equally harsh but less capable son. The son executed his brother, hugely increased the army's pay, and was murdered in his turn, beginning a long period of political instability and military rebellions. Successive emperors kept bidding for the army's favor by raising its pay even more, covering the expense by debasing the coinage and causing inflation that lost the army's favor again. Meanwhile, on the eastern frontier, the Parthian Empire was replaced by a new, stronger, and more aggressive Persian Empire under the Sassanid dynasty. While the Persians raided from the east, the Germans raided from the north.

In 251 a new epidemic broke out, this time probably measles, which was far more deadly than it later became because the population had no immunity to it. Now both Germans and Persians began not merely to raid but to invade and sometimes to conquer Roman territory. Scarcely any part of the empire escaped foreign invasion or civil war, and most of the East suffered from both. From 211 to 285, besides a large crop of unsuccessful usurpers and rebels, Rome had about twenty-six emperors who were generally recognized as such, more than in all of its previous history. Of these one died of the epidemic, another died fighting the Germans, a third was captured by the Persians and died in captivity, and twenty-three died violently at the hands of Romans. So matters stood in 285, when the general Diocles defeated and killed the last of his predecessors and became sole emperor under the name of Diocletian.

Among several grave problems Diocletian faced when he took over the empire, probably his greatest worry was remaining emperor. Most of his predecessors had lasted less than two years before being killed. While staying alive was doubtless a high priority for Diocletian personally, political stability was also a prerequisite for any lasting solution to the empire's other problems. No long-term initiative at home or abroad could be taken without some continuity in government, and constant fear of imminent death had long led emperors to take short-sighted measures like their ruinous increases in military pay. Civil wars were themselves damaging to the empire's security and costly for its economy, and as long as the empire's neighbors saw it wracked by chronic anarchy they would be tempted to raid and invade again.

Even apart from its civil disturbances, the empire faced serious military threats. Most of the lost Roman territory had been recovered except for Dacia in the region of today's Romania, evacuated under barbarian pressure. But the Persians remained powerful and bellicose on the eastern frontier, and an uninterrupted chain of barbarian tribal confederacies remained just across the northern frontier. Both borders had weak natural defenses, consisting of rivers and mostly low mountains, which the empire's enemies had learned how to cross easily. No further withdrawal, except perhaps for a drastic abandonment of several provinces, could have made the frontiers significantly more defensible. Roman troops could hardly retreat into the empty center of the empire, the Mediterranean Sea. The only means of keeping the enemy out was to station large armies all along the vulnerable frontiers. To be effective against the enemy, these armies had to be so strong that they could raise an effective revolt against the emperor himself as well.

The empire also had major economic and fiscal difficulties. The two epidemics, which had recurred after their initial outbreaks, had caused very substantial loss of life, which the civil wars and foreign invasions had compounded. Although few precise figures are available, we can scarcely doubt that the Roman population decreased appreciably between 165 and 285. The more Romans died, the more difficult it became to maintain tax revenues and recruitment for the army. The inflation caused by debasing and overminting the coinage had damaged trade, reduced the value of government tax receipts, and left the soldiers not only discontented but poorly supplied and equipped. The coinage was so debased that the standard silver coins finally became almost all bronze, so that they could scarcely be adulterated further.

Besides such concrete and tangible problems, the Romans were suffering from a crisis of religious confidence that no emperor could ignore. Most people at the time believed that political and military reverses and natural disasters were signs of divine anger. Several emperors had persecuted the rapidly growing Christian Church on the theory that it angered the pagan gods. Yet these persecutions had brought no apparent improvement, and in any case many pagans had become dissatisfied with paganism itself. Although the disasters of the time had encouraged a general return to religion, the old Olympian gods, the subjects of many unedifying and contradictory stories, no longer commanded much faith or respect, offering neither a moral example nor hope of a satisfactory afterlife. The mystical philosophy that we call Neoplatonism was too abstract to have very wide appeal. Although the emperors' ability to do anything about religion was limited, they ranked as high priests and were blamed for religious disunity.

Most Romans did share some ideas about moral behavior, however little their religion helped to reinforce it. No one seriously argued that the pederasty of Zeus, the thievery of Hermes, or the drunkenness of Dionysus were admirable. Most Romans had always disapproved of divorce, sexual promiscuity, and homosexual acts, except for some of the Roman elite, who without having a different moral code behaved as if no morality applied to them. Roman law punished adultery and rewarded childbearing, though it allowed divorce by mutual consent. A few aberrant practices in the provinces, such as brother–sister marriage in Egypt, had gradually succumbed to Roman condemnation. The overall trend seemed to be toward more strictness in sexual matters, and Neoplatonists even went so far as to regard virginity as superior to marriage. Christian morality had anticipated this trend, and remained more rigorous than ordinary pagan morality. Nevertheless, some pagans, assuming that Christian rejection of the majority's gods implied rejection of the majority's morals, believed and spread rumors of cannibalism and incest among Christians.

Religion had a special importance for the Romans because the pagan gods, for all their deficiencies, were almost the only cultural element that the whole empire had in common. Unlike the western part of the empire, where the Romans had introduced cities, literacy, and the Latin language among largely uncivilized peoples, the lands that the Romans conquered in the East had already had their own civilizations and languages, except in the north along the Danube River, which was the only part of the East that became Latin-speaking. Nor did the eastern empire form a cohesive cultural unit even within itself. Since the time of Alexander the Great the Greeks had made some efforts to Hellenize it, but outside the Greek peninsula they had truly succeeded only in western Anatolia. The majority languages remained Coptic in Egypt, Syriac in Syria, a medley of native languages in eastern Anatolia, and Thracian and Illyrian to the north of Greece. The peoples of these regions had their own cultural traditions to go with their languages, and most lived in relative isolation from outsiders.

On the other hand, the Roman Empire of 285 had some undeniable strengths. Despite all the trials of the preceding century, it had held most of its land and was still stronger than any of its enemies, including the Persians. Throughout the third-century crisis the empire also seems to have maintained its army at about the same strength, and at a fairly high level of military effectiveness. Roman cities were still relatively large; Roman trade seems not to have decreased greatly; and the central and provincial governments had not broken down. By now nearly every Roman wanted political stability to return, and the army had begun to discover the futility of nominal pay increases. The empire had at least learned how to live with many of its weaknesses, even if its emperors had not yet learned how to survive them.

The eastern part of the empire weathered the third century in rather better condition than the western part, despite serious incursions by the Persians and many revolts, including an interval of virtually independent rule in Syria and Egypt by the Roman client state of Palmyra. Much of the reason for the better state of the eastern empire was that the eastern Mediterranean lands had always been more prosperous, urbanized, and cultured than the regions to the west, and so had greater resources to marshal in times of trouble. Unlike the Germanic barbarians, the Persians and Palmyrenes had mainly sought to conquer, not just to plunder, so that they had inflicted considerably less destruction on Roman cities and territory than if they had been interested only in movable property.

At least partly because of the more developed condition of the eastern part of the empire, during the second and third centuries the Greek culture of the East showed much more vitality than the Latin culture of the West. Though in the first century before Christ Latin literature had advanced while Greek literature declined, in the second century AD Greek literature had revived while Latin literature seemed to be succumbing to the general crisis. Both trends continued into the third century, when for the first time most of the major authors in the Roman Empire were writing in Greek rather than in Latin. Apart from the biographies of Plutarch and the satires of Lucian, most of the secular Greek literature of the second and third centuries is too artificial and rhetorical to have much appeal today; but it nonetheless reveals a sizable community of well-educated authors and readers or auditors. Moreover, the Neoplatonist philosopher Plotinus and the Christian theologian Origen, who both lived in the third century, showed a subtlety and sophistication on which Greek culture could build in the centuries to come.

The best reason for thinking that in the third century the eastern part of the Roman Empire had a vigorous society, culture, and economy is that it developed into the remarkably resilient Byzantine Empire. By contrast, the western part of the Roman Empire, after a short-lived recovery, resumed its decline and soon fell. Although the respective fates of the East and the West could hardly have been foreseen in detail in the late third century, especially before the two parts of the empire received separate administrations and emperors, the East had at least the potential to become a strong state. Diocletian, who proved to be a ruler with ideas and talents well suited to tackling many of the problems that confronted him, surely deserves some of the credit for the temporary recovery of the whole empire and for the future durability of the East.

2

THE FORMATION OF BYZANTIUM (285–457)

Diocletian the Refounder

Diocletian, like most of the short-lived emperors of the previous half-century, was a soldier from the Balkan peninsula, then called Illyricum. Level-headed and shrewd, Diocletian commanded the respect of those who knew or met him. His original name Diocles meant "Zeus's Glory," and he took it seriously, showing a special devotion to the king of the gods throughout his life. It was also a Greek name, though he Latinized it to Diocletian. Apparently he felt at ease speaking either Latin or Greek, the one the language of the army and government and the other the common tongue of the polyglot natives of the eastern part of the empire. In 284, at the age of about forty, he was head of the imperial bodyguard when he seized power in the East, while claiming someone else had murdered his predecessor. The next year, in a bloody battle in Illyricum, Diocletian disposed of his last rival, the brother of the emperor he had succeeded.

No sooner had Diocletian conquered the western part of the empire than he assigned it to his fellow officer and friend Maximian. Without a son of his own, Diocletian adopted Maximian and appointed him Caesar, or junior emperor, the usual title for the son and heir of the Augustus, or senior emperor. Yet from the first Diocletian seems to have meant for Maximian, who was only a little younger than himself, to become the permanent ruler of the West. A year later Diocletian made his purpose clear by promoting his colleague to Augustus. By both his loyalty and his ability, Maximian proved worthy of Diocletian's

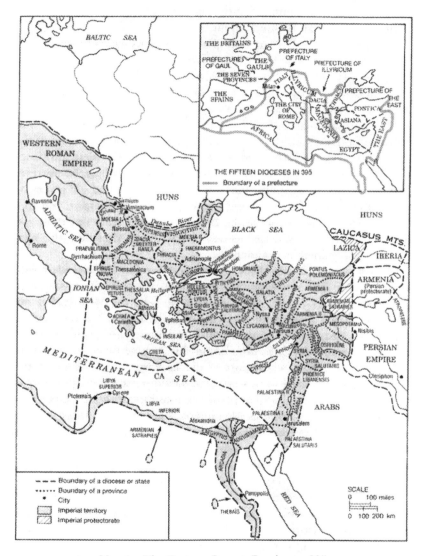

Map 1　The Eastern Roman Empire *ca.* 395

trust, though he had the difficult task of defending the poorer and less
defensible half of the empire with only about a third of the army.
Diocletian also kept ultimate authority throughout the empire, where
all his measures had the force of law.

While some past emperors had given their sons control over part of
the empire as an emergency measure, Diocletian's division of the
empire was revolutionary, not just because it was formal and permanent
but because it recognized his own eastern part of the empire as the more
important. Diocletian made this unmistakable by styling himself Jovius
and styling Maximian Herculius, thus comparing himself to Zeus and
Maximian to Zeus's son Hercules. No doubt since the beginning of the
empire the East had produced more revenue than the West, and since
the second century the eastern army had been larger than the western.
Before this the historic importance of Rome and Italy had still given the
West an advantage in power and prestige within the empire. Yet to a
Greek-speaking military man like Diocletian, what mattered most was
the armies and the resources needed to pay them. After him, the West
never truly regained its dominance.

The eastern lands that Diocletian ruled for himself included four
main regions. The westernmost, Illyricum, where Latin was spoken
about as much as Greek, could have gone with the West had it not
been Diocletian's homeland. Illyricum was the largest but the poorest
part of the East, underpopulated and undercultivated, with no really
large urban center and a frontier along the Danube River vulnerable to
barbarian raids. The richest part of the East was Egypt, the empire's
main granary, not hard to defend, and including the great port city of
Alexandria. Syria was almost as prosperous as Egypt, and its chief city of
Antioch was about as large as Alexandria, though the country was less
populated and less defensible, with the Persians just across the desert
frontier in Mesopotamia. The most central, most defensible, most Hellenized, and probably the most populous region was Anatolia, though it
lacked a metropolis of the size of Alexandria or Antioch.

As emperor Diocletian traveled all over his domains, but he spent
more time at Nicomedia in Anatolia than anywhere else. While he may
have favored the city because he had first become emperor there, it also
lay conveniently on the main route joining the two problem frontiers of
Illyricum and Syria. For several years he found shuttling between them
a tiring job, while in the West Maximian had even more trouble holding
both his borders on the Danube and Rhine. In 293 Diocletian therefore
tried a solution as bold as his original division of the empire. Each

Augustus gave responsibility for one of his two threatened frontiers to a new Caesar, who in each case became his son-in-law. Maximian's Caesar Constantius took the Rhine, and Diocletian's Caesar Galerius originally took the Syrian desert, with his headquarters at Antioch. Though this system is often called the tetrarchy – the rule of four emperors – the main division remained that between East and West, with each Augustus and Caesar cooperating and Diocletian keeping his authority over the whole.

Before and after appointing these two Caesars, Diocletian implemented additional reforms. Convinced that for most purposes bigger was better, he thought the empire needed not only more emperors but more soldiers, more officials, and more revenue to pay for them. The task of raising money was complicated by the continuing inflation of the coinage, which had made monetary taxes absurdly low and left the government dependent on more or less arbitrary requisitions in kind, especially of grain to supply the army. The problem was to adjust taxes to the taxpayers' ability to pay without relying on assessments in an unreliable currency. Even though Diocletian tried minting undebased gold, silver, and copper alloy coins, their values and those of earlier coins continued to fluctuate.

Diocletian ovecame this obstacle by inventing two artificial but stable units of assessment, the *caput* ("head") and the *jugum* ("yoke"). In a new census, probably begun in 292, the resources of each taxpaying household were assessed at a certain number of *juga* and *capita*, the first measuring the household's ability to pay taxes in grain and the second its capacity to pay other taxes in kind or coins. These household assessments were then added to give totals for each city and its surrounding territory. Every year the government told the city councils how much grain to collect for each *jugum* and how much money (or its equivalent in goods) to collect for each *caput*. Thus the government could adjust its annual requisitions not only for inflation but to meet its needs. Naturally most adjustments were upward.

While the defensive problems of the West forced its two emperors roughly to double their army, in the East Diocletian and Galerius only increased their forces by about a quarter. Their enlarged armies had about 311,000 soldiers and their fleets about 30,000 seamen, with most of the additions going to the army on the Syrian frontier. Most soldiers served not under provincial governors as before but under new regional commanders called dukes (*duces*), of whom there were eighteen in the East. The dukes' commands lay along the frontiers, and consisted

mostly of infantry on garrison duty. The structure of the system shows
that Diocletian's main interest was in preventing military revolts and
foreign invasions, not in making foreign conquests.

To help the four emperors keep their territories and soldiers under
control, Diocletian increased the size of the bureaucracy. Earlier emperors had had a central bureaucracy under an administrator called a
praetorian prefect, subordinate provincial governments under governors, and within provinces city councils to administer each city and
its region. Now each of the four emperors received his own praetorian
prefect for the lands he governed. The emperors and prefects also had
new subordinates called vicars (*vicarii*) to administer parts of their lands
called dioceses. Under the vicars were the provincial governments, now
multiplied as the older provinces were divided. The overall number of
officials seems roughly to have doubled, to about 15,000 in the East
alone. Since the pay of both the army and the civil service remained at
the same low rates, with monetary pay reduced by inflation but supplemented by rations in kind, the added expense came from the increased
numbers of soldiers and officials.

Expensive though these measures were, they succeeded in restoring
the empire's stability. Eventually Diocletian and his colleagues put down
every rebellion against them and repelled every invasion. Despite some
reverses, Diocletian and Galerius defeated the Persians and sacked their
capital of Ctesiphon in 298, forcing a peace treaty that secured imperial
control over the buffer states of Iberia (modern Georgia) and Armenia.
Diocletian then transferred Galerius from the Syrian frontier to
Illyricum, where he made his headquarters at Thessalonica in northern
Greece and fought several successful campaigns against the barbarians
across the Danube. Still based at Nicomedia, Diocletian personally ruled
Anatolia, Syria, and Egypt, enjoying nearly universal respect as the
restorer of the empire.

With the return of stability, Diocletian turned to less pressing matters.
His efforts to restore the coinage failed, because he minted too few gold
and silver coins to bring them into wide circulation and minted so many
copper alloy coins that they kept falling in value. Not realizing that the
overminting was causing the inflation, in 301 Diocletian declared
the value of his copper alloy coins to be doubled and posted long lists
of the maximum legal prices for all sorts of goods. When merchants
refused to sell at the posted prices, the edict became a dead letter,
though a splendidly informative one for modern scholars. At least
Diocletian's system of assessment protected government revenues

from inflation, and the soldiers were partly protected by receiving their supplies in kind. Most people had long since learned to live with the inflation, which was moderate by modern standards, and the benefits of peace and order offset the increased burden of taxation.

Prodded by Galerius, Diocletian then took measures against Christians. As the laws against Christianity were seldom enforced, it had been spreading dramatically, especially in the East, where the cathedral of Nicomedia stood in front of the imperial palace. In an edict of 303, Diocletian outlawed the Christian liturgy and ordered the destruction of all churches and the confiscation of their property. The next year he commanded all his subjects to sacrifice to the pagan gods, exempting Jews but not Christians. These edicts, though they had little effect in the West, were at least partly enforced throughout the East. Some Christians sacrificed, more evaded the edict, thousands were imprisoned and tortured, and several hundred were executed. This persecution, without really threatening the existence of the Church, forced it to become less visible, and that limited result was probably what the emperors had mainly intended.

In 305, after a successful reign of twenty-one years, Diocletian took the extraordinary step of abdicating voluntarily, persuading his fellow Augustus Maximian to do the same. The former Caesars Galerius and Constantius became the new Augusti of the East and West; each adopted a new Caesar, Galerius his nephew Maximin and Constantius a close friend of Galerius named Severus. In the East Galerius kept Illyricum and took over Anatolia to increase his power to suit his higher rank, leaving Syria and Egypt to his new Caesar Maximin. Evidently the empire was to go on being ruled by cooperating Augusti and Caesars of the East and West, with the Caesars succeeding the Augusti in due course and being replaced by new Caesars. Diocletian himself resumed his old name of Diocles and retired to a palace so immense that it later became a city called Spalatum ("Palace"), the modern Split in Croatia.

While Diocletian himself must have seen that some features of his system would need adjusting in the future, many of them lasted a long time. His division of the empire into two persisted. His single system of tax assessment, unlike the haphazard taxes of the old Roman Empire, shaped taxation through the whole Byzantine period. Most of his provincial boundaries lasted for centuries; so, somewhat modified, did his system of prefects and vicars. His preference for a large army and bureaucracy with low pay held for the next two centuries, and though it eventually fostered corruption it did help make the empire stronger and more stable than it had been during the third-century crisis. Diocletian had averted a real danger that the empire might be overcome by invaders and rebels. His reforms were the reason for much of his success, though events after his abdication showed that much had also been due to the force of his personality.

Constantine the Fortunate

As the new Augustus of the East and a close associate of Diocletian and the two new Caesars, Galerius hoped to inherit Diocletian's old position of leadership throughout the empire. At first the only emperor without close ties to Galerius was the western Augustus Constantius, away in the far West and in poor health. But when Constantius died in 306, his army proclaimed his son Constantine an Augustus as his father's heir. Though the succession should actually have been determined by the other emperors, to avoid a civil war Galerius agreed to recognize Constantine as Caesar of the West, promoting the West's other Caesar, his friend Severus, to Augustus.

Constantine accepted this compromise, but his proclamation proved contagious. It inspired Maxentius, son of the recently retired Augustus Maximian, to take over the territory of Severus, who killed himself. Constantine and Maxentius made an alliance, with Constantine marrying Maxentius' sister. Both of them, and even the eastern Caesar Maximin, now called themselves Augusti. An expedition by the indignant Galerius failed to replace Maxentius with another friend of his, Licinius. Licinius had to share Illyricum with Galerius, and was still doing so when Galerius died miserably of bowel cancer in 311. On his deathbed, thinking the Christian God might be punishing him, Galerius finally ended the persecution of Christians.

At this point the empire had four Augusti, each on bad terms with his immediate neighbor or neighbors. In the East Licinius held Illyricum, but was hostile to Maximin, who had seized Anatolia to add to his portion. In the West Constantine and Maxentius also quarreled, after Constantine forced Maxentius' father Maximian to commit suicide. Licinius and Maxentius had been enemies for years. On the principle that an enemy's enemy made a likely friend, Licinius and Constantine joined in an alliance against Maximin and Maxentius. Although Constantine had the smallest army and Maxentius the largest, Constantine made the first move by marching against Maxentius.

Apparently during this march, Constantine claimed that he had a vision of a cross of light over the sun, followed by a dream in which Christ told him to adopt the cross as his army's standard. The combination of the sun and the cross is intriguing, because Constantine's mother Helen was a Christian, while his father Constantius, who had divorced Helen to marry Maximian's daughter, had passed on to his son a special devotion to the sun god. Constantine did begin using the Christian standard, and with it defeated and killed Maxentius in a battle outside Rome, gaining control over the whole western part of the empire.

From this time on, Constantine favored Christianity, though without openly abandoning his attachment to the sun god, which reassured pagans. Constantine took Christian priests as his advisers, restored confiscated church property in his territories, and started to build churches. In 313, he met at Milan in northern Italy with his ally Licinius, who agreed to restore the church property in his own lands. At this point Maximin, who was persecuting Christians again, invaded Illyricum, forcing Licinius to march against him. Licinius won a clear victory, and Maximin committed suicide, leaving the entire East subject to Licinius as the West was subject to Constantine.

The West was however not enough for Constantine, who invaded Illyricum three years later. When Constantine had the better of the civil war, Licinius ceded most of Illyricum to him, keeping only Thrace in the southeast. Even so, the Christian emperor seemed to have the wrong part of the empire, because Christians were far more numerous in Licinius' territories than in Constantine's. Licinius had more and more trouble with his Christian subjects, which led Constantine to invade Thrace in 324. This war ended with a naval victory by Constantine's son Crispus and a victory on land by Constantine himself, both near the town of Byzantium. Though Licinius surrendered on a promise of immunity, Constantine soon executed him.

When Constantine won the remainder of the empire he was just over fifty. Born in the Latin-speaking part of Illyricum, he had served under Diocletian and Galerius in the East while his father was Caesar in the West, then gone west just in time to replace his father. Constantine had enjoyed unbroken and sometimes improbable success. He had defeated his former allies Maxentius and Licinius despite their having larger armies, and had managed to prosper as a convert to Christianity, the religion of a small minority in the empire and a particularly tiny minority in the West and the army. Constantine was impatient, ambitious,

Figure 2   A colossal head and hand of Constantine I (reigned 306–37), the first Christian emperor, from a statue in his basilica in the Roman Forum. Constantine ruled the whole Roman Empire from 324, when he conquered its eastern part in a battle near Byzantium and refounded that city as Constantinople. (*Photo*: Musei Capitolini, Rome)

and not outstandingly clever, but either truly inspired or very lucky. Christians might well think God was on his side.

One of Constantine's peculiar decisions, made just after his victory over Licinius, was to refound Byzantium as a capital called New Rome, or alternatively Constantinople ("Constantine's City"). Both the city of Rome and the idea of a capital seemed almost obsolete at the time, when the real seat of government was wherever the peripatetic emperors happened to be. Though at Rome the senate and the grain dole for the poor seemed relics of the Republic that no one would have reinvented, Constantine created both a senate and a grain dole for his new capital. Nor had anyone founded a city on the scale planned by Constantine since Alexandria and Antioch more than six hundred years before. Constantine might more cheaply have enlarged and renamed Diocletian's Nicomedia, which as he knew shared the main advantages of Byzantium. Each city lay midway on the road between the Persian and Danube frontiers, had a good port, and could serve as an administrative center for both Anatolia and Illyricum. Constantine appears to have chosen a new place mainly to distinguish himself from Diocletian, and to have chosen Byzantium mainly because he had defeated Licinius nearby.

The city took vast resources and many years to build, but thanks to Constantine's determination and posthumous prestige it eventually became what he had intended, the capital of the East. This had consequences that he probably had not foreseen. It gave the eastern empire a more Hellenized identity, centered on Greek-speaking Anatolia and Thrace rather than Egypt, Syria, or the Latin-speaking northern Balkans, where Constantine had resided before defeating Licinius. Though not naturally well defended, Constantinople lay on a peninsula that could be cut off by a fairly short wall, which Constantine began to build. The city's natural hinterland was the Anatolian peninsula, protected by high mountains and provided with enough men and farmland to support itself. Anatolia became the heartland of the Byzantine Empire as Constantinople turned into its metropolis.

Constantine had four sons, Crispus by his deceased first wife and the others by his second. Evidently he meant for all of them to succeed him in a fraternal tetrarchy. He had already entrusted his original portion of the empire in the far West to Crispus as Caesar with a separate praetorian prefect. Now Constantine divided the remainder into three regional prefectures intended for his much younger sons. In the East the emperor appointed one prefect for Illyricum, including

Constantinople, and another for Anatolia, Syria, and Egypt. But Constantine also kept a senior prefect attached to himself, along with a central army separate from the armies on the frontier. The emperor deprived the praetorian prefects of their military powers and put the armies of the prefectures under new commanders called masters of soldiers (*magistri militum*). He also created his own corps of guardsmen and agents known as the Scholae, replacing the Praetorian Guard that had existed since the early empire.

Having disposed of the last pagan emperor Licinius, Constantine naturally extended his favor to Christians over the whole empire. He preferred Christians in making administrative and military appointments, and took some measures favored by Christians, such as ending gladiatorial shows, restricting grounds for divorce, and penalizing rape and adultery. He had already made Sundays holidays, somewhat ambiguously because the day was sacred both to Christ and to the sun god. He also forbade pagan sacrifices and divination, without making much effort to enforce his prohibitions, and confiscated the treasures of pagan temples, which met most of the expense of building Constantinople. Constantine used the gold from the temples to mint a much more abundant gold coinage, as pure as that of Diocletian though weighing somewhat less. While the copper alloy coins continued to suffer from inflation, the new gold coin, called the *nomisma* in Greek and the solidus in Latin, became common enough to be used for large payments and savings, simplifying government finance and wholesale trade.

The empire's overwhelmingly pagan population accepted a Christian emperor passively, and many pagans began to turn to Christianity. Some wanted to gain government favor. More thought that Constantine's victories and his rivals' defeats showed Christianity was right. Some had already admired the Christians' morality, care for the poor, or steadfastness under persecution, and were ready to join them as soon as it was safe and easy. But while admiring the morals that the Church demanded of its baptised members, many converts emulated Constantine, who postponed baptism so as to be able to sin without performing the strict penances the Church demanded afterward. Some failed to realize that Christianity required giving up all pagan gods and practices, and many had only a nebulous idea of Christian theology. Exactly how many Christians there were was therefore very hard to say, though for years to come they were surely a minority of the population.

The wave of new converts after the end of persecution in 313 coincided with a dispute over Christian doctrine. Arius, a priest in Alexandria, tried to clarify the relations between God the Father and Christ by declaring that the Father had existed before his Son, whom he had created. This doctrine, Arianism, was unacceptable to most Christians with a firm grasp of theology, who believed that the Son was fully God, begotten from the Father's own essence. Led by Athanasius, first a deacon and then Bishop of Alexandria, a large party of clergy objected that Arius was denying the unity of the Godhead by turning the Son into a different and inferior god. But to polytheists none too familiar with Christianity the idea of greater and lesser gods was unobjectionable; and even many Christians were not quite sure how the Father and the Son could be distinct and yet a single God.

When Constantine discovered the Arian controversy soon after overcoming Licinius, he wanted it resolved before it became an obstacle to converting more pagans. As the recipient of a divine vision and the most powerful Christian in the empire, Constantine felt a personal responsibility. Once he realized the extent of the disagreement, he resorted to the usual arbiters of church disputes, a gathering of bishops. With the general consent of church members, he called the first council of bishops from all over the empire, a body known as an ecumenical council. It met in 325 at Nicaea in Anatolia, not far from the construction site of Constantinople.

About three hundred bishops, most from the East but some from the West, deliberated at Nicaea. Encouraged by Constantine, who was present, some produced a creed that excluded Arianism, specifying that the Son was "of the same substance as the Father," and therefore not inferior to him. Some objected that this could mean the Son had simply been the Father in a human body, a doctrine condemned a century before as the Sabellian heresy. But Athanasius and the majority insisted it meant only that the Son, while a separate person from the Father, was wholly God. In the end, with Constantine's approval, all but two bishops accepted the creed referring to Father and Son as "of the same substance," which became known as the Nicene Creed, and condemned Arianism as a heresy.

In the years after the Council of Nicaea, Constantine began to lose his sense of direction, having already attained the summit of his ambitions. In 326 he executed first his son Crispus and then his wife Fausta, allegedly because Fausta had accused her stepson of trying to seduce her and was then found actually to have tried to seduce him.

Constantine was also disturbed to find many bishops grumbling that the Nicene Creed either condoned Sabellianism or was unduly harsh to Arians. Without repudiating the creed, the emperor seized on the farfetched argument of the Arian bishop Eusebius of Nicomedia that Christ's being "of the same substance as the Father" could mean merely that Christ came from the Father. Intermittently influenced by Eusebius and obviously wishing that the whole problem would go away, Constantine vacillated between pro-Arian and anti-Arian measures without adopting any coherent policy, in turn exiling and recalling Bishop Athanasius of Alexandria.

In 335 the emperor distributed the prefectures among his sons the Caesars, who were to inherit them as Augusti on their father's death. His eldest surviving son Constantine II had already replaced the dead Crispus in the far West, though this was hardly the most important part of the empire. Italy, including Rome, went to the youngest son Constans, while the middle son Constantius II received Anatolia, Syria, and Egypt, which was the richest part. Since Constantine had four prefectures and just three sons, he proclaimed his nephew Dalmatius a fourth Caesar, oddly assigning him Illyricum, with the still expanding capital of Constantinople and perhaps even the central field army. The emperor had still stranger plans for his other nephew Hannibalianus, whom he crowned king of Armenia to replace a king killed by the Persians the previous year. While planning a campaign to put Hannibalianus on the Armenian throne, in 337 Constantine died near Nicomedia, baptised on his deathbed by the city's Arian bishop Eusebius.

Constantine shares with Diocletian only a little of the credit for restoring order to the empire. He began disrupting Diocletian's system the year after the older emperor retired, and stopped attacking his colleagues only when he had none left. His arrangements for the succession risked more civil wars unless his sons and nephews could be counted upon to cooperate, as they could not. Constantine used the army Diocletian had expanded without strengthening it much himself, though he built many frontier forts and seems to have converted many infantry on the frontiers into cavalry. By taking some of the best troops for his standing field army, he began to reduce the prestige and efficiency of the garrison armies on the frontiers. Late in his reign he had to campaign repeatedly on the Danube, where the garrison armies seemed unable to keep the barbarians out. Constantine was a good general, or at any rate a victorious one, but his finest campaigns were fought against his colleagues.

Constantine wisely left Diocletian's governmental machinery much as he had found it, even continuing its four prefectures after three of the emperors who had ruled them were gone. He liked to legislate, and created a new minister of justice, the Quaestor. Otherwise, apart from depriving the prefects of their military powers, his main administrative innovations were in finance. He added two new financial officials, the Count of the Sacred Largesses to manage state expenditures and the Count of the Private Estate to manage the large revenues from crown lands. His confiscation of the temple treasures let him spend extravagantly, encouraging habits of corruption and overspending that could never again be paid for in that way.

Constantine's adoption of Christianity for the empire, though doubtless a matter of religious conviction rather than political policy, turned out well for the empire. Christianity had a spiritual, moral, and organizational rigor that many contemporaries found missing from paganism. Paganism lacked the leadership or theology to change itself, and even had it done so would have lost the appeal to tradition that was its only clear advantage over Christianity. By Diocletian's time extinguishing Christianity was impossible, persecuting it only caused trouble, and merely tolerating it satisfied nobody. While Constantine's conversion may have seemed premature, especially for the West, it won so much favor and provoked so little opposition that it may actually have helped him win his civil wars, and certainly did not hurt him. On the other hand, his mishandling of the Arian controversy, which might have ended promptly if he had defended the decisions of his own Council of Nicaea, showed how poorly Constantine understood his adopted faith.

Constantinople, which must have seemed an extravagance at the time, also prospered in the long run. Its foundation soon brought the mixed blessing of the virtual independence and dominance of the eastern part of the empire. While the West was poorer and weaker without the East, the East was richer and stronger without the West, though both might have been better off if they had cooperated more closely than they were to do. Scarcely any city in the empire could have been made as thoroughly defensible as Constantinople, and its impregnability was to be vital to the eastern empire's survival. Admittedly, Constantine cannot have anticipated anything of the sort. As with the other triumphs of his career, his refoundation of Byzantium was not so much prudent or provident as fortunate. Much of the rest of his legacy became a burden to his successors.

Five Struggling Emperors

Constantine's plans for the succession came to almost instant grief. Although none of his sons was close to Constantinople, where his body was brought for burial, his nephew Dalmatius, allotted the capital along with Illyricum, was either in the city or nearby. But the soldiers, who favored the great man's sons, lynched most of his other relatives, including Dalmatius and the titular Armenian king Hannibalianus. The first son to arrive at Constantinople was Constantius II, who came from Antioch, followed by his younger brother Constans, who arrived from Italy. The two agreed to divide Illyricum between them, with Thrace and Constantinople going to Constantius and the rest to Constans. Though splitting the rulerless prefecture between the two rulers on either side of it made geographical sense, it left their older brother Constantine II with the smallest and poorest portion of the three. Each new Augustus ruled his lands as a single prefecture, maintaining his own field army and acting for most purposes as an independent ruler.

Constantius II, just twenty when he took over much the largest part of the East, showed himself quite competent, less charismatic than his father but also less erratic. Constantius' main aim was to make his father's expensive and unwieldy system work. He had inherited a war with Persia over Armenia, which he fought cautiously and not unsuccessfully from his base at Antioch. Though Constantinople was of little use to him, he kept building it at a reduced pace. Unlike his brothers, he continued his father's attempts to accommodate critics of the Nicene Creed, most of whom were in his portion of the empire. While no Arian himself, Constantius did support some Arians, notably his father's friend Eusebius of Nicomedia, whom he made bishop of Constantinople. Eusebius was unpopular there, but took his chance to begin spreading Arian Christianity among the Goths, the Germans living across the Danube frontier.

Constantius fared better than Constantine II, who died fighting Constans, or than Constans, who was killed by the usurper Magnentius in 350. Like his father, Constantius wanted to keep imperial power in the family, but after Constans' death he had just two surviving male relatives, his younger nephews Gallus and Julian. Before marching west to avenge his brother, he named Gallus Caesar of the East and left him to govern at Antioch. In a hard-fought campaign, Constantius disposed of Magnentius and claimed the whole West by 353. But in the meantime

Gallus ruled the East with such irresponsible savagery that Constantius had to have him executed. Seeing that the empire was too big for one man to rule, Constantius made his other nephew Julian Caesar of the West with the task of fighting the Germans on the Rhine.

As the only Augustus in the empire, in 356 Constantius promulgated a law closing all pagan temples and forbidding all pagan rites, going well beyond what his father had been able to do but provoking no overt opposition. Constantius also tried to impose his toleration of Arianism on the whole empire, arousing widespread confusion and hostility by exiling some staunchly anti-Arian bishops, including Athanasius of Alexandria. The Augustus then moved to Constantinople, from which he directed the ever more costly government and army. To meet his expenses, he not only raised taxes but confiscated the extensive lands that endowed the empire's cities, aggravating the budgetary problems of the city councils.

In 359 the Persians invaded the empire in earnest. In massing his field forces against them, Constantius decided he needed more men. He therefore asked for part of the army serving in the West under the Caesar Julian, who had defeated the Germans smartly. But since the troops were as reluctant to leave Julian as he was to relinquish them, they proclaimed him Augustus. Both sides prepared for a civil war, but while Julian was marching east Constantius fell ill on the march west. As he lay dying, he received baptism and, having no son, forgave Julian and declared him his heir.

What Constantius did not know was that Julian had secretly rejected his Christian upbringing and turned to paganism, in particular his grandfather's cult of the sun god. Cerebral and enthusiastic at age twenty-nine, Julian knew that the empire's pagans still outnumbered its Christians, and hoped that by some judicious measures he could revive the old religion. He legalized paganism again, reopening the temples and restoring their lands. Aware of the advantage a clear hierarchy of bishops gave Christians, he appointed a parallel hierarchy of pagan priests. He condoned some pagan violence against Christians, and to encourage Christian dissension he recalled Athanasius and the other anti-Arian bishops exiled by Constantius. Julian also dismissed some palace servants and returned the civic lands Constantius had confiscated.

Although the mostly pagan army and many pagan civilians backed Julian, and no Christians rebelled against him, he was disappointed to find how weak paganism had become in the empire. Constantinople and Antioch, both probably majority Christian by this time, received him without enthusiasm. Since the empire was at war with the Persians, Julian hoped to win a great victory against them to vindicate his faith. Though the Persians were ready to make peace, he continued Constantius' preparations for war, and assembled a vast army of some 65,000 men, probably including most of the field armies of the whole empire. Julian planned to lead the main force against the Persian capital at Ctesiphon, while a detachment under his relative Procopius was to collect some Armenian allies and link up with him from the north.

The expedition set out in 363, and Julian advanced as far as Ctesiphon, carrying all before him. But Ctesiphon looked impregnable, and Julian, uncertain what to do, turned north to look for Procopius. Dogged by the Persians, who stripped the country of supplies, the army had already become exhausted when Julian received a wound, probably from a Persian spear, and died of it. His generals offered the throne to the pagan prefect Salutius, a friend of Julian's, but his refusal, nominally because of old age, may have shown his judgement that with the expedition's failure the pagan cause had become hopeless.

The soldiers then proclaimed the Christian guardsman Jovian. Eager to extricate the hungry and demoralized army from Persia safely, he made a moderately unfavorable peace with the Persians, ceding part of the border zone in Mesopotamia and the protectorate over Armenia and Iberia. He rescinded Julian's anti-Christian measures and set out for Constantinople. But in 364 Jovian died suddenly in the middle of Anatolia, and the army had to choose an emperor once again. It proclaimed another Christian guardsman, Valentinian, but also insisted on his naming a colleague as insurance against another open succession. Valentinian chose his brother Valens, assigning him the East as far as Thrace, the portion Constantius II had ruled early in his reign. Valentinian kept the rest of Illyricum, the homeland of both brothers, which was enough to make the West the larger part of the empire.

In his mid-thirties and relatively inexperienced, Valens had middling abilities but showed the fraternal loyalty Valentinian expected. The emperors amicably shared the field armies between them, replacing the losses suffered in Persia. Alarmed by the empire's burgeoning taxation, bureaucracy, and corruption, the brothers tried to reduce them, making up for the lost revenue by repeating Constantius' confiscation of the lands of pagan temples and city councils. Valens, though not his brother, reinstated Constantius' sentences of exile for Athanasius and the anti-Arian bishops, which aroused even more opposition than before.

Valens weathered some serious challenges. He put down a rebellion by Julian's relative Procopius, and fought a campaign to punish the Goths who had backed the usurper. Valens drove the Persians from most of Armenia and Iberia and reestablished the empire's protectorates there. When the Goths asked for refuge in imperial territory to escape the Huns, fierce nomads recently arrived from Asia, Valens began settling Goths in Thrace. When too many Goths arrived and began raiding Thracian farms, Valens marched against them with most of his field army of some 40,000 men. In 378 he attacked them near Adrianople.

In a confused but finally devastating battle, Valens and two-thirds of his army lost their lives. His brother Valentinian had died not long before, leaving a young son, Gratian, with more than enough problems in the West. Rather than name his even younger brother Valentinian II as eastern emperor to face the rampaging Goths, Gratian chose a well-qualified general, Theodosius. Theodosius received not only the dominions of the late Valens but the central part of Illyricum, which he needed because its field army remained intact. The eastern field armies were shattered, while the garrison armies were needed for defense and had become too inured to it to take the field.

Aged thirty-three at his accession, a Spaniard with considerable military experience, Theodosius accepted his difficult assignment with grim determination. Desperate to rebuild the eastern field armies, he recruited any fit and willing soldiers he could find, most of whom turned out to be Germans. Even with his new recruits, he had to call for help from Gratian before he could win some modest victories over the scattered Goths who had begun raiding central Illyricum. At least Theodosius forestalled the immediate danger that the empire's Balkan defenses would collapse entirely. Luckily for him, at this time the Persians had a weak king unready to exploit the empire's troubles.

In 380 Theodosius fell gravely ill and, fearing he was dying, received baptism. He recovered to find himself the first Christian emperor to rule as a full member of the Church, and felt his added Christian responsibilities. Taking up residence at Constantinople, in 381 Theodosius summoned an ecumenical council that unequivocally condemned Arianism as a heresy. This Council of Constantinople affirmed the full divinity of all three persons of the Christian Trinity, the Father, the Son, and the Holy Spirit. The decision gained rapid acceptance in both parts of the empire, though, ominously for the future, outside imperial territory the Goths and other Germans remained Arians. The council also

declared that the bishop of Constantinople, henceforth called a patriarch, ranked next after the Pope, because Constantinople was the New
Rome.

The year after the council, Theodosius and Gratian made a treaty
with the Goths, who were to settle down in imperial territory in two
different groups and serve with the imperial army in allied units. The
group of the Visigoths held part of northern Thrace, while that of the
Ostrogoths held part of western Illyricum in the western empire. This
treaty gained the empire both peace and an alliance, without giving the
Goths more land than they already occupied and the empire was unable
to take from them. To show his confidence that the emergency had
passed, Theodosius then returned control over central Illyricum to
Gratian.

In 383 Gratian was killed by the usurper Maximus, who seized the far
West while Gratian's brother Valentinian II retained Italy and western
and central Illyricum. Perhaps still unsure of the strength of his army,
Theodosius reluctantly accepted this division until Maximus drove out
Valentinian entirely. At that Theodosius marched west with his somewhat stronger forces and Gothic allies, and killed the usurper. He
reinstated Valentinian in the West but transferred not just central Illyricum and its army but some additional western forces to the East.
While still in the West, Theodosius ordered all pagan temples to be
closed and outlawed all pagan rites. Legally this was no more than
Constantius II had done, but Theodosius enforced his measures more
strictly.

Valentinian lasted several more years in the West until he lost his life
and throne to the pagan German general Arbogast, who chose as
emperor the professor Eugenius, a nominal Christian sympathetic to
paganism. Again Theodosius marched west with his Goths, leaving in
Constantinople his elder son Arcadius, designated as the future eastern
emperor. After an initial reverse in Italy, Theodosius prevailed and
killed Eugenius, while Arbogast killed himself. The victorious emperor
planned to return to the East, leaving his younger son Honorius as the
prospective western emperor. But before Theodosius could return he
died, in 395.

Theodosius had handled foreign and domestic emergencies skillfully,
but by his time they had grown alarmingly frequent. Although Julian
could be blamed for his failure against the Persians and Valens for his
defeat by the Goths, neither emperor had been a bad general, and no
imperial commander during this time had won victories as important as

those defeats. While all the usurpations had ultimately failed, several revolts in the West would have succeeded without costly intervention from the East. Taxes in both parts of the empire could seldom be collected in full, and the city councilors responsible for collecting them were constantly trying to escape their ruinous duties. Corruption was by all accounts spreading. Despite the best efforts of capable emperors, the government and army seemed to have grown both bigger and weaker.

Three Weak Emperors

Theodosius' partition of the empire in 395 proved to be permanent. It roughly corresponded to the division between the two main languages, Greek and Latin. The Hellenized part, inherited by Theodosius' elder son Arcadius, included an arc of territory from Thrace to Egypt, known as the Prefecture of the East, plus Greece and the rest of central Illyricum, hereafter simply called the Prefecture of Illyricum. Along with these two prefectures Arcadius was to inherit five field armies: the Army of Illyricum, the Army of Thrace, the Army of the East that faced the Persians, and two armies called "praesental" because they were supposed to be present wherever the emperor was. These field armies, the bulk of which had gone west with Theodosius to fight Eugenius, had a strength on paper of 104,000 men, probably less than the combined forces of the Goths and Persians. The remaining 200,000 or so troops in the East were second-class garrison forces, pinned down guarding cities and frontiers.

When Arcadius became eastern emperor he was only eighteen, and unusually dull and inert. Earlier Theodosius had given each of his feeble sons a capable adviser: the Prefect of the East Rufinus for Arcadius, and the half-German general Stilicho for Honorius. Yet Stilicho alleged that the dying Theodosius had named him guardian of Arcadius as well. Rufinus rejected this unlikely claim, and a fateful quarrel began. For the moment Stilicho had the advantage, because most of the eastern field armies were still in his power.

Within the year the eastern empire came under attack from the Huns, who raided across Armenia into northern Syria, and the Visigoths, who migrated into southern Thrace under their chieftain Alaric. Blocked by the walls of Constantinople, Alaric looted his way to northeastern Greece. Stilicho advanced against him with the eastern field armies, only to receive orders from Arcadius to return the eastern armies and leave the East. Aware that Rufinus had dictated the orders, Stilicho sent the armies back under a Visigoth in imperial service, Gaïnas, who on his arrival murdered Rufinus.

Power over the docile Arcadius passed to the eunuch Eutropius, a friend of the emperor's new wife Eudoxia. But Eutropius also distrusted Stilicho. When Stilicho returned to Greece to fight Alaric, he found himself not only sent away but outlawed by Arcadius. The eastern government rashly named Alaric commander of the Army of Illyricum, with permission to occupy northwestern Greece. Having allied himself with the Visigoths, Eutropius drove out the Huns. Soon Eutropius too fell victim to Gaïnas, who in 400 forced the eunuch's execution and his own appointment as commander of one of the prae-sental armies.

Backed by the largely German soldiers of those armies, Gaïnas made Arcadius his figurehead and took charge of the government in Con-stantinople, where he ruled for several months. If Gaïnas had been more adroit, he might well have turned the eastern empire into a Ger-man puppet state. But he enraged the already restive people of Con-stantinople and their patriarch John Chrysostom by trying to open a single Arian church for his troops. As the Germans tried to withdraw from the city, a mob massacred many of them. Arcadius' officials per-suaded the commander of the Army of the East, the pagan Visigoth Fravitta, to attack Gaïnas and his men, who fled across the Danube and were slaughtered by the Huns.

After this German interlude, a shadowy group of anti-German but short-sighted officials enjoyed the favor of the empress Eudoxia and dominated Arcadius. They rid themselves of Alaric and his Visigoths by encouraging them to invade the western empire, and had John Chry-sostom exiled over the protests of the Western Church. By the time Eudoxia died and Arcadius finally found a satisfactory adviser in the Prefect of the East Anthemius, the East had utterly antagonized the West. Stilicho tried to ally with Alaric to take Illyricum from the East, but the parlous state of the West kept Stilicho from mounting his campaign.

In 408 Arcadius died and was succeeded by his supposed son, the seven-year-old Theodosius II. Though some thought his real father had been an adviser of Eudoxia's, Theodosius soon showed an incapacity strikingly reminiscent of Arcadius. At first Anthemius continued ruling for the boy emperor, and made up the quarrel with the West that had damaged both sides. When the Visigoths marched unchallenged into

Italy and sacked Rome in 410, the East sent reinforcements that helped Honorius hold his new capital of Ravenna. When the Huns invaded Illyricum and Thrace, Anthemius built new walls for Constantinople so strong as to be almost impregnable by assault.

Anthemius seems to have died in 414, leaving young Theodosius in the hands of his sixteen-year-old sister Pulcheria and some officials and barbarian generals allied with her. This regime bought off the Huns and fought an inconclusive war with Persia. It also intervened in the West after Honorius' death, helping suppress a western emperor not related to the Theodosian dynasty. The western emperor whom the eastern forces installed was Valentinian III, a young grandson of Theodosius I, who was engaged to marry the young daughter of Theodosius II to confirm the friendship between the eastern and western empires. Pulcheria's government also endowed professorships at Constantinople to train future bureaucrats, and began compiling the first official collection of Roman laws, which became known as the *Theodosian Code*.

Figure 3 The Theodosian Walls of Constantinople, seen from the southwest before the recent restorations. Begun in 413 by the Prefect of the East Anthemius for the underage emperor Theodosius II (reigned 408–50), these formidable double walls shielded Constantinople from attack on the land side of the peninsula on which the city is built. (*Photo*: Warren Treadgold)

In 431 the eastern government called another ecumenical council at
Ephesus in western Anatolia to judge the Patriarch of Constantinople
Nestorius, who objected to calling the Virgin Mary the Mother of God.
Nestorius' argument was that Mary had borne Christ's human nature,
but obviously not his Godhead. Yet to many opponents, led by Bishop
Cyril of Alexandria, Nestorius seemed to be making far too drastic a
distinction between Christ's divinity and his humanity. To the emperor's
dismay but his sister's satisfaction, the council declared Nestorianism a
heresy because it divided Christ into two persons, though Nestorius
denied that he meant to do anything of the sort. While Nestorianism
never spread much within the empire, it found a good many adherents
among Christians in Persian Mesopotamia.

Eventually Pulcheria lost her influence over Theodosius to a new
adviser, the eunuch Chrysaphius. Chrysaphius had to deal with ambitious barbarian generals still friendly to Pulcheria, frantic appeals for
help from the collapsing western empire, another Persian invasion, and
an ever-growing threat from the Huns under their new king Attila. The
western empire had to fend for itself, and lost its rich African provinces
to the German confederacy of the Vandals.

The Huns, after years of being bribed not to attack the East, made a
devastating raid on Illyricum and Thrace and extorted still higher
tribute. Luckily for Chrysaphius, the defeats inflicted by the Huns discredited the empire's barbarian generals, while incursions by the White
Huns of Central Asia forced the Persians to make peace with the empire.
But Attila's Huns kept raiding Illyricum and Thrace and defeating
imperial armies, forcing the empire to evacuate northern Illyricum
and pay still more tribute in 447.

The somewhat muddled condemnation of Nestorius by the Council of
Ephesus led to a new dispute over whether Christ had both divine and
human natures or only one nature. The doctrine that Christ had a
single nature, known as Monophysitism, raised the question of whether
this nature was fully human, since the Council of Nicaea had already
declared that Christ was fully divine. Chrysaphius followed the extreme
Monophysite opinion that Christ's nature was unlike that of ordinary
men.

The eunuch persuaded the emperor, who earlier had favored the
quite different opinion of Nestorius, to call another ecumenical
council at Ephesus in 449 to settle the question. Under the direction
of the Bishop of Alexandria Dioscorus, the council became disorderly, expelled some of its bishops including Bishop Flavian of

Constantinople, and finally deposed Flavian and declared that Christ had only one nature. Though the Pope and the Western Church protested, Chrysaphius seemed to have carried his point. The same year he gained Attila's permission to reoccupy northern Illyricum.

In 450 Theodosius died after a fall from his horse, and Chrysaphius' enemies closed in. The emperor's sister Pulcheria allied herself with one of her former supporters, the barbarian general Aspar. She alleged that her brother had named as his heir Aspar's lieutenant Marcian, whose claim she secured by marrying him. Though not as weak as Arcadius and Theodosius II had been, Marcian deferred to the empress and general who had made him emperor. Executing Chrysaphius, he repudiated both Monophysitism and Chrysaphius' treaty with Attila. Instead of retaliating, Attila turned to plaguing the western empire, until his sudden death led to the Huns' disintegration.

Marcian and Pulcheria called yet another ecumenical council, which met at Chalcedon, an Asian suburb of Constantinople, in 451. The Council of Chalcedon endorsed the first Council of Ephesus but disowned the second, deposing Bishop Dioscorus of Alexandria, who had presided over it. The bishops at Chalcedon declared that Christ had two natures, one divine and one human, which however acted together in one person. Though incompatible with extreme Monophysitism, this formula amounted to much the same thing as the moderate Monophysite position that Christ's single nature was both fully divine and fully human.

The council also completed a century-long process of recognizing that the Pope and four eastern bishops, now commonly called patriarchs, had wide authority over the bishoprics surrounding their own. The Pope had long had such jurisdiction over the western empire, including Illyricum even after it had been attached to the East. Egypt had likewise been subject to the Patriarch of Alexandria, and Syria to the Patriarch of Antioch. The bishops at Chalcedon now gave the Patriarch of Constantinople similar authority over Anatolia and Thrace, while the Patriarch of Jerusalem received the same prerogatives in Palestine.

Since this new status for Constantinople and Jerusalem had no basis in church tradition, the Pope objected – but not very strenuously, because he was scarcely affected and he approved of the council's condemnation of Monophysitism. The main beneficiaries, the patriarchs of Constantinople and Jerusalem, accepted all the decisions of Chalcedon with enthusiasm. In the patriarchates of Alexandria and Antioch, however, displeasure at the promotion of the other patriarchates at their expense helped discredit the council's theology, which had moreover caused the deposition of a Patriarch of Alexandria. Many of the clergy and laity of Egypt and of Syria north of Palestine made moderate Monophysitism their rallying point against the Council of Chalcedon. Monophysitism quickly became yet another problem for the weak government of the eastern empire.

Marcian outlived Pulcheria, and died in 457 without leaving or adopting an heir. His death made it plain that real power in the eastern empire lay with his mentor, the veteran general Aspar, an Arian barbarian leading a predominantly Arian and barbarian field army. In the tottering western empire another Arian barbarian general held similar power after the murder of Valentinian III, and had yet to name a puppet emperor for himself. The West was never to have another emperor in full control, and the East had scarcely had one since 395. Aspar was much cleverer and better established than Gaïnas, the other barbarian general who had virtually ruled the East.

Aspar's interest in maintaining his own power over a mostly anti-Arian and anti-barbarian people was best served by ruling behind the throne. Yet he also had an interest in preventing anyone on the throne from gaining such prestige as to be able to dispose of Aspar. The mighty commander therefore had an incentive to keep the government weak at a time when outside enemies still threatened the frontiers. The army and bureaucracy lacked the cohesion and independence to lead the empire themselves, and their members too could benefit from having a ruler too feeble to curb their own influence and corruption. So in 457 it was an open question whether the East would ever have a strong emperor again, or could last much longer in relative security.

A New Society

Despite growing barbarian influence, corruption in the bureaucracy and army, and some military reverses, between the reigns of Diocletian and Marcian the eastern empire was in many ways successful. It evolved from a mere administrative jurisdiction into a diverse but distinct society. Peoples who before had had little in common but being ruled by Rome came to share the Christian religion, a single system of taxation and administration, a mostly self-contained economy, and a better-defined culture. The East became practically independent of the West, and unlike the West proved to be a viable state. Although in the fourth century that state is best called the Eastern Roman Empire, by the fifth century it can reasonably be called the Byzantine Empire, or Byzantium for short.

During this period the eastern empire kept almost all its land. It ceded a little border territory in Mesopotamia to the Persians after the failure of Julian's Persian expedition, and, without any formal cession, let some borderlands in Illyricum fall under the temporary control of first the Visigoths and then the Huns. The eastern empire's only major loss on the map, western Illyricum, was only the result of a series of administrative shifts in the boundary between the eastern and western empires. The subtraction of western Illyricum however left Byzantium lopsidedly divided between a reduced Prefecture of Illyricum and a far larger, richer, and more populous Prefecture of the East. The seven dioceses, two in Illyricum and five in the East, were more evenly distributed and represented better defined regions. Since all of them had at least a short seaboard, a ship traveling along the coast from western Illyricum to Constantinople and on to Egypt would have touched on each diocese in turn.

Of the poor and vulnerable Prefecture of Illyricum, the Diocese of Dacia in the mid-Balkans was the poorest and most vulnerable part. The Visigoths and Huns had ravaged it, as other barbarians had done in the third century. Though it contributed to the army some of the men it was unable to support otherwise, who were stationed there to defend it, the government mainly bothered to garrison Dacia because raiding there kept barbarians from raiding more valuable places. The rest of the Prefecture of Illyricum, the Diocese of Macedonia, was the old Greek homeland. Its glorious past notwithstanding, the prolonged effort of colonizing and Hellenizing the whole eastern Mediterranean basin had left Greece somewhat exhausted, and recent barbarian raids had not helped. Yet neither of these dioceses was much worse off in the mid-fifth century than it had been in the mid-third. Both remained joined to the western empire under the ecclesiastical authority of the Pope, and Dacia was still partly Latin-speaking.

Within the huge Prefecture of the East, the Diocese of Thrace and the dioceses of Asiana and Pontica in Anatolia were the core of the new Byzantine Empire. They formed the empire's geographical and political center and the natural hinterlands of its new capital of Constantinople, which as it grew in size and wealth was already becoming the hub of the empire's trade routes. With the decline of the native Thracian and Anatolian languages and the spread of Greek, Anatolia and Thrace had also become the real center of the Greek world, richer and more populous than Greece itself and linked to the Hellenized coastlands of Syria and Egypt. All three dioceses fell under the ecclesiastical jurisdiction of the Patriarch of Constantinople. These were relatively secure territories, though barbarians occasionally raided Thrace. Anatolia, divided between Asiana and Pontica, was especially safe, with fertile agricultural land and good communications by road and sea with the rest of the empire.

Also parts of the Prefecture of the East were the confusingly named Diocese of the East, consisting of Greater Syria with Palestine and Byzantine Mesopotamia, and the Diocese of Egypt. The boundaries of the Egyptian diocese were the same as those of the Patriarchate of Alexandria, though the patriarchates of Antioch and Jerusalem now divided the Diocese of the East between them. Syria and Egypt, civilized and urbanized long before Greece and Rome and speaking Semitic and Hamitic languages unlike Indo-European Greek and Latin, had always been anomalous parts of the Roman Empire. Diocletian had finally brought them into his revised versions of the empire's administrative and fiscal systems, in the process forcing some Egyptians and Syrians to learn more Greek to deal with the government. Both Egypt and Syria remained prosperous; their trade with Persia and India was as lively as ever, and Egypt was still the biggest exporter of grain in the Mediterranean. Yet within the empire Anatolia was gaining political, economic, cultural, and ecclesiastical importance at their expense, and in particular Alexandria and Antioch had become less important than the upstart city of Constantinople.

The Byzantine Empire owed its distinctiveness not just to Diocletian's division of the Roman Empire and his successors' perpetuation of the division, but to Constantine's foundation of Constantinople and his successors' promotion of it. As the city became the real capital of the East, it enhanced the prominence of the Greek-speaking lands that extended as far west as the Adriatic and as far east as Antioch. While the eastern empire grew less Latinized and more Hellenized, knowledge of the Greek language spread further into inland Thrace and Anatolia and along the Illyrian, Syrian, and Egyptian coasts. Most of the exports of the East began to flow not to Rome but to Constantinople. By 457 Constantinople, with perhaps 200,000 people, had surpassed the older metropolises of Rome, Antioch, and Alexandria in size, wealth, and power. Anatolia, previously a mere geographical expression, had acquired a regional identity like those of Syria or Egypt, with an export economy and a Hellenized culture of its own.

Like Alexandria and Antioch before it, Constantinople had been planned as a capital and a showplace, with market squares decorated with monuments and main streets lined with covered colonnades and shops, though most of the city was an untidy jumble of tenements and small houses. Except for an acropolis that had been the whole ancient city of Byzantium, Constantinople was more up to date than its eastern rivals, with appropriate buildings for the new government and religion and for the latest amusements, and large open spaces within the walls for future growth. The central square, the Augustaeum, fronted on the Great Church of the Holy Wisdom ("St Sophia"), the Great Palace of the emperors, a large public bath, and a huge Hippodrome for the chariot racing that after Constantine's ban on gladiatorial shows had become the empire's most popular sport.

Constantinople owed most of its importance to the growth of the empire's government. Although by the fifth century the eastern empire was about a quarter smaller than in Diocletian's time, mainly because of the transfer of western Illyricum to the western empire, the eastern army and bureaucracy were about as big as they had been under Diocletian, and much larger than before him. The bureaucrats based in the capital numbered some 2500, around a sixth of the total number of officials. About one in twelve of the empire's adult males served in the army, navy, or civil service, nearly twice the proportion in the third-century empire. The main task of the bureaucrats was to raise money to pay the much more numerous soldiers. Neither group was particularly well paid, and both therefore tended to resort to embezzlement and extortion.

The government tried to reduce the cost of the army without reducing its size. With the inflation of the copper coinage the soldiers' pay dwindled to nothing in the course of the fourth century, though the large donatives distributed on the accession of an emperor and every fifth year thereafter kept their value because they were paid in gold. The government largely compensated the soldiers for their lost pay by providing allowances in gold for their rations and fodder. As the division between the field armies and the garrison armies became sharper, the field soldiers came to receive twice the ration allowances of the garrison soldiers. These allowances afforded a living wage for the field soldiers, many of whom were barbarians, and a very low wage for the garrison soldiers, who became a part-time force with other sources of income. Such pay resulted in an inferior garrison army and a middling field army that was often discontented.

The system of taxation established by Diocletian was highly flexible, and accordingly easy to abuse. For a time taxes rose steadily; but in the later fourth century they apparently stopped rising, and by the fifth the allotments of each city and region seem to have become fixed, not to be raised and to be reduced only in case of an enemy invasion or a natural disaster. Corruption persisted, since the tax collectors could embezzle for themselves and charge individual taxpayers more or less to make up the overall totals. The stabilization of the totals nonetheless indicates that, though tax increases had been necessary during much of the fourth century, by the fifth the existing rates met the government's needs. Apparently the economy was improving somewhat, while both corruption and the growth of government had come under some control.

That the emperors after Constantine succeeded each other by legal means in the East was partly a matter of luck, which the West did not share. Although no eastern emperor seized power by force during these years, Julian and Valens died violent deaths, Constantius II might well have been overthrown had he not died of natural causes first, and none of the fourth-century emperors could rest easy. The main reason the frequent power struggles after 395 never threatened Arcadius, Theodosius II, or Marcian is that those figureheads stayed out of the way of the squabbling functionaries and generals who really ruled. On the other hand, the lengthening tradition of orderly imperial successions in the East, accidental or not, kept political unrest within bounds, and discouraged future conspiracies.

The chief civil and palatine officials and generals, like Rufinus, Eutropius, or Aspar, were usually the most powerful men in the empire after the emperor, and sometimes ahead of him. Appointment by the emperor to a high office, whether a real one or an honorary one like the consulate, was the regular means of admission to the senate. Though the senate had little power as a body, and the eastern senators were not nearly as rich or well-born as the western, the privileges and prestige of a senator were significant and coveted. The 2000 or so eastern senators formed a ruling class, assuming an aristocratic air but by no means closed to meritorious or ambitious outsiders. While most of those who obtained senatorial rank were already rich, any who were not soon became so. Even some bureaucrats who never became senators gained wealth and influence through the power of government.

The next class down from the senators were the decurions, the members of city councils outside the capital, since the senate itself served as the council of Constantinople. The eastern cities, somewhat fewer than a thousand, would have had around 50,000 decurions. The richest men of each city, except for those who were exempt as senators, other officials, or clergy, had to sit on the councils, administering local affairs and collecting taxes. Most decurions were landholders, traders, and professional men, and of fairly modest means. Though in earlier times most decurions had been happy to serve their cities, the expanding central government had taken over most of their power and much of their prestige. They now found their responsibilities for collecting the taxes burdensome, and even ruinous when they personally had to pay whatever they could not collect from others. Their burdens increased as some of their colleagues gained exemptions, especially when the richest and most influential became senators or clergy.

The clergy of course had their own hierarchy, and bishops, often with substantial funds to distribute for charity, became civic leaders in their own right. The decurions had no interest in competing with them, and by and large the charitable works of the bishops met needs that pagan society had neglected. Bishops and priests did sometimes clash with government officials over theological controversies, in which the majority of the clergy seems from early on to have been on the side that eventually prevailed. Yet the resistance of the clergy to official paganism and to toleration of Arianism also shows that most clerics cared little for secular power, which they could best have obtained by conforming to the government's wishes. In purely secular matters the clergy was generally passive, because its interests lay elsewhere.

The cities and their councils administered the countryside around them, as they had done since many of them had been city-states. Most of the territory assigned to the cities was rural, and most of their nominal citizens lived in the country. In the eastern empire around 450 probably only the conurbations of Constantinople, Antioch, and Alexandria had more than 100,000 people, only another thirty or so cities had more than 10,000, and the populations of all of these totaled only about a million. Perhaps another million lived in nine hundred or so smaller cities, which today we would call small towns, averaging around a thousand people. The rest of the people, something like fourteen million, were peasants, living in villages in the rural parts of city territories. Despite the preponderance of villagers, the government paid more attention to townsmen, who lived alongside at least some officials and could riot if they were seriously discontented.

A slow but steady migration from the countryside showed that city life had its charms, especially in the three great metropolises. The larger cities had their own hippodrome, theater, cathedral, churches, monuments, waterworks, public baths, and private schools, and many shops and a forum with a large and varied market, though they also had their dangers, particularly disease. Even the small towns had a cathedral, a public bath, fountains, a schoolmaster, and a few shops and a market. Townsmen were relatively lightly taxed, but many were poor or even destitute, and the only ones who were truly rich drew their income from estates outside the city. Manufacturing and luxury trade remained on a small scale. The main trade in bulk, transporting grain from the country to feed the cities and the armies, was too strictly regulated by the government to be very profitable.

The peasants who formed about nine-tenths of the empire's subjects almost all lived in villages of at least a few dozen people, not on isolated farms. They spent most of their time raising what they and their families consumed. Some, though not many, were slaves, and many were tenants on the estates of large landholders or the government. Scattered evidence indicates that imperial estates amounted to around a fifth of the land, and that all private estates amounted to no more. So a majority of peasants evidently owned their own farms. Life was doubtless hard for many of them, especially in the often ravaged lands along the Danube frontier in Illyricum, and enemy raids or bad weather could reduce any farmer to bankruptcy and famine. The tax system could be harsh to the poorer peasants, and in bad years might force them to sell their land and become tenants. Yet most of the time most peasants in the eastern empire appear to have been reasonably well off, and to have paid their taxes without great trouble. Taxation provided an incentive to produce a surplus, and when that surplus was distributed to feed the army it helped support the poorer regions along the frontiers where most soldiers were stationed.

In an economy dominated by subsistence farming, and with plenty of agricultural land, population should have been a good index of economic growth. A rising population would indicate an expanding economy, and a falling population a contracting one. Between 285 and 457 the absolute level of the population is hard to gauge. The frequently raided frontier regions showed signs of depopulation, but they were not typical of the empire as a whole. Scattered figures and archeological evidence suggest that the cities grew somewhat, as Constantinople certainly did; but this may show migration from the countryside rather than overall growth. In the fourth century we find complaints of over-taxation, uncollected taxes, and abandonment of land, but these become rarer in the early fifth century. The equivocal evidence probably means that there was no dramatic change in population one way or the other.

Scholars still dispute whether the eastern empire was in decline between the late third and the early fifth centuries. The empire's military expenses evidently fell, because the army barely grew, its pay in copper alloy coins kept inflating, and its donatives and allowances failed to make up for the lost pay. Since other expenditures remained fairly stable and the treasury amassed only a moderate surplus, revenues must also have fallen. Growing corruption probably reduced state income by no more than rising tax rates increased it. The economy that produced the revenue therefore seems to have shrunk, perceptibly though not disastrously, and this probably reflected a decline in the productive population.

Yet evidence from many different archeological sites suggests that the worst demographic decline had begun with the epidemic of the late second century and was over by the late fourth century. At some time around the year 400 the population seems to have begun to grow again, though by midcentury it was probably still no larger than it had been under Diocletian. If so, the empire's military and political fortunes roughly reflected its demographic and economic development. In both it suffered a gradual decline during the fourth century, and made a partial recovery in the fifth.

A New Culture

The great cultural unifiers of the Byzantine Empire were the government, Christianity, and the Greek language. The three were related. From Constantine's time, the emperors generally recognized church authority in religious and moral matters. The Church, which had long recognized the legitimacy of the Roman state in the secular sphere, gladly accepted it as an ally. The newly intrusive eastern government used Greek more than Latin, though Latin continued to be the empire's official language. Greek was already the language of the Christian New Testament and the most common forms of the eastern Christian liturgy. Before Diocletian, the majority in the eastern empire had little contact with the government, scarcely knew what Christianity was, and lived in places where Greek was seldom heard. By the mid-fifth century, most people in the empire had to deal with the government on a regular basis, were at least nominal Christians, and had learned to cope with Greek, if not necessarily to speak more than a few words of it.

Christianity was a very different sort of religion from paganism. What we call paganism, which lacked even a proper name for itself, was a body of disparate beliefs and cults without any definite theology, morality, or organization of its own. The list of its multiple gods was conventional and fluid, and many gods were loosely identified with others, as the Greek Zeus was with the Roman Jupiter and the Semitic Baal. According to tradition, the gods committed adultery, incest, rape, theft, and murder; Zeus himself was an adulterer and pedophile who had killed his father and married his sister.

Since the gods bestowed favors on men in return for worship and sacrifices rather than moral conduct, the ideas of morality that most pagans had were based on tradition rather than on obeying or emulating the gods. The leading philosophy of the third and fourth centuries, which we call Neoplatonism, maintained that the traditional gods were unimportant anyway, subordinate to an omnipotent and perfect God ("the One") far greater than they. Shaped by society rather than shaping it, paganism at most reflected whatever unity society already had. Unless the state provided pagans with leadership, as it did under Diocletian, Maximin, and Julian, they were scarcely capable of resisting the advance of Christianity.

Beginning as the religion of a small though rapidly growing minority when it won over Constantine, Christianity spread quickly throughout the empire. State support helped, though the state never passed laws against paganism as stringent as the former laws against Christianity. The government harmed paganism most by simply withdrawing its patronage, which was vital to the argument that one should worship the gods because almost everyone else did, including the emperor. Only philosophers were comfortable defending paganism on its merits, and they did so by invoking a God so exalted that he seemed above most human concerns, as the Christian God did not. Julian's attempt to combine such philosophy with traditional paganism was too superstitious for many Neoplatonists and too philosophical for many ordinary pagans. By the time of the Council of Chalcedon, Christians were in the majority throughout the empire.

Despite old rumors that Christians engaged in cannibalism and incest, pagans soon found that Christians not only behaved respectably but, like Jews, gave religious reinforcement to morality that pagans could not. Most pagans, while disapproving of adulterous and homosexual behavior, had hesitated to reject the myths that attributed it to the gods. Philosophers, even if they followed Plato in rejecting the myths and condemning homosexuality, could hardly find examples of self-discipline in the gods, who included deities of wine, thievery, and erotic love. But Christians could unreservedly condemn license and luxury as distractions from the only God in whom they believed. The Christian ideals of organized charity for the poor, forgiveness for enemies, and preferring martyrdom to apostasy, though all alien to traditional pagan morality, gradually gained the admiration of many pagans and contributed to the spread of Christianity.

After Constantine's conversion, Christianity came increasingly to influence both public and private life. Christian charitable institutions for the poor grew. Public entertainments became much less violent with the abolition of gladiatorial combat and mock battles. Curiously, church disapproval of public nudity led to closing gymnasiums rather than to clothing athletes. The Church grudgingly permitted public baths segregated by sex, and chariot racing in hippodromes. While it denounced prostitution and the popular theatrical performances of nearly naked actresses, both remained legal.

Basil of Caesarea uneasily reconciled the Church's condemnation of killing with the demands of warfare by barring soldiers who killed in battle from communion for three years. Christian approval of sexual continence led to restrictions on divorce and the growth of groups of monks and nuns consecrated to chastity. Adultery by husbands, homosexual acts, abortion, and infanticide, which pagans had long tolerated with misgivings, came to be considered selfish, cruel, and abhorrent. Since most people found celibacy difficult, a decrease in abortion and infanticide probably helped counteract the decline in population that had begun in the early Roman Empire.

Christianity also advanced the position of women in society to some extent. The reason all Christian priests were male was that they were taken to represent Christ himself, while pagan priests and priestesses were only the servants of gods. The Church took the example of the Virgin as proof that women could be men's spiritual equals, and some Christian abbesses, nuns, and other women won moral recognition far beyond most Christian priests or any pagan priestess. The Church made saints of Constantine I's mother Helen and Theodosius II's sister Pulcheria, and the ecumenical Council of Ephesus upheld Pulcheria's insistence on calling the Virgin the Mother of God. The political influence of women of the imperial family, which in Roman times had been hidden and exceptional, now became open and usual, as Pulcheria, Eudoxia, and other empresses and princesses contributed to setting policy.

While Christianity developed from a persecuted minority sect into a majority religion, monasticism grew from nothing to a large and prestigious movement. It began in the early fourth century with attempts by individual ascetics to lead a perfect Christian life of devotion to God and indifference to almost everything else, which the hermit Anthony pioneered in the Egyptian desert. Because only a person of iron will like Anthony could succeed in such a quest without human aid and guidance, aspiring monks and nuns soon gathered together in monastic communities, with a director and rules for conduct.

The experienced monk Pachomius founded the first such monasteries and convents in Egypt, serving as their head and composing rules for them. In the later fourth century the theologian, scholar, and former hermit Basil of Caesarea composed rules that in various versions have been used by eastern monks ever since, prescribing a common life of obedience to an abbot, prayer, physical labor, some reading, and moderation in self-denial. Yet some monks remained hermits, and could be found standing on pillars, living in caves, or practicing other forms of asceticism.

Although pagans had begun the revival of Greek culture in the second century, Christians soon embraced it. Origen had already used elements from Neoplatonism to create a sophisticated Christian theology, but because he failed to clarify the nature of Christ his work could be used to defend Arianism. The working out of the implications of the anti-Arian Council of Nicaea was largely the work of Basil of Caesarea, with his brother Gregory of Nyssa and their friend Gregory of Nazianzus. Rejecting the Arian belief that Christ was inferior to God the Father, they first distinguished between God's single substance, proclaimed in the Nicene Creed, and his three persons, the Father, Son, and Holy Spirit. In particular, Gregory of Nazianzus went on to distinguish between the single person of the Son and his two natures, one fully human and one fully divine. After Basil and the Gregories had convinced most theologians that these seemingly paradoxical concepts were compatible, Arianism became discredited among Romans and accepted only by barbarians without intellectual pretensions.

The distinction between the natures of Christ however failed to prevent the later controversy over Monophysitism. The most moderate form of Monophysitism, which agreed that the Son's nature was fully human and fully divine, was so close to orthodoxy that it was almost impossible to prove unorthodox. One problem was that the controversy over Nestorius had led some theologians to exaggerate their defense of Christ's divinity to refute a caricatured Nestorianism which no one really professed. A worse problem was that at the Council of Chalcedon the question of Monophysitism became confused with jurisdictional rivalries among the five patriarchates. For whatever reason, no theologian of the stature of Basil and the two Gregories emerged in time to reconcile the disputants. While in doctrinal terms the Monophysite dispute was a fairly minor one, it became a symbol for almost irreconcilable discord between the patriarchates of Alexandria and Antioch and the rest of the Church.

In this period Christians made their first contributions to the writing of formal history. Under Constantine, Bishop Eusebius of Caesarea compiled a chronicle of short entries from pagan, Jewish, and Christian sources which, though lost today in its original form, served later Byzantine scholars as a source and a model. Eusebius also composed a widely read history of the Church from the time of Christ to his own day, which won a wide readership and survives, along with continuations of it by three fifth-century historians.

While Eusebius also inaugurated Christian biography with a life of the emperor Constantine, the model for that genre became Athanasius of Alexandria's life of the hermit Anthony, a more inspired treatment of a more obviously admirable subject. Although Eusebius and Athanasius were merely competent stylists, theologians like Basil of Caesarea and Gregory of Nazianzus were well versed in classical Greek rhetoric and ranked among the finest writers of their day. The Patriarch of Constantinople John Chrysostom, also a classically trained orator, first raised the Christian sermon to a polished and effective literary form.

Given that for centuries all Greek literature, education, and philosophy had been pagan, educated men remained disproportionately pagan for some time. If anything, competition with Christians seems to have stimulated pagans to write more and to write better than before. Though few authors of any kind wrote literature of much distinction in the days of Diocletian and Constantine, later a whole circle of Christians and pagans began writing with subtlety and refinement, including the emperor Julian himself. The most important Latin history of the fourth century was the work of a Greek-speaking pagan, Ammianus Marcellinus of Antioch, who settled in Rome.

Most secular orators continued to be pagan, even those who praised Christian emperors. Yet the leading pagan orator Libanius of Antioch taught not only the pagan Julian but the very Christian Basil of Caesarea, Gregory of Nazianzus, and John Chrysostom. Even in the fifth century, the philosopher Proclus put Neoplatonism into its definitive form, creating a complex pagan theology that was influenced by Christianity and was to influence Christian theologians in its turn. While Christianity was obviously winning over the cultural elite, it converted them more slowly than it did others, and in the meantime pagans participated along with Christians in the renewed vitality of Greek culture.

This vitality is apparent from the revival of the groups of schools in several eastern cities that had long functioned as something like universities for the Greek world. The traditional university towns were Athens, where Proclus headed a philosophical Academy that claimed Plato as its founder; Antioch, where Libanius taught rhetoric; and Alexandria, best known for its schools of philosophy and medicine. After the government endowed thirty-one professorial chairs at Constantinople in 425, the capital took its place beside the older cities as a center of higher education. The capital's schools concentrated on teaching aspiring officials the practical and prestigious skills needed to rise in the bureaucracy. In contrast to the older institutions, only one of the professors at Constantinople taught philosophy, and almost as many taught in Latin, still the language of the law, as in Greek, the language of most people in the city and its hinterlands.

While the importance of Greek grew in both the government and the Church, inhabitants of the eastern empire began writing extensively in Coptic, Syriac, and Armenian for the first time. Most of the literature in these languages consisted of translations of Greek Christian texts, including the Bible and the liturgy, and showed a greater penetration of Hellenism and Christianity into the native cultures of Egypt, Syria, and Armenia rather than any cultural separatism. A few writers also composed original works in Coptic, such as Pachomius' monastic rules, and in Syriac, including elaborate hymns for the liturgy.

This writing in languages seldom used for literature before may well reflect an increase in literacy in regions where scarcely anyone had ever known Greek. Notwithstanding a modest spread of Hellenization, if most of the people of Egypt, Syria, and Armenia were to understand what they heard in church it could only be in their native languages. Yet Greek remained the language of the principal cities and their bishops and clergy. Even Egyptians and Syrians who embraced Monophysitism were simply accepting the judgement of their Greek-speaking patriarchs in Alexandria and Antioch that Monophysitism should be the doctrine of the whole Church. A century earlier no one in the Greek metropolises could have exerted such influence over the Egyptian and Syrian countryside.

The extension of Roman government, Greek culture, Christianity, and general prosperity also had effects on art and architecture. Luxury building and art, which because they are expensive can be signs of wealth, showed a definite expansion and improvement from a low point in the late third century to a much higher one in the early fifth. The palace Diocletian built for his retirement is essentially an enormous fort. Constantine decorated Constantinople by plundering other cities, and built churches that soon started to collapse. Many churches must have been built during the rapid spread of Christianity in the fourth century, but remarkably few survive, probably because most were of shoddy construction. A real boom in luxury building appears to have begun at Constantinople and resumed in other eastern cities only during the reign of Theodosius I. The first large and elegant churches in most eastern cities date from the early to middle fifth century.

Painting, textiles, and smaller objects followed a similar pattern of multiplication and improvement, which probably began in the capital but soon reached the provinces. The decoration of churches and other monuments developed along with their architecture. In representational art, the advance from the crude portraits of the tetrarchs to the refined ones of the Theodosian dynasty is obvious. To look for separate traditions of popular art at this time would as a rule be anachronistic, because even the lowliest craftsmen seem to have been trying to imitate the most skilled. Though artists who fell short of their intentions can be found in every period, the general impression at this time is of some advance at every level of achievement. The quality of the materials of artists and architects also seems to have risen.

The Byzantine Empire of 457 certainly had its strengths. Although it defended itself somewhat feebly against the Goths and the Huns, it managed to survive with its armies more or less intact until the Germans became less threatening and the Huns passed from the scene. Its new Christian culture impressed most barbarians; it at least helped to convert many Germans to Arian Christianity, and some Persian subjects in Mesopotamia to Nestorian Christianity. Byzantium remained much more prosperous and cultured than its barbarian enemies, and seemed to be in the early stages of a broad economic expansion.

Yet Byzantium still had serious problems. These included threats by Germans and Persians to its frontiers, internal corruption and inefficiency, and domination by barbarian generals with an interest in keeping the emperors and their Roman officials weak. Byzantine prosperity was by no means unqualified, thus far hardly touching Illyricum, and without necessarily strengthening the empire's defenses Byzantine wealth tempted the empire's enemies to invade and plunder it. The Western Roman Empire was also far richer and more cultured than the barbarians who were overrunning it, and was nonetheless being overrun. Before Byzantium could safely enjoy its new prosperity and culture, it needed to deal with the Germans on its frontiers and in its army.

3

RECONQUEST AND CRISIS (457–602)

The Survival of the East

The eastern senate offered to elect Aspar emperor, which might have been the best way to assure his downfall. He cautiously declined, passing the crown on to his subordinate officer Leo. Like Marcian, Leo was in his late fifties, without a hereditary claim to the throne, a power base, a son to succeed him, or much of a reputation. In an attempt to enhance his frail legitimacy, Leo had himself crowned by the Patriarch of Constantinople, a ceremony that made a good enough impression to set a precedent for emperors in the future. Though Leo had the wits and will to be more than a figurehead, his barbarian master was far more powerful than he. Aspar commanded one of the two praesental armies, Aspar's son Ardabur commanded the Army of the East, and Aspar's ally Theoderic Strabo led the empire's Ostrogothic allies in Thrace.

Cautious though Leo was about standing up to Aspar, the emperor began to create a counterweight to his powerful general by recruiting soldiers from the Isaurians, a pugnacious people native to the mountains of southeastern Anatolia. The emperor found a particularly valuable ally in the leader of the Isaurian recruits, Zeno, who soon showed a talent for intrigue. By providing Leo with proof that the Persians were plotting with Aspar's son Ardabur, Zeno helped Leo to remove the son from his command. The grateful emperor created a new imperial guard corps of the Excubitors and made Zeno commander of it. Next Leo married Zeno to his daughter Ariadne and made him commander of the Army of Thrace.

52

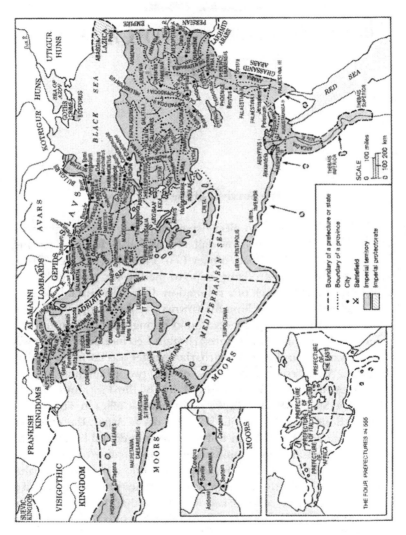

Map 2 The Empire *ca.* 565

In 467, Leo sent a great expedition to help the Western Roman Empire reclaim its richest region, northwestern Africa, from the Vandals who had seized it. Victory would have enhanced Leo's reputation and restored the western empire as a viable partner. At Aspar's insistence, Leo gave the African command to his own brother-in-law Basiliscus. After hugely expensive preparations, Basiliscus managed to be defeated by the Vandals, damaging the eastern army, nearly bankrupting the eastern treasury, and leaving the western empire in ruins. So many thought that Aspar and Basiliscus had purposely bungled the campaign in order to weaken the emperor that resentment of Aspar increased.

When Leo's daughter Ariadne bore Zeno a son, who became his grandfather's namesake and presumptive heir, Aspar grew impatient with his loss of influence. A mutiny in the Army of Thrace, probably instigated by the Alan general, forced Zeno to abandon his command. Next Aspar forced Leo to marry his younger daughter to Aspar's younger son Patricius, and to name Patricius Caesar and heir to the empire. This marriage, however, so outraged popular opinion in Constantinople that it actually harmed Aspar. The emperor was soon able to name Zeno commander of the Army of the East. In 471 the emperor finally contrived to have Aspar and his elder son Ardabur assassinated.

Enraged by Aspar's murder, the Ostrogoths in the imperial army deserted, and joined their fellow Ostrogoth Theoderic Strabo in ravaging Thrace. Meanwhile the Ostrogothic allies in the neighboring part of the western empire invaded the East, and raided its part of Illyricum. After two years of devastation of his Balkan provinces by both groups of Ostrogoths, Leo made peace. He granted the western Ostrogoths lands in central Illyricum and Strabo's Ostrogoths lands in central Thrace, and gave Strabo nominal command of one of the praesental armies. But the emperor appointed Zeno to the other praesental command with real power over both armies, in which Isaurians replaced many of the Ostrogoths.

By conspiracy and murder, after several reverses and the virtual cession of part of the Balkans to the Ostrogoths, Leo had at last purged his field armies of disloyal barbarians and become undisputed ruler of the eastern empire. He was even able to send a few troops to help a new western emperor take unsteady control over Italy. Soon after making these advances, which were of vital importance for the empire's future, Leo died in 474. He left the throne to his seven-year-old grandson Leo II, whose father Zeno was to serve as his regent. Yet little Leo died before the year was out, and Zeno succeeded him.

Now nearing fifty, Zeno was an accomplished plotter, but widely disdained for combining Isaurian gruffness with un-Isaurian deviousness. Unpopular in Constantinople, he had seemed better cast as the power behind the throne than as emperor. He had barely been crowned when his mother-in-law Verina, her brother Basiliscus, and the Ostrogoth Theoderic Strabo mounted a conspiracy against him. They put Basiliscus on the throne, sending Zeno and a band of loyal Isaurians fleeing into Anatolia. Though the conspirators probably expected Basiliscus to be a compliant ruler, he proved to be foolish and willful. He offended most Constantinopolitans by favoring Monophysitism, and gave the command against Zeno to Zeno's fellow Isaurian Illus.

Illus joined Zeno, and with his help the deposed emperor regained the capital the year after he had lost it. Having promised not to execute Basiliscus, Zeno imprisoned him and let him starve to death. The emperor reconciled with his mother-in-law Verina, and her daughter the empress soon bore him another son. But he dismissed the disloyal Theoderic Strabo from his titular command and replaced him with the leader of the western Ostrogoths, Theoderic the Amal. Zeno had the Amal move his Ostrogoths to a part of Thrace not far from Strabo's Ostrogoths, hoping to pit the two Theoderics against each other.

While Zeno was precariously reestablishing himself in the eastern empire, in 476 the barbarian general Odoacer deposed the impotent western emperor Romulus at Ravenna. Rather than appoint another puppet, Odoacer declared his allegiance to Zeno as emperor of both East and West, and asked him for recognition as his commander in Italy. Zeno declined, because he still recognized another western emperor in the West's remnant of Illyricum, but he was much too busy to fight Odoacer. In the following years Theoderic the Amal looted the Balkans again, and Theoderic Strabo joined him after another failed plot against Zeno. These raids continued through 480, when Odoacer seized the lands of the last western emperor, Nepos. Now the only part of the Roman Empire that remained Roman was the eastern, or Byzantine, empire.

As the sole emperor, Zeno tried to deal with the persistent religious dispute over Monophysitism. Realizing that even most of those who rejected the Council of Chalcedon agreed with it that Christ was fully human, the emperor looked for a way to unite the vast majority of Christians who used different language to mean the same thing. In 482, with the approval of his Patriarch of Constantinople Acacius, Zeno issued a deliberately ambiguous edict, the *Henoticon* ("Act of

Union"). Without confirming or repudiating the Council of Chalcedon, the *Henoticon* followed it in rejecting the extreme Monophysite doctrine that Christ was not fully human. This formula won grudging acceptance from many on both sides, but not from all.

In the meantime Theoderic Strabo had died in a riding accident. Theoderic the Amal, adding Strabo's Ostrogoths to his own, raided once more. Zeno mollified him by reappointing him praesental commander and granting his people new lands in northeast Illyricum and northwest Thrace. When Zeno's general Illus proclaimed a rebel emperor at Antioch, Zeno defeated him with an army reinforced by these Ostrogothic allies. Though Theoderic and his Ostrogoths resumed plundering Thrace soon after helping subdue Illus, they later agreed to a truce. The Pope condemned the *Henoticon* and excommunicated the Patriarch Acacius, but this breach with the Papacy, known as the Acacian Schism, posed no serious threat to Zeno.

The wily emperor now conceived the cleverest of his many schemes for ranging his enemies against each other. In 488 he persuaded Theoderic to lead his Ostrogoths into Italy, ostensibly to punish Odoacer for overthrowing the Western Roman Empire. Theoderic ultimately succeeded in conquering Italy and founding an Ostrogothic Kingdom there, but Zeno achieved his real aim of securing Thrace and eastern Illyricum as soon as the Ostrogoths left Byzantine territory. He enjoyed three years of unaccustomed peace and security before dying of disease in 491.

Though both Leo I and Zeno had remained in power with great difficulty, they left Byzantium much strengthened. Between them they reduced the barbarian element in the field armies to tractable size, while making no more than a moderate reduction in the total number of soldiers. Zeno finally rid the empire of the Ostrogoths, giving it control over all of its Balkan possessions for the first time in more than a century. Despite Leo's losses in his African expedition and the many Ostrogothic raids, the treasury remained solvent. Though without the skills of Leo and Zeno Byzantium might well have succumbed to barbarian domination or bankruptcy and anarchy, their success also suggests that it was sustaining its demographic and economic recovery. The two emperors always seemed able to recruit new troops and to raise the money to pay them.

Since Zeno's second son had died shortly before his father, the widowed empress Ariadne, daughter of Leo I, determined the succession by marrying the chamberlain Anastasius, who became emperor with the senate's consent. Just over sixty, Anastasius was cultivated, intelligent, a good administrator, and, unlike nearly all his predecessors, from a Greek-speaking family. Although the new emperor was known as a moderate Monophysite, this doctrine was compatible with Zeno's *Henoticon*, and as a condition of his coronation the patriarch forced him to promise not to repudiate the Council of Chalcedon.

Anastasius faced opposition from the Isaurians and from the clubs of the Blues and the Greens, which sponsored the chariot races and theatrical shows that had grown in popularity when more bloodthirsty sports were outlawed. Most Isaurians in the army wanted Zeno's brother Longinus for emperor and raised a rebellion. Anastasius sent an army that drove them back to Isauria, and he later had them deported to Thrace. The Blues and Greens never much liked Anastasius, largely because his rival Longinus had been a patron of theirs, and they showed an increasing fondness for rioting and mayhem. Though Anastasius soon crushed the Isaurian rebels, he had intermittent trouble with the Blues and Greens throughout his reign.

Anastasius gave priority to some long-neglected administrative problems, and took an interest in economics that was quite atypical of Byzantine emperors. Whenever possible, he substituted cash for goods in government requisitions and payments; this change made accounting easier, helped reduce embezzlement, and eliminated the expense and waste of carting and storing supplies all over the empire. The emperor levied in cash many taxes formerly levied in kind, and repealed an inconvenient tax on urban commerce that had been levied every five years. He replaced the field soldiers' issues of arms and uniforms with generous monetary allowances that let them buy their supplies with money left over. Anastasius also replaced the unstable copper alloy coinage with a stable and pure copper coin, the *follis*. *Folles* and their fractions provided convenient small denominations for both the government and private citizens for the first time since the early third century. Without these smaller coins to add flexibility to the monetary system, Anastasius' program of monetarization would have worked much less well.

The success of these measures and others taken against official corruption seems to have been dramatic. The state gained revenue while taxpayers often paid less than before. The burden that the government imposed upon the economy shrank, while the workings of government continued unimpaired or actually improved. In particular, though the garrison army remained an inferior force, the higher pay of the field army began to attract an ample pool of suitable recruits, most of them native Byzantines. No longer was the government dependent on impoverished and discontented barbarians and Isaurians to keep its army up to strength.

In 502 the Persians invaded Syria for the first time in sixty years, while the Bulgars, a federation of tribes akin to the Huns, raided Thrace. In the reigns of Leo I or Zeno, such attacks could have been disastrous, and might even have let Aspar or the Ostrogoths seize power permanently at Constantinople. As it was, the Persians sacked several major cities near the border. But Anastasius mustered 52,000 men, almost as many as Julian had massed for his Persian expedition when he could draw upon the armies of both East and West. Within two years the Byzantines had pushed out the Persians and started raiding Persian territory, and the third year the Persian king agreed to a truce. Anastasius built a great fortified base at Dara on the frontier to keep the Persians out in the future.

The emperor's successes emboldened him to promote his Monophysitism more openly. In 512 he deposed the Chalcedonian Patriarch of Constantinople and replaced him with a Monophysite, setting off riots in the city. The next year the Chalcedonian general Vitalian raised a rebellion in Thrace and defeated an imperial army. When Vitalian marched to the gates of the capital, Anastasius named him commander of the Army of Thrace and opened negotiations with the Pope to heal the Acacian Schism. Two years later, however, an imperial army defeated Vitalian and forced him to flee to northern Thrace. The aged emperor was firmly in power by the time he died suddenly in 518.

Even after his expensive wars, reductions in taxation, and increases in military pay, Anastasius left in his treasury a reserve of 23 million nomismata, almost three times the empire's annual budget and more than three times the treasury reserve in 457. The size of this reserve shows the efficacy of Anastasius' efforts to reduce corruption and waste, as well as the pervasiveness of both before his reign. Yet such a sum probably shows something else as well: the growing prosperity of Byzantium. Like Leo I and Zeno, Anastasius faced stubborn rebels and powerful invaders, but he defeated them much more easily than his predecessors had done. Under Anastasius the eastern empire seemed healthier than it had ever been before in its separate existence.

Justinian the Reconqueror

Since Anastasius' wife Ariadne was dead and he had never named an heir, his courtiers chose the Count of the Excubitors Justin as the next emperor. In his late sixties, Justin was uneducated, inactive, and poorly qualified to rule. But he had an adopted son, his trusted nephew Justinian, who was thirty-six, with enough education and more than enough ability and ambition to run the empire. Justin and Justinian came from peasant families in northern Illyricum, spoke Latin as their native tongue, and were firm Chalcedonians. While Justinian felt at home in Constantinople, he never forgot the lost provinces of the western empire that shared his Latin language and Chalcedonian faith. To Justinian the large gold reserve and efficient army left behind by Anastasius were tools that should be put to good use. At first, however, Justinian was only a very powerful adviser, though he soon became commander of one of the praesental armies.

Justin and Justinian promptly endorsed the Council of Chalcedon, and negotiated an end to the Acacian Schism with the Pope and the Western Church. They rid themselves of the Chalcedonian rebel Vitalian by appointing him commander of the other praesental army and then having him killed. They managed to impose Chalcedonianism on the hierarchy throughout the empire except Egypt, where Monophysitism was so strong that they allowed most of the Monophysite bishops to remain. The pious emperor and his nephew also started a war with Persia by accepting a protectorate over the Christian kingdom of Lazica, which had been a Persian vassal.

As Justin aged, Justinian gradually assumed the power of a ruler. A partisan of the racing and theater fan club of the Blues, he soon became enamored of one of the Blues' actresses, Theodora, who was known for her beauty and her thoroughness in displaying it. Although a law forbade senators to marry former actresses because of the obscenity of their performances, Justinian had his uncle exempt actresses who repented, and married Theodora. She became a faithful wife and a close collaborator, sharing with Justinian a lowly background and a strong will, though she was a Monophysite. Not long after their marriage, Justin crowned Justinian co-emperor and died, in 527.

At the beginning of Justinian's reign the Persian war occupied much of his vast energy. He nearly doubled the strength of the field army fighting the Persians by creating a separate Army of Armenia in the northern part of the frontier. In the southern sector, he put the Army of the East under the command of Belisarius, who had proved to be a talented subordinate in the praesental army Justinian had led. With the Army of Armenia so new, the war continued indecisively for several years. But Justinian was able to send a small land and sea expedition to annex the Crimea, whose king had been murdered after converting to Christianity. The conquest of the Crimea was small but significant, because for a long time emperors had shown no interest in conquering anything but lands that the empire had recently lost.

Justinian appointed a commission to codify the empire's laws, which had been piling up for centuries without being properly collected. The one earlier compilation, the *Theodosian Code* of Theodosius II, had not been designed to include every valid law on every subject, as Justinian meant his *Justinian Code* to do. Besides collecting older laws and repealing those that were obsolete, Justinian promulgated many new ones. He tried to reduce corruption in the bureaucracy, made pederasty punishable by castration, and banned pagans from public teaching. Pleased by his legal commission's work, Justinian made its chairman John the Cappadocian his main adviser on domestic matters and Prefect of the East.

The Byzantine armies of Thrace and Illyricum handily repelled raids by the Bulgars and their western neighbors the Slavs, but the armies of Armenia and the East did rather less well against Persia, though they gained ground in Armenia. In 530, when the Vandals of northwestern Africa deposed their king, who had been friendly to Justinian, the emperor began planning an expedition against them. This was a far larger project than conquering the Crimea, and much more aggressive than the expedition that Leo I had sent against the Vandals to help the western empire while it still existed. In order to free his hands for campaigning in the West, Justinian began negotiating a permanent peace with the Persians. In 532 they agreed, in return for a large cash payment.

Justinian was preparing to send his favorite general Belisarius against the Vandals when the clubs of the Blues and Greens united in rioting against him. At first they only wanted pardons for some of their members who had committed crimes; but as they felt their power, the rioters rallied to some senators who wanted to overthrow Justinian and replace him with a nephew of the emperor Anastasius. The Blues and Greens burned and looted much of the center of Constantinople, shouting *Nika* ("Win!"), as they did for their favorite charioteers. Belisarius finally put down the uprising by massacring most of the rioters.

Justinian took the destruction as an opportunity to rebuild the capital on a grander scale. Among many lavish buildings, his most splendid and expensive was a daring, original, and enormous replacement for the city's main church of St Sophia.

This uprising of the Blues and Greens, known as the Nika Revolt, failed to deter Justinian from trying to conquer the Vandal Kingdom. In 533 Belisarius sailed for Africa with an expeditionary force of some 18,000 soldiers. His landing took the Vandals by surprise. When he came upon their army near their capital of Carthage, he put it to flight and marched into the city. The Vandals regrouped, but he crushed them in a second battle. After a siege of their last stronghold, the Vandals' king Gelimer and his remaining men surrendered. Within a year Belisarius had captured the entire Vandal Kingdom, including Sardinia, Corsica, the Balearic Islands, and almost the whole Mediterranean coast of Africa west of Byzantine Egypt.

Belisarius had shown himself a superb commander, and the Byzantine army had proved its superiority to the larger force of the Vandals. Most of the African population had disliked the Vandals and welcomed the Byzantine conquest. Northwestern Africa was an important producer of grain and relatively defensible, though the Moors in the interior sometimes raided it. The Vandals' treasury alone probably covered the costs of Justinian's expedition, and Justinian expected the revenues of his new African provinces to cover the payroll of his new Army of Africa plus a sizable surplus to forward to Constantinople.

This triumph over the Vandals in Africa made Justinian eager to attempt the more difficult task of taking Italy from the Ostrogoths. In 535 the murder of their queen gave him a plausible pretext. On his orders Belisarius seized Sicily with a small force, and the Army of Illyricum, after an initial reverse, took western Illyricum from the Ostrogoths the next year. Meanwhile Belisarius landed in southern Italy and marched north, capturing first Naples and then Rome itself. But with too few men to advance further, he found himself besieged in Rome by the Ostrogoths. A mutiny by the new Army of Africa, which the African revenues had proved insufficient to pay at once, also showed that Justinian was trying to do too much in the West with too few men and too little expenditure.

Realizing his mistake somewhat tardily, the emperor sent reinforcements in several stages to Belisarius, who then advanced as far north as Milan. The reinforcements that arrived in 537 would probably have been enough to finish the war if the general sent with them, the eunuch

Narses, had not refused to follow Belisarius' orders. Disputes between the two generals allowed the Ostrogoths to retake and sack Milan. Then Justinian recalled Narses and the Byzantine advance resumed. By 540 the Byzantines had conquered all of Italy south of the Po River except for the capital of Ravenna, where Belisarius was besieging the Ostrogothic king Vitigis. The Ostrogoths sued for peace.

Justinian now wanted Belisarius back in the East because the Persians seemed about to break their treaty and invade Syria. The emperor therefore offered the Ostrogoths undisturbed possession of Italy north of the Po in return for Ravenna and half their treasury. Belisarius, reluctant to leave his conquest of Italy unfinished, persuaded the Ostrogoths to submit to him by pretending that he would rule with their support as an independent western emperor. He took possession of Ravenna and the Ostrogoths' king and treasury, but then embarked for the East. Except for some dismayed Ostrogoths in a few forts in the far north, he had conquered Italy.

As Justinian had feared, the Persians did invade Syria during Belisarius' absence. Sweeping past the lightly defended frontier, they tore through the countryside and surprised and sacked the Syrian metropolis of Antioch. The Byzantine client King of Lazica transferred his allegiance from the Byzantines to the Persians. Yet when Belisarius arrived in Syria with many of his soldiers and some newly enlisted Ostrogoths, he halted the Persian advance and raided Persian Mesopotamia in retaliation. The Persian invasion seemed to have come to nothing more than a raid in force.

Thus the Byzantines had made their wide conquests in Africa, Illyricum, and Italy without losing anything in the East but their protectorate over Lazica. Justinian had promulgated a final version of his *Justinian Code* and completed St Sophia and many other impressive buildings. He had even imposed orthodoxy on the Egyptian Church by detaining its Monophysite bishops in Constantinople and preventing them from consecrating more bishops. John the Cappadocian had reduced the size and improved the efficiency of the civil service. John ended the sale of governorships and abolished the whole bureaucratic tier of the dioceses before he fell foul of Theodora and was dismissed in 540.

Such achievements seem to confirm that Byzantium was continuing to grow in wealth and strength. While Justinian was more ambitious than his predecessors, he also had more freedom to act and better instruments to employ. He spent liberally but not wildly, given the huge reserve left by Anastasius and the large treasures that he captured from the Vandals and Ostrogoths. Africa and Italy were both valuable conquests, though Italy was somewhat more impoverished and less defensible than Africa. In any event, Justinian took the reasonable position that the empire's interest in the West should continue despite the disappearance of a western emperor. Without neglecting the lands and subjects he already ruled, Justinian had made an appropriate use of his resources in the West before shifting them back to the East when the Persians broke the peace.

Justinian and the Plague

Justinian might well have attempted more conquests in Visigothic Spain or elsewhere in the West after settling with the Persians, if an unforeseeable disaster had not struck late in 541. The bubonic plague, previously unknown in the Mediterranean lands, arrived in Egypt, reportedly from Ethiopia. Carried by fleas on rats, the disease usually followed the routes for transporting grain, which the rats ate. The contagion spread by ship, through farmland, along with armies, and especially in cities, though it mostly spared drier regions with little food for rats, like the interior of Syria or the parts of Egypt a little away from the Nile. By early 542 the plague had attacked most eastern cities and the opposing Byzantine and Persian armies on the frontier.

The mortality was on a staggering scale. About three-quarters of those who caught the disease died. One historian put Constantinople's death toll at over 230,000, probably more than half the city's people. Another historian who was in the capital at the time thought that of the empire's whole population about as many died as survived, including those who caught the plague but recovered. Because the infection would have affected the countryside less than the cities, the overall loss of population was probably nearer to a quarter, about the proportion who were to die from the same disease in the thirteenth century.

Justinian himself caught the plague, leaving Theodora in effective control of the government and presumptively of the succession. When this news reached the Army of the East, its officers discussed proclaiming Belisarius emperor if Justinian died. Learning of their plans, Theodora had the great general removed from his post. As a Monophysite, she also allowed the deposed Monophysite bishops to consecrate more bishops from their detention in Constantinople. One of the men they consecrated, Jacob Baradaeus, traveled throughout the East, ordaining priests and setting up separate Monophysite congregations, which became known after him as the Jacobite Church.

When the emperor regained his health late in 542, he found everything he had worked for in jeopardy. The Monophysites were stronger than ever. The plague must have reduced government revenues as drastically as it had the empire's population, at a time when government spending on wars and buildings had soared. The Ostrogoths, whose inland positions and more primitive organization were less affected by the plague, rallied under their new king Totila and began retaking Italy from the poorly led Byzantine troops. The Moors bordering the new Byzantine provinces in Africa had similar advantages, and soon began raiding in force. Though the Persians also suffered from the plague, they had fewer enemies than the Byzantines. Because of Theodora's interference, Justinian faced these financial and military crises without John the Cappadocian or Belisarius, his best administrator and his best general.

The emperor found a passable replacement for John in the Count of the Sacred Largesses Peter Barsymes, who became Prefect of the East. To meet government expenses despite the loss of revenue caused by the plague, Peter resumed the sale of governorships, and raised large sums from wealthy senators by confiscations and compulsory loans. He postponed and eventually canceled the meager pay of the less important garrison troops, and delayed the much larger pay of the field armies as long as he could. Naturally the garrison army became even weaker, while the field armies suffered from mutinies, and even from desertion to the Ostrogoths in Italy and to the Moors in Africa. Though the plague abated in 544, it was followed by a famine that took still more lives.

Seeing that Jacob Baradaeus had frustrated the government's attempt to suppress Monophysitism, Justinian now tried to conciliate the moderate majority of Monophysites, whose views were nearly orthodox in any case. Their most potent argument against the Council of Chalcedon was that its doctrine was tainted with Nestorianism, and one of their key points was that it had failed to condemn three bishops who had been symphathetic to Nestorius. To blunt this argument, Justinian explicitly condemned the pro-Nestorian doctrines of all three men in a careful document known as the Edict of the Three Chapters. The Chalcedonian patriarchs of the East reluctantly accepted this edict, but the Pope found its posthumous condemnations excessive and rejected it. Jacob Baradaeus continued his mission.

Figure 4 Mosaic of Justinian I (reigned 527–65) and his court from the Church of San Vitale, Ravenna. The bearded man at Justinian's right is probably his great general Belisarius, who reconquered northwestern Africa from the Vandals and most of Italy from the Ostrogoths. This mosaic probably dates in its original form from 544–5, when it commemorated the betrothal of Belisarius' daughter to the grandson of the empress Theodora (probably the young man to Belisarius' right), though it was reworked *ca.* 548 to substitute Archbishop Maximian of Ravenna (labeled "Maximianus") for his predecessor Victor. (*Photo*: Irina Andreescu-Treadgold)

As Totila's Ostrogoths advanced further, Justinian sent Belisarius back to Italy. With neither enough men nor enough money nor the emperor's full confidence, the long-victorious general was barely able to hold his own. He lost Rome to Totila and then took it back again, but the Ostrogoths continued to hold almost all the rest of Italy except Ravenna. The Moors overran much of Africa, whose Byzantine troops not only mutinied but at one point raised a full-blown revolt. The Bulgars and Slavs repeatedly raided Illyricum.

Finally in the East the Persians agreed to a truce, only excluding Lazica, which they still held. Lazica's king soon asked Justinian to restore the Byzantine protectorate and drove the Persians out of most of his kingdom. In Africa the Byzantine commander inflicted a decisive defeat on the Moors and restored order. The worst of the emergency was over by 548, when Theodora died. Although Justinian seems to have been fond of her to the end, she had in several ways frustrated his plans, which he pursued with renewed vigor shortly after her death.

The emperor recalled Belisarius and made preparations for a great new expedition to Italy under his cousin Germanus. Yet various obstacles delayed the campaign until 550, when Germanus died. The next year the emperor prepared to send an enlarged army into Italy under Narses, Belisarius' co-commander of twelve years before. If Justinian's confidence in his plans for conquest in the West had ever flagged, he had now regained it. When rebels against the Visigothic king in Spain asked for Byzantine help, the emperor agreed, and arranged to send a small force to Spain on top of his commitment in Italy.

In 552 Narses marched through Illyricum and into northern Italy with about 20,000 men. He met Totila in a battle between Ravenna and Rome and won a shattering victory, in which Totila was fatally wounded. Narses reoccupied Rome, which the Ostrogoths had retaken, and managed to surround most of the remaining Ostrogothic army near Naples. There he killed most of them, along with the king who had replaced Totila. These two defeats reduced the Ostrogoths to a few small garrisons and wandering bands, without a king and far inferior in strength to Narses' army. Meanwhile the Byzantine forces landed in Spain and defeated the Visigothic king. They established themselves in the southern part of his kingdom, which they soon turned into a Byzantine province.

As Jacob Baradaeus consecrated more Monophysite priests and even bishops for his Jacobite Church, the emperor became so determined to win acceptance of his Edict of the Three Chapters that he called an ecumenical council at Constantinople for 553. The overwhelmingly eastern bishops at this Second Council of Constantinople duly endorsed the emperor's edict. The Western Church, which had resisted the edict, disliked the council, which seemed a disproportionate response to a minor issue. The Pope, whom Justinian had detained at Constantinople, accepted it after a long resistance. But the council appears to have done nothing to slow the growth of the Jacobite Church.

The Byzantines were completing their conquest of Italy, extending their winnings in Spain, and holding Lazica against the Persians when the bubonic plague struck again in 558. This outbreak, if less severe than that between 541 and 544, probably wiped out any demographic recovery since that time, and caused another drop in government revenues when expenses were still very high. Justinian reappointed

Peter Barsymes as Prefect of the East and let him use some of the same rough and unpopular methods as before to keep the budget shakily in balance.

As the effects of the plague spread, the Byzantine advances in Italy slowed and those in Spain stopped. Because, as before, the epidemic afflicted nomads far less than it did the settled Byzantines, it helped the Bulgars, Slavs, and some leftover Huns known as the Kotrigurs to raid far into the Balkans. The Kotrigurs defeated a Byzantine army and advanced on Constantinople, which was poorly defended at the time. Justinian called on the retired general Belisarius, who repulsed them. The emperor then took the command himself in time to take some credit for the Huns' departure, though he simply paid them to withdraw. He also paid a larger and stronger group of Huns, the Avars, an annual subsidy not to invade.

In 561 the Persian king at last agreed to a fifty-year peace treaty, recognizing the Byzantines' protectorate over all of Lazica and ceding a few outposts in it in return for a small annual tribute. Justinian had thus recovered all the places that the Persians had taken. The same year Narses completed the Byzantine pacification of Italy when the last bedraggled Ostrogoths departed across the Alps. After a slow but steady and thorough reconquest, Narses administered the whole peninsula with the title of Patrician, also commanding the new Army of Italy. Yet the long war with the Ostrogoths had done grievous damage to Italy and particularly to Rome, which had changed hands five times.

With his empire and conquests secure at last, the elderly Justinian made one more attempt to conciliate the Monophysites. This time he unrealistically hoped to win over even the extreme Monophysites, who believed that Christ's fully divine nature made him incapable of sinning or of suffering pain. In 565 the emperor issued an edict embracing both this belief and the apparently incompatible Council of Chalcedon, which had affirmed Christ's full humanity. The obvious explanation for Justinian's bizarre behavior is that at age 83 his mind was no longer as keen as his ambitions. Most of his church hierarchy managed to delay taking a position on this edict until the emperor died, later the same year.

Justinian had a high opinion of his accomplishments, and it was justifiable. His buildings and his law code have won him well-deserved fame from his time to ours. His conquests in Italy, Africa, Illyricum, Spain, and the Crimea were vast. All except the Crimea were strictly speaking reconquests, because they had been part of the Western Roman Empire of which Byzantium was the eastern counterpart and institutional heir. Yet all of them had been lost before Justinian was born, and his undertaking to reclaim them was an act of both vision and audacity. Though his own advisers had doubted his African expedition could succeed, the emperor correctly guessed that the Vandal, Ostrogothic, and Visigothic kingdoms were much weaker than Byzantium, and could be defeated at an affordable price. He also understood that Africa, Italy, and Spain could be major assets for the empire.

Yet many of Justinian's plans miscarried. His long effort to bring Monophysites back into the Church came to nothing after Theodora interrupted it when it seemed about to prevail. He abandoned much of his campaign to reduce corruption in government when he returned to selling offices under dire but temporary fiscal pressure. Because his law code was in Latin, most eastern jurists could use it only with difficulty or not at all. By the end of his reign, though Byzantium was much larger than it had been at the death of Anastasius, its strength and prosperity were shaken.

Some rough calculations of the state budget show what had happened. Around 540, when Justinian already held almost everything he was to conquer, his building program and additions to the army appear to have brought his budget to some 11.3 million nomismata, larger than Anastasius's by about a third. By 565, when Justinian had conquered a little more but had canceled the pay of his frontier troops and finished most of his building, his budget appears to have been about 8.5 million nomismata, a quarter smaller than it had been in 540 and almost the same as that of Anastasius. A quarter of the empire's wealth seems simply to have disappeared.

The evident explanation for this decline in state spending is the same as that for most of Justinian's failures: the effects of the plague after 541. These were so different from most historical events in magnitude and kind that they were inevitably underestimated by most Byzantine observers, as indeed they have been by most modern historians. Not even the return of the plague in the thirteenth century wreaked such havoc, because it recurred less often and reduced a denser population. If the first outbreak had killed Justinian, as it almost did, it might well have brought on the fiscal and military collapse of the empire that he barely averted. Had the plague not occurred, Justinian's reconquests would surely have left Byzantium greatly strengthened.

As it was, the plague changed the empire profoundly, mostly for the worse. Unable to economize much more on their army, the Byzantines once again found themselves burdened by their state apparatus.

Byzantine cities shrank. The city councils, long struggling under their responsibilities for tax collection, apparently became unable to discharge them at all after the plague. The decline of the cities affected education, literature, and art, which were mostly supplied and demanded by city dwellers. This sort of harm to education was probably far greater than that caused by Justinian's forbidding pagans to teach, a measure that appears not to have been very effective.

For all its tribulations, however, Byzantium remained a much greater power than any of its neighbors. After Justinian's reconquests, it probably had twice the population and resources of Persia, its only serious rival, which also suffered sorely from the plague. The fact that the great majority of Byzantines had become Christians offset their division over the fine points of Monophysitism. Especially because the empire's economy had always been overwhelmingly rural, the modest decline of its cities was of limited importance. The Byzantine bureaucracy and army still functioned reasonably well, and the field army of 150,000 men was more than half again as big as it had been under Anastasius. If the empire was not much stronger than it had been before Justinian, neither was it much weaker.

Justinian's Successors

According to a chamberlain who had attended the dying Justinian, the old emperor named as his heir his nephew Justin, who had married Theodora's niece Sophia. This story sufficed to secure Justin's claim, since he was the most obvious successor and had made important friends during long service as supervisor of the Palace. Yet his uncle, perhaps doubting his ability, had given him quite restricted duties. In his mid-forties at his accession, Justin II naturally wanted to emerge from his uncle's shadow, and promptly reversed some of Justinian's more unpopular measures. He wisely abandoned the recent edict on Monophysitism, sensibly repaid the forced loans from senators, and foolishly stopped sending the subsidy to the Avars.

The Avars made no immediate attack on Byzantium because they were busy expanding to their west. To get out of their way, the Lombards, a German tribe living northwest of Illyricum, migrated in 568 into Italy, where Justin had for some reason relieved Narses of his command. Without Narses the Byzantine Army of Italy proved unable to halt the advance of the Lombards, who conquered the northern region that has been called Lombardy ever since. Meanwhile the Visigoths invaded Byzantine Spain, and the Moors attacked Byzantine Africa. Justin, who had become obsessed with saving money, did scarcely anything to defend the western possessions that Justinian had labored so hard to conquer.

Justin was more interested in the East, where he saw an opportunity to reconcile the moderate Monophysites. Some extreme Monophysites had begun to insist that just as Christ, as one person, necessarily had one nature, so the Trinity, with three persons, necessarily had three natures. Moderate Monophysites denounced this doctrine as Tritheism, belief in three gods. Yet in order to refute it, they had to accept the Chalcedonian argument that person might differ from nature, so that Christ could conceivably have two natures and one person at the same time. After several conferences organized by Justin, the moderate Monophysite bishops, led by Jacob Baradaeus himself, actually acknowledged that Chalcedonians were orthodox, and in 571 accepted an edict of union. Almost at once, however, their enraged priests and laity forced them to recant. Indignant at their repudiation of the union, the emperor outlawed Monophysitism, making the schism worse than before.

Instead of defending Italy against the Lombards, Africa against the Moors, or Spain against the Visigoths, in any of which a few reinforcements might have made a crucial difference, the emperor's eastern interests led him to break Justinian's carefully cultivated peace with Persia. Justin encouraged an Armenian revolt against the Persians, withheld their annual tribute, refused to negotiate, and invaded their territory. The Persians retaliated in 573 by besieging and capturing Dara, which since Anastasius' reign had been the anchor of the Byzantine frontier. The fall of Dara awoke Justin so painfully to his folly in attacking Persia that he lost his sanity and attempted suicide. His wife Sophia put his friend the Count of the Excubitors Tiberius in charge of the empire.

Tiberius, whom the demented emperor soon agreed to name Caesar, became effective ruler of the empire in his mid-thirties. Of Illyrian stock like the family of Justinian, he was a military man of some talent, with more common sense than Justin II. But Tiberius felt honor bound to recover Dara, which meant pursuing a costly and perilous war. He used some of Justin's accumulated savings to buy four years of truce from the Persians, though they refused to extend it to Armenia, where the war raged on indecisively. During this truce Tiberius not only transferred many troops from the armies of Illyricum and Thrace to the Persian frontier, but permanently increased the Army of the East with 15,000 new recruits. These measures burdened the budget and endangered the Danube frontier, but Tiberius hoped that they would insure a quick victory against Persia. When the truce expired in 578, Tiberius' general Maurice won some significant victories. The same year the mad Justin II died, and his Caesar succeeded him as Tiberius II.

Tiberius offered to exchange the land that Maurice had taken from the Persians in Armenia to regain Dara, but the Persians refused the terms. Though with a little help from Tiberius the Byzantines improved their positions slightly in Italy and Spain and greatly in Africa, in the poorly defended Balkans the Avars began threatening the border, and Slavic tribes began migrating across the Danube as far south as Greece. Maurice won further victories, at one point even approaching the Persian capital of Ctesiphon, but the Persians would not yield. The general interrupted his campaign in 582, when the ailing Tiberius summoned him to the capital. Before dying, the emperor married Maurice to his daughter and made him heir to the throne.

Maurice looked like the emperor Byzantium needed. A native of central Anatolia, aged forty-three, with a good education and a fine military record, he was intelligent and honest, and resolute to the point of obstinacy. As he well knew, he faced urgent and intractable problems. The Persian war was far from won, and reducing the army in the East was likely to prolong the war. But much of that army was desperately needed against the Avars and Slavs in the Balkans, not to mention the Lombards in Italy. Tiberius' increased spending on the army and tribute had so depleted the treasury that Tiberius had begun to delay paying the eastern army. This military and fiscal predicament offered no easy escape.

Obviously Maurice wanted an early victory in the East. For two years he sent large armies into Persian territory, but they failed to gain any decisive advantage. The emperor then transferred some troops to the Balkans, where the Avars and Slavs had become too troublesome to be ignored. After this transfer, the Byzantines kept on defeating the Persians and raiding their lands, but still could not force them to make peace. The soldiers who arrived in the Balkans barely held their own against the Avars occupying most of the Danube frontier and the Slavs holding much of the interior.

As the expense of both wars mounted, in 588 Maurice tried to save money by declaring that the government would begin supplying soldiers with arms instead of giving them the generous arms allowances established since Anastasius' day. Outraged by this cut in their real income, the eastern armies rose in mutiny. They ousted their commander Priscus, elected a commander themselves, and plundered the Syrian countryside. The delighted Persians crossed the frontier to raid. As it happened, however, the commander elected by the troops was loyal and responsible. He restored order, defeated the Persians, and drove them out of Byzantine territory. The mutiny ended after Maurice restored the army's pay, but in the confusion the Persians had seized the border city of Martyropolis, which the Byzantines failed to retake. In the meantime the Avars moved on to raid Thrace.

While the hardships of the war were straining Byzantium, they put even more pressure on Persia. By 590, the eighteenth year of the war, some Persians were exasperated enough to mount two separate revolutions. The first overthrew their king and replaced him with his son Khusrau II. The second expelled Khusrau himself and replaced him with a rebellious general. Escaping to Byzantium with some attendants, Khusrau declared that he would give up Martyropolis and Dara, and the Persian protectorates over Iberia and most of Armenia, in return for Byzantine aid in regaining the Persian throne. His usurping rival offered Maurice Martyropolis, Dara, and the long-lost border city of Nisibis simply for not interfering.

Those aware of what would happen later might say that Maurice should have chosen the usurper, preferring a favorable peace at no cost and an unstable and illegitimate Persian government. Not knowing the future, Maurice backed Khusrau. Presumably the emperor thought, with some reason, that Armenia and Iberia were more valuable than Nisibis, and that a stable and friendly Persia would be more likely to keep the peace. He sent a large Byzantine force under his general Narses along with Khusrau, who attracted support as he went. The allies took Martyropolis and Dara for Byzantium, reinstated Khusrau in the Persian capital of Ctesiphon, and crushed the usurper's army before the end of 591. Khusrau surrendered Iberia and Armenia as he had promised.

Maurice had concluded the Persian war triumphantly, winning Byzantium its most favorable eastern border since Julian's day and an apparently reliable peace with Persia. His prestige was so great that he managed to win over the Iberian Church and much of the Armenian Church from Monophysitism to Chalcedonianism. The emperor now shifted large numbers of troops from the East to the Balkans, beginning the laborious task of driving the Slavs out of Byzantine territory and restoring the Danube frontier.

To shorten this process, Maurice decided to attack the Slavs in their homeland north of the Danube, where the Byzantine army defeated them twice. To reduce the campaign's expense, in 593 he ordered the army to remain north of the Danube through the winter, living off the country. But this prospect was so disagreeable that the men were about to mutiny when their commander Priscus, who had fled the mutiny in the East five years before, agreed to lead them to safer and pleasanter winter quarters in Thrace. The Slavs resumed raiding northern Illyricum, and the emperor angrily dismissed Priscus.

The next year, still bent on economizing, Maurice declared that he was canceling the soldiers' allowances not only for arms but also for uniforms, all of which would now be provided in kind. To compensate the soldiers for their lost income, he guaranteed that those who died in battle would be replaced by their sons and that those disabled in battle would continue to receive their allowance for rations as a pension. The men still threatened to mutiny. Their new commander had both to pay the old allowances and to confirm the costly provisions meant to make up for them. Maurice dismissed him in his turn and replaced him with Priscus.

However expensive or discontented they were, the soldiers fought creditably. Priscus defeated the Slavs, faced down the Avars, and secured most of Illyricum and Thrace. But while he was chasing off the Slavs, the humiliated Avars struck back. In 597 they swept through northern Illyricum and into northern Thrace, threatening Constantinople. The Avars only withdrew the next year after catching the plague, which had recurred in the empire. Priscus counterattacked a year later, invading the Avars' territory north of Illyricum and inflicting repeated defeats on them. Maurice had now practically won his Balkan war, but warfare and plague had exhausted the Byzantines as well.

In 602 the emperor renewed his order to have the Balkan armies winter north of the Danube and live off the land. With little more to fear from the Slavs, the soldiers might have obeyed, had the weather not taken a turn for the worse. Their commander, Maurice's brother Peter, could still have averted a mutiny by rescinding the order; but he would not, knowing that such concessions had always brought dismissal. Rather than obey him, his exasperated men openly rebelled, chose a junior officer named Phocas as their commander, and marched on Constantinople.

Maurice had few troops in the capital, and found that his parsimony had left him unpopular there as well. The rebels offered the throne to

Maurice's eldest son Theodosius, who declined, then to Theodosius' father-in-law Germanus, who hesitated. As Maurice and his family fled the city, the rebels proclaimed their leader Phocas emperor. Phocas captured and executed Maurice along with his brother and his five younger sons. The only son to escape was Theodosius, who had been sent to beg the Persian king Khusrau to help Maurice, as Maurice had once helped him. Both Khusrau and the eastern commander Narses, who had once restored Khusrau to power, refused to recognize Phocas and prepared for war.

Phocas was the first eastern emperor since Diocletian to take full power without any hereditary or legal claim, and his was the first violent takeover of the East to succeed since Constantine's defeat of Licinius. Though Basiliscus had temporarily displaced Zeno, and several western emperors had lost their thrones with ruinous consequences for the West, one of the East's greatest assets had been its tradition of stable succession. It came to an end at a time when the empire had long been struggling to maintain its balance and could ill afford an internal crisis.

No doubt the three successors of Justinian could have managed the empire better than they did. Justin II was right to feel remorse at the fall of Dara: his war with Persia was unnecessary and unwise, and his resources would have been better used to defend Italy against the Lombards. The best course for Tiberius and Maurice would probably have been to accept the loss of Dara and end the Persian war before it emptied the treasury and let the Slavs and Avars overrun the Balkans. In any event, no matter how straitened his treasury was, Maurice should have learned from his three earlier experiences with mutinous soldiers not to provoke the revolt that destroyed him.

On the other hand, until the obviously avoidable fall of Maurice, Byzantium suffered no absolute catastrophes. Its new African provinces maintained themselves against all the attacks of the Moors. It held the main cities and much of the best land of Italy with very little commitment of men or money, and with slightly more effort could probably have driven out the Lombards entirely. About half of the Byzantines' Spanish province survived despite the emperors' almost total neglect. The Byzantines won their ill-considered war with Persia, then decisively defeated the Avars and Slavs. The soldiers who mutinied against Maurice had reason to think that they had fought well, and deserved to keep all their perquisites. Evidently the empire still had some reserves of strength.

A Fractious Society

From the mid-fifth to the mid-sixth century, Byzantium enjoyed great prosperity, and triumphed over its enemies at home and abroad. Byzantine political, economic, and military advances multiplied and built upon each other. Leo I's freeing the army and government from barbarian control was an important advance, as were Zeno's recovery of the northern Balkans from the Ostrogoths and Anastasius' filling the treasury and strengthening the army. Justinian's reconquests were the most striking achievement of Byzantine history, and went together with sweeping legal and administrative reforms and a splendid building program. Beginning with the later reign of Justinian, however, the army and government had to go to greater and greater lengths to support the enlarged empire.

Meanwhile the imperial government, Christianity, and Greek culture failed to make much more progress in unifying Byzantine society. This was perhaps to be expected. By now the provinces had fully adapted to the more pervasive administration introduced by Diocletian. Once nearly all Byzantines had become Christian, as they had by the late sixth century, Christianity had done most of what it could do to unify the empire. By the end of the sixth century knowledge of Greek had reached its natural limits, almost entirely replacing its fellow Indo-European languages in Thrace and Anatolia but unable to overcome less compatible Hamitic or Semitic languages like Coptic or Syriac. Moreover, Justinian had reconquered several million Latin speakers who knew hardly any Greek and were unlikely to learn much more. So sixth-century Byzantium had three parts: a well-Hellenized center, an only superficially Hellenized east, and a Latinized west.

The central part consisted of Greece, Thrace, and Anatolia, which were later to form the whole of the Byzantine Empire and were already becoming its core. Almost all the inhabitants of this region came to speak Greek by the end of the sixth century, though a good deal less than half their ancestors had been Greeks. The only significant linguistic minorities to remain were Armenians in the far east, Latin-speakers in the north, and some Illyrians in the west who had escaped Hellenization and Latinization by being isolated in the mountains between the two linguistic zones. The metropolis of the whole region was Constantinople, now the empire's unquestioned capital and by far its largest city. The Patriarchate of Constantinople included most of this Greek-speaking territory, though not all, because Greece itself was subject to the Papacy. The region's Christians were overwhelmingly Chalcedonian, but not necessarily hostile to limited efforts to win over moderate Monophysites.

Most emperors, generals, and bureaucrats came from this heartland, though its Latin-speaking north, a major recruiting ground for the army, produced a disproportionate number of emperors and generals, including Leo I, Justinian, Belisarius, Tiberius, and Maurice, not to mention Phocas. Despite these men's efforts to defend their native lands, northern Illyricum and Thrace remained almost as impoverished and endangered as before. Many peasants joined the army because their prospects at home were so bleak, and the main consumers of their small surplus of food were probably the soldiers on the Danube frontier. To the south, Greece was almost as poor, especially after the Slavs raided it in the later sixth century. Southern Thrace suffered less from invasions and benefited from the market provided by Constantinople. Anatolia, which was as well located as Thrace to profit from the economic stimulus of the capital, enjoyed peace except for occasional outbreaks of brigandage, and grew richer until the arrival of the plague. The population of Constantinople probably approached 400,000 in the early sixth century. Then the plague devastated it along with the other cities of Anatolia and Greece, depressing the economy almost everywhere.

The eastern region consisting of Egypt and Syria had never been homogeneous. Limited knowledge of Greek and partial rejection of the Council of Chalcedon set Egypt and Syria apart from the Greek core without joining them to each other, since Coptic and Syriac, their main languages and the languages of their Monophysite churches, were mutually unintelligible. As Justinian's attention shifted toward the West, and Constantinople eclipsed Antioch and Alexandria, Syria and Egypt occupied somewhat less of the government's attention than before. Because the plague hit hardest at cities and coastlands, where ships carried infected rats and fleas, it depopulated the Greek-speaking parts of Syria and Egypt more than the countryside and interior, leaving the region less Hellenized than before. Yet if archeology is any guide, the fifth and early sixth centuries were a time of extraordinary demographic and economic growth in Syria and Palestine, when both agriculture and trade expanded. The plague almost spared the interior of Syria, though the interior of Egypt must have suffered a good deal because of the boat traffic up and down the Nile.

The West of the empire – Justinian's reconquests in Africa, Italy, and Spain – was always the poorest part, and soon became poorer still. While the three reconquered lands had the Latin language in common, they were geographically isolated from each other and from the East. Although up to 540 Belisarius took Africa and most of Italy without causing much disruption or damage, the later wars with the Moors, Ostrogoths, and Lombards, and again the plague, did much more harm. Africa was the most fortunate of the reconquests, because the Byzantines finally overcame the Moors and established real peace there. Byzantine Spain was never much more than a set of embattled outposts. In Italy the Byzantines had barely defeated the Ostrogoths when the Lombards invaded, beginning an endless war and soon conquering more than half the peninsula. Italy became badly depopulated and ruralized, and Rome shrank to the size of a small town. Justinian's successors, preoccupied with their problems in the East, mostly let their western possessions fend for themselves.

Through all these military struggles, the Byzantine army performed better than it had in the previous period. Not only did it conquer vast new lands in the West, but it fought stoutly in its various defensive campaigns, despite sometimes inadequate support from the emperors. The crucial change was evidently Anastasius' raising the pay of the field armies enough to improve their morale and to attract enough native volunteers to match the barbarians. The numbers of the field soldiers swelled from some 95,000 to 150,000 with Justinian's creation of the four new field armies of Armenia, Africa, Italy, and Spain.

Yet the garrison armies, already of limited value, continued to decline. Anastasius raised their pay only slightly, and Justinian stopped giving them any regular pay at all, leaving them only some allowances. Although Justinian kept the field armies' pay at the level set by Anastasius, when financially pressed he delayed the payrolls, provoking serious mutinies in Africa and Italy. Later Maurice did try to reduce the field soldiers' pay, finally provoking them to overthrow him. Effective and loyal if paid in full and on time, the sixth-century field army had also become expensive, and as the century wore on became hard to afford.

Along with the field army's performance, another striking improvement after 457 was the end of the succession of weak emperors. Though the weakness of the three previous monarchs and the length of their reigns may have resulted from accidents of heredity and longevity, the reversal of the trend was the hard-won achievement of Leo I and Zeno. Except for the young Leo II and the aged Justin I, who had Zeno and Justinian to rule for them, not one of the emperors of this period was inert or inept. Beginning with Leo I, the emperors not only broke the power of their barbarian generals but subdued insubordinate native commanders like Illus and Vitalian. The rulers seem also to have asserted their control over their other courtiers and bureaucrats, reducing corruption and improving efficiency. After reclaiming this control when times were good, the emperors maintained it under less prosperous and peaceful conditions.

The system of taxation seems to have improved along with the bureaucracy. Anastasius' monetarization of many levies and payments in kind surely helped. As the class of the decurions continued to decline, Anastasius largely superseded them by appointing officials for each city who served as tax farmers. These kept revenues at a high level, assisted by the remaining decurions, who could still be constrained to pay what they could not collect. That Anastasius could raise spending and accumulate a record surplus demonstrates that revenues were rising.

Although the higher revenues must also have reflected economic expansion, such expansion alone would merely have led to more tax evasion if the collectors had slackened their efforts. When the plague arrived, the success of Justinian's officials in keeping up receipts by fair means or foul is particularly notable. While poor taxpayers doubtless suffered, the government apparently devoted its most strenuous efforts to collecting from decurions and senators. Justinian in particular tended to choose officials from humble backgrounds, like John the Cappadocian, who would be loyal to the emperor rather than to rich and powerful friends and relatives.

In the later fifth century the government appears to have managed to stop the remaining decurions from escaping their duties by becoming senators. Membership in the senate ceased to be hereditary and became limited to those who had held high office. Former decurions, struck from the roll of the senate, had to resume their duties on city councils, unless they became too impoverished to fulfil them. Justinian, who with his peasant origins had little use for aristocrats anyway, was quite ready to tax and confiscate the wealth of senators, especially after some senators backed the Nika Revolt against him. In the West the decline of Italy and the city of Rome ruined the fortunes of the western senators. The eastern senators, formerly poorer than western ones, by the end of the sixth century were the richest men in the empire, but growing fewer, poorer, and more dependent on the emperor than they had been. Meanwhile the power of the bishops and the resources at their disposal increased, as they gained a voice in choosing provincial governors and their courts received jurisdiction over some civil cases.

This whole period saw considerable urban and even rural unrest. Sometime in the fifth century the government gave the racing clubs of the Blues and Greens responsibility for staging public entertainments, perhaps to keep the honorary officials who had formerly staged the games and shows from courting popularity. The unintended result was to make the clubs themselves popular and powerful. They often led riots in Constantinople and other cities, usually out of pure rowdiness but sometimes with grievances against the government. The Blues and Greens aggravated a trend toward rioting that had been evident before them and included brigandage in the countryside. New prosperity, new poverty, and the many dislocations of the plague led to an awareness that the present distribution of wealth and power could be changed, perhaps by violence.

Archeology reveals a strong growth of cities up to the time of the plague, a general contraction afterwards, and throughout the period gradual changes in the patterns of urban life. New buildings encroached upon the wide and regular streets and large open squares laid out in Hellenistic and Roman times. In particular, uniform shops lining market squares gave way to disorderly shops lining narrowed streets. The many new churches were built wherever land was available, with little regard for the earlier city plan. After the plague, as raiders and invaders threatened more of the empire, new city walls went up, with reduced circuits that doubtless reflected reduced populations.

In most cities not just pagan temples and gymnasiums but hippodromes, theaters, and baths began to be abandoned or adapted to other uses. As the old city councils disappeared, so did the need for large public buildings and public spaces. Church disapproval continued to take its toll on entertainments involving violence or nudity, and finally closed the hippodromes, theaters, and large baths in most towns. Though private houses may not have been smaller or less comfortable than before, most city dwellers presumably had a more limited selection of goods and amusements to choose from. Only the largest cities, like Constantinople, Alexandria, and Thessalonica, resisted the trend.

After the plague, cities became not just smaller but somewhat fewer. In Italy and Illyricum, constant warfare turned some cities into ghost towns, while most of the rest dwindled to insignificant villages. Antioch never really recovered from being devastated by earthquakes and sacked by the Persians. Despite Justinian's reconquest of so much territory, the number of cities in the empire with populations over 10,000 might have declined from thirty or so to about twenty. In the

West, Carthage may have been the only city of that size after the ruin of Rome. In Illyricum, Thessalonica was probably the only such city after the Slavs sacked the ancient cities of Greece. The change was less pronounced for the great majority living in villages, which were less tempting to invaders, less dependent on imported food, and less vulnerable to the plague. In inland Syria, where the land can never have been very fertile, villagers were building large new houses up to the end of the sixth century.

Trade, whose main purpose was to bring food to the cities from the countryside, would have expanded before the plague and contracted after it. The economic expansion of the fifth and early sixth centuries would first have given people more money to spend on imported goods of all kinds. The silk trade seems to have boomed to supply the rich, and a native silk industry developed under Justinian, using silkworms brought from China. Poorer people who produced a surplus would have wanted spices from India to preserve their food and to improve its taste when it began to spoil. In fact, the growth of the spice trade from India through the Red Sea to Egypt probably speeded the arrival of the plague, which first appeared in Egypt and reportedly came from Ethiopia.

No doubt the demographic and economic contraction after the plague had widely varying impacts on the survivors. As the empire's economy became even more concentrated on subsistence farming, trade would have declined even more sharply than the economy as a whole. Because any demographic decline makes labor more valuable and land less so, it tends to benefit the working poor at the expense of the landed rich, and rural producers at the expense of urban consumers. Less surplus wealth would therefore have remained for large landholders and for the state, and both large estates and government revenues evidently shrank. The natural result was that by the end of the sixth century senators, decurions, and other landholders and traders were growing poorer and less powerful, and that the Byzantine state was struggling to meet its expenses.

A Diverse Culture

By the end of the sixth century, with the aid of very little persecution, the Church had practically extinguished paganism. While some vestiges of pagan practice remained as popular customs, especially in the countryside, these had ceased to have much religious significance, though preachers denounced them from time to time. Except for Jews, who were widely dispersed through the empire's cities with a small concentration in northern Palestine, practically everyone in the empire was a baptized Christian. Arianism and Nestorianism had almost disappeared from the empire. The only heresy with a significant following among Byzantines was Monophysitism, primarily in a moderate form that differed from orthodoxy in little but semantics. Even if Christians often failed to live up to the demands of their faith, the Church, with its doctrine of Original Sin, had never had many illusions about human perfectibility in this life.

The wealth of the Church came from the voluntary donations of its members. Most donors were private citizens, though Christian emperors and officials also contributed, occasionally from public funds. Since donors gave money not only to build churches, monasteries, and charitable institutions but to maintain them in the future, the Church acquired property that produced rents and other income independent of current donations. Much of this money went to relieving the needy, especially the poor in the cities. Donors also liked to display their munificence by financing large and elaborate buildings for the Church, which almost always accepted them.

The Church supported its bishops, priests, deacons, and secular employees with pay ranging from miserable to princely. As bishops and priests gained a measure of comfort and a certain position in society, some began to pay bribes for their ordination, despite a long-standing prohibition of any such payments as simony. While clerical corruption seems not to have been rampant, naturally a number of the hundreds of thousands of clergy and monks strayed from the strict but sometimes inconsistent rules and precepts that governed their behavior.

Inevitably, an organization as large, influential, and rich as the Church developed its own internal politics. On the one hand, the Church distrusted personal ambition, suspecting that anyone who coveted ordination was unworthy of it. On the other hand, bishops and priests had legitimate ambitions to defend what they thought was orthodoxy, and often wanted to defend or extend the traditional prerogatives of their sees. The Council of Chalcedon had helped clarify the rules for episcopal and patriarchal jurisdiction, but these remained a jumble of Christian traditions and imitations of the civil administration.

As a rule, every city with a city council also had a bishop. The bishop of the capital of every civil province had the title of metropolitan with jurisdiction over the other bishops of the province. Yet these principles had their exceptions and ambiguities, and exactly what the jurisdiction meant could also be ambiguous. Everyone agreed that the Pope had some sort of authority over all bishops, but this authority did not necessarily go beyond a precedence of honor and a limited right to hear appeals from the decisions of other bishops.

The enrichment and politicization of the Church hampered its efforts to settle the bickering over Monophysitism. Justin II's momentary success in reconciling the moderate Monophysites showed that a solution was possible in theory but virtually impossible in practice. Although theological terms could be found to resolve the schism, no churchman emerged with enough authority to impose them in the years after the Council of Chalcedon. Finally the two sides became almost irreconcilable, each stubbornly defending its doctrines for the sake of tradition.

The rise of Monophysitism coincided with the final victory of Christianity over paganism and the end of the age of the great Church Fathers like Saints Athanasius and Basil. These three phenomena were probably related. By the sixth century the Church no longer had clear enemies to combat. While expecting it to care for the poor, pay its bills, and maintain its buildings, and criticizing it if it failed to do any of these, many also grumbled that the Church handled too much money. As churchmen became comfortably established, they came to seem less like saints and more like politicians, and consequently lacked the prestige they needed to resolve the Monophysite controversy.

Monks too lost some of their earlier fame. This was an age of respect for the dead saint rather than for the living holy man, as an attentive reading even of the period's encomiastic hagiography will show. The most popular saints remained the early Christian martyrs, the first hermits, and the confessors persecuted for opposing Arianism. Contemporary monks and ascetics were too numerous, and their opportunities for heroism too limited, to allow them to gain comparable notoriety and adulation. Moreover, the great mass of the people never saw a living hermit, while practically everyone had heard of the earlier saints and many had visited their shrines. Monks therefore had only a little more chance than bishops of winning over Monophysites to Chalcedonianism or Chalcedonians to Monophysitism.

After Zeno and Anastasius had followed the precedents of Constantine, Constantius II, and Valens by trying to ban discussion of the theological issues, Justinian moved more aggressively to fill the gap in church leadership. During his early military and political successes he had almost enough prestige to suppress Monophysitism; then his best efforts failed, undermined by Theodora and the troubles of his later reign. He and Theodora did however add further Christian features to civil law. Theodora, whose mother had prostituted her as a child, persuaded Justinian to legislate against forced prostitution and the sexual abuse of children. Justinian also abolished the longstanding Roman practice of divorce by mutual consent, though Justin II bowed to popular demand and reinstated it. Sometimes Justinian legislated for the Church itself, as when he gave the custom that bishops should be celibate the force of law.

The Church demanded more than mere compliance with civil laws, though it partly relaxed its old penitential rules for sins committed after baptism. Now sinners could undergo less demanding penances, and go through them more than once before the deathbed repentance that had always been admitted. By the sixth century various clerics compiled collections of canon law, drawn from the canons passed by ecumenical and local church councils. Yet in the absence of a single definitive collection of canons in both Latin and Greek, church practices began to diverge from region to region, with the jurisdiction of the Pope particularly differing from the eastern patriarchates.

Thus the Western Church prohibited the ordination of married men, while the Eastern Church permitted it, only forbidding marriage after ordination. The Western Church forbade divorced persons to remarry, but the Eastern permitted those who divorced an adulterous husband or wife to remarry. The Western Church allowed the widowed unlimited remarriages, while the Eastern set a limit of three marriages even for the repeatedly widowed. While the Western Church sometimes granted full dispensations from its canons, the Eastern Church more often granted an indulgence, which declared the exception permissible but still sinful. Such condemnation with permission applied to all second and third marriages in the East. Similarly, the Western Church allowed killing in battle, while the Eastern Church maintained Basil of Caesarea's position that such killing was sinful though necessary. Such divergence between Eastern and Western practices developed without much awareness by either side of the other's position.

In higher culture, throughout the empire the dominance of classical Greek became less widespread. In the West the old tradition that every educated man should know the Greek Classics had been waning even

before the barbarian invasions, and by the time of Justinian's reconquests few westerners read Greek. The only ones who commonly spoke
it were descendants of ancient Greek colonists in Sicily and southern
Italy. In the East, where some of the last pagans were professors, many
Christians worried that traditional higher education might be keeping
paganism alive. Among the worriers was Justinian, who in 529 tried to
ban pagans from teaching, as before him Julian had tried to ban Christians from teaching classical texts. Although Justinian's edict was spor-
adically enforced, it probably hastened the disappearance of the class of
pagan professors, who had shared the religious beliefs of the authors
they taught.

By itself, the extinction of paganism need not have had much impact
on education. The empire had long had many Christians with a thorough education in the ancient Classics. Christian professors knew the
pagan texts as well as pagan professors did, and taught them in much
the same way. Success in the civil service still required a good classical
education in writing and speaking, and practically all senators, most
decurions, and many bishops and priests had had such training. The
most ambitious authors, pagan and Christian alike, continued to write in
the artificially correct classical Greek that their readers expected of
them. Yet the decurions and even the senators were becoming fewer
and less important, while a decreasing number of bishops, priests, and
laymen saw the need for the traditional school curriculum and literary
style.

At first traditional literature proved hardy. Up to the middle of the
sixth century a literary golden age produced a series of first-rate historians and poets, both secular and religious, though today not all their
work has survived complete. The last pagan historian was the unexceptional Zosimus around 500, but in the next generation a Christian from
Palestine, Procopius of Caesarea, ranked as one of the great historians of
any age. Drawing on his experience as secretary of Justinian's general
Belisarius, Procopius wrote a gripping and panoramic account of Belisarius' wars with the Persians, Vandals, and Ostrogoths, supplemented
by a scathing unpublished attack on Justinian and Theodora, *The
Secret History*. His work was continued by a succession of similar classicizing histories down to the end of Maurice's reign. The immediate
continuer of Procopius' history, Agathias of Myrina, was also one of a
circle of classicizing poets. A classicizing Latin poet from reconquered
Africa, Corippus, made his name first at Carthage and then at Constantinople.

While such authors could write as if they had scarcely heard of Christianity when they wanted to imitate the ancient Classics, they could also use their talents in the service of the Church. Agathias and his friends wrote both erotic and religious poetry, and the most talented Greek poet of the age, the Syrian Romanus the Melode, composed only Christian hymns. Around the turn of the fifth century, an extraordinary theologian made extensive use of Neoplatonist philosophy, enhancing his work's reputation by using the name of St Paul's disciple Dionysius the Areopagite. As his pseudonym suggests, Pseudo-Dionysius would have been more at home in the age of the Fathers, who had often drawn on philosophy to write original theology. Most contemporary theologians, whether Chalcedonian or Monophysite, were more conventional and less learned.

Late in the sixth century, a falling off in the quality and quantity of all literature became unmistakable. The feeling spread that Christians should learn the Bible rather than the pagan Classics, and should write the comparatively simple Greek of the New Testament, and of the Septuagint translation of the Old Testament. A literature grew up in something approaching spoken Greek, including not only hagiography and other inspirational works but a world chronicle by John Malalas of Antioch. Some saints' lives and Christian chronicles were also composed in Syriac, though most works in Syriac, Coptic, and Armenian continued to be translations of Greek religious works. By the late sixth century, what little was still written in the Latin-speaking part of the empire was also overwhelmingly religious in content. As secular literature became less common in Greek, it practically disappeared in other languages. All over the empire secular schools were dwindling, and literacy was apparently declining. The golden age that had peaked under Justinian had passed.

Art and architecture followed a pattern similar to that of literature, with an advance followed by a plateau and a decline. The years from the middle of the fifth to the middle of the sixth century saw a flowering of early Byzantine art, which reached its apex during the early reign of Justinian. At Constantinople the lavish building of churches and monuments of the early fifth century proceeded apace. Under Zeno elaborate churches went up even in his remote and primitive homeland of Isauria. St Sophia remains an indisputable masterpiece, with its gigantic size, its structural complexity, and its imposing effect. Yet it was only the most famous of Justinian's many churches, fortifications, and other buildings, which transformed Constantinople and many other places all over the

Figure 5 The interior of the Church of St Sophia, Constantinople, showing the dome and apse. St Sophia (more accurately, the Holy Wisdom, meaning Christ as the Word of God) was the largest and most sumptuous Byzantine church ever built. Though the architecture is Justinian's, many of the mosaics are later Byzantine work, and the furnishings shown are Turkish. (*Photo*: Dumbarton Oaks, Washington, D.C., © copyright 1999)

empire. Though paintings and mosaics have survived less well than architecture, those that remain are of comparable quality and appear to be the work of a large group of highly productive artists.

After Justinian the building boom was over, and his successors left few monuments. Even in much more humble private construction, like houses in the Syrian countryside, the strong growth that had begun in the fifth century slowed markedly in the mid-sixth. As already noted, when the cities became smaller new building in them became more slipshod and less monumental. These changes in art, architecture, literature, and education can all be considered declines, because the total production of each contracted, and what was still produced showed less versatility, virtuosity, and competence.

In some cases, particularly in literature, some Christians may have thought that greater simplicity was a virtue. In most cases, however, as with smaller and wobblier houses and churches, no one is likely to have thought the change was for the better. Everyone simply had to make do with whatever was available and affordable. If Christian moralists believed that less wealth was good for people, few of those who became impoverished are likely to have agreed with them. Ignorance, though less unpopular than poverty, was more often the incidental result of seeking holiness than a positive goal in itself.

As the seventh century began, Byzantium was in many ways over-extended. Although its borders had become almost as far-flung as those of the whole fourth-century Roman Empire, it held much less territory in the West than it had held then, with a much smaller population, economy, and army with which to defend itself. Byzantium faced defensive threats on nearly all its frontiers from Persians, Avars, Lombards, Visigoths, Moors, and others. The cities that had long been the empire's administrative, economic, and cultural centers had begun to shrink, and defending them and maintaining their monuments was becoming more and more burdensome. After 602, with far less than its third-century resources, the empire was to face an internal and external crisis as serious as the one that in the third century had almost brought it down.

4

CATASTROPHE AND
CONTAINMENT (602–780)

Heraclius the Defender

Phocas' reign was practically doomed from the start. Aged fifty-five, a simple soldier from the Balkans as several of his predecessors had been, he had enough cunning to make up for his inexperience with the workings of government, but not to compensate for his lack of a legal claim to the throne. Any members of the old government whom he left alive were liable to plot against him; but the more of them he killed, the more he frightened the rest and their supporters into hostility. At first, apart from Maurice and his closest male relatives, Phocas executed only two officials. The year after his accession, when Maurice's widow Constantina plotted to proclaim her son's father-in-law Germanus, Phocas merely forced them both to enter the Church. But two years later, when Constantina and Germanus conspired again, Phocas executed them.

Phocas declared that he had found and killed Maurice's eldest son Theodosius, but the eastern commander Narses claimed that Theodosius had found refuge with him. Which story was true is hard to say, though Narses seems to have had less reason to lie than Phocas. The Persian king Khusrau recognized the supposed Theodosius, on whose behalf he attacked Phocas' armies in the East. Phocas brought in troops from the Balkans, opening the way for the Slavs to invade there. In several fierce campaigns, Phocas' forces finally captured and killed their fellow Byzantine Narses, but lost repeatedly to the Persians, who destroyed the border stronghold of Dara. Phocas gained nothing when the alleged Theodosius died, because Khusrau, with no legitimate

88

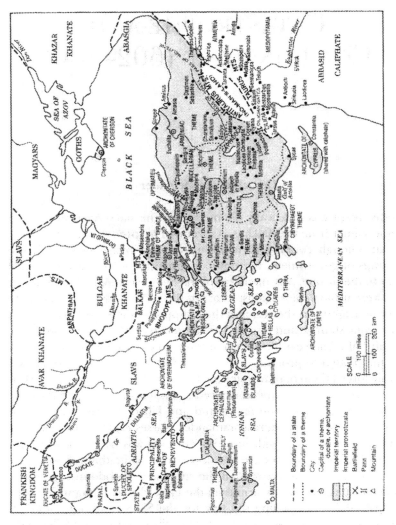

Map 3 The Empire *ca.* 780

heir to help, began conquering border territory for himself, including most of Armenia.

Since the late sixth century, Byzantine Africa and Italy had become increasingly autonomous under civil and military commanders known as exarchs. In 608 the Exarch of Africa Heraclius rebelled against Phocas. The Exarch sent his nephew Nicetas overland to Egypt, which after a bitter fight with Phocas' forces he secured. Nicetas' rebels then advanced into southern Syria, while the Persians took eastern Syria and raided Anatolia up to the Asian suburbs of the capital. The Slavs overran northern Illyricum, and the Blues and Greens began fighting each other in several of the empire's remaining cities. Finally the Exarch Heraclius sent a naval expedition to Constantinople under his son, also named Heraclius. In 610, the younger Heraclius landed in the city, captured and executed Phocas, and became emperor in his place.

The new emperor, however, seemed unequal to the tremendous task of righting the foundering empire. In his mid-thirties, of Armenian stock but familiar with not much more than Africa, Heraclius had limited military and political experience and only such legitimacy as he could claim for having overthrown a usurper. Khusrau considered him no more legitimate than Phocas. On the other hand, no one living had a better right to the Byzantine throne, and Heraclius possessed a melancholy doggedness and strategic sense that allowed him to survive and grow in office.

Heraclius kept his cousin Nicetas as commander of his men in Egypt and Syria, and made Maurice's old general Priscus commander of the larger army in Anatolia. In 611 a Persian force drove a wedge between the two by seizing Antioch and the rest of northern Syria, while other Persians eluded Priscus to raid central Anatolia. The emperor dismissed Priscus and himself took charge of the Anatolian army. As the first reigning emperor to fight an enemy since Theodosius I, Heraclius attacked the Persians near Antioch in 613. After a struggle, they drove him off, advanced into Palestine, and took Jerusalem. There they seized the relic believed to be the True Cross of Christ, deported most Christians from the city, and allowed Jews to resettle it. By this time the Avars had assumed leadership over the Slavs and joined them in overrunning nearly all of Illyricum except the coasts.

Now that almost half the empire had been lost, in 616 Heraclius halved the army's pay, probably substituting free issues of arms and uniforms for money as Maurice had tried to do more than twenty years before. Although mutinous soldiers had frustrated Maurice, the emergency had grown so dire that the troops apparently accepted the same measure from Heraclius without protest. Heraclius also halved the salaries of his civil officials, evidently without compensation. Soon the emperor also stopped the grain dole for Constantinople that dated back to Constantine I. Even with these drastic economies, Byzantium remained on the verge of bankruptcy.

While the northern Persian army plundered Anatolia, the southern Persian army began conquering Egypt. As the Persians incorporated Egypt and Syria into their empire, they curried favor with the local Monophysites by forcing the Jews out of Jerusalem. The Persians completed their conquest of Egypt in 620 when Nicetas surrendered Alexandria to them. Since Khusrau refused to discuss peace even after making such vast conquests, his plan must have been to go on conquering, taking Anatolia and possibly even Constantinople.

Heraclius realized that his only chance was to attack. To collect the money he needed for an all-out offensive against the Persians, he obtained permission from the Patriarch Sergius to borrow and melt down gold and silver plate from the empire's churches. Heraclius seems to have concentrated on preserving as much of the army as possible, because about three-quarters of it had survived all his catastrophic defeats. Leaving the last of Byzantine Spain to the Visigoths, and withdrawing most of his troops from Thrace under a truce with the Avars, Heraclius massed some 50,000 men in Anatolia.

In 622 the emperor led his army to eastern Anatolia, where the main Persian army was raiding under the Persians' best general, Shahrvarāz. After prolonged maneuvering, Heraclius brought Shahrvarāz to battle and defeated him. While not overwhelming, this was the first real Byzantine victory of the war, and it revived Byzantine morale and forced the Persians to evacuate Anatolia. The emperor was ready to advance into Armenia, but the Avars broke their truce and invaded southern Thrace. After negotiations in which the Avars almost captured him, Heraclius bought another truce from them.

Now the emperor prepared for a decisive strike at Persia itself. He returned to his army in Anatolia in 624, taking his wife Martina along and leaving the Patriarch Sergius to rule at Constantinople. Heraclius marched right through Armenia and into the Persian province of Atropatene (modern Azerbaijan). Though Khusrau gathered an army to resist him, even after summoning Shahrvarāz the king found himself outnumbered, and Heraclius chased him out of Atropatene. The Byzantines then wintered in the Caucasus, where they hired local mercenaries. The next year the Persian forces were larger than before, but in a lengthy campaign in Armenia Heraclius defeated them three times.

Khusrau responded vigorously by allying with the Avars for a joint attack on Constantinople. In 626 Shahrvarāz made his way around Heraclius' army and reached the city's Asian suburbs, though only after the emperor had reinforced the city itself. The Avar khan besieged the city walls and sent his Slavic allies in canoes to ferry Persians across the strait; but on the return trip the Byzantines sank the canoes with both Slavs and Persians. Then the Byzantines intercepted a letter from Khusrau ordering the execution of Shahrvarāz. They passed it on to the general, who withdrew his forces to plot his revenge. Without Persian support, the Avars and Slavs also gave up the siege.

The tide now turned in the Byzantines' favor. Refusing to obey his king, Shahrvarāz held Syria and Egypt for himself with his army. The Avars and Slavs fell out and began fighting each other. Heraclius made an alliance with the Khazars, a Turkish people to the north of the Caucasus, and defeated the Persians in Iberia. By 627, reinforced by troops no longer needed at Constantinople, the emperor is said to have had some 70,000 Byzantine and allied troops. With these he marched through Armenia and Atropatene, making for the Persian heartland in Mesopotamia. At the end of the year, near the ruins of Nineveh, he inflicted a sharp defeat on the king's only remaining army. By early 628 he was threatening the Persian capital of Ctesiphon. When Khusrau still refused to make peace, his own son Kavād II deposed and killed him.

The new Persian government agreed to surrender all the captives it had taken and all the conquests it had made since the beginning of the war. These concessions amounted to less than they seemed, because nearly all the conquests were in the hands of the rebellious Shahrvarāz. But in 630, after Kavād had died, probably of the plague, Shahrvarāz agreed to hand over Egypt, Syria, and the True Cross in return for Byzantine recognition as king of Persia. He seized the Persian throne, only to be assassinated after two months. Meanwhile Heraclius restored the prewar frontier and brought the Cross back to Jerusalem. At last he returned in triumph to his capital with his faithful wife Martina.

History has seen few reversals of fortune as dramatic as this. Much of the reason for the reversal is that at first the Byzantines were divided by the usurpation of Phocas and overextended, while later in the war their enemies were the ones who were overextended and divided between Khusrau and Shahrvarāz, and between the Avars and the Slavs.

Steadfast defenders have advantages against reckless attackers, and the treasures of the Church and the walls of Constantinople were particular assets for the Byzantines. But Heraclius deserves much credit for keeping his head, choosing to save soldiers rather than land, and finally making a well-timed and skillful counterattack.

The emperor made good use of the glory he had won to tackle the maddening Monophysite schism. He and his Patriarch Sergius proposed a compromise doctrine known as Monoenergism, according to which Christ had two natures but one "energy," a purposely nebulous term. With the victorious emperor's prestige behind it, Monoenergism quickly reconciled most of the empire's Monophysites and Chalcedonians. Because Heraclius had recovered most of the empire's lost land and kept paying the army and civil service at half the previous rate, he managed to balance his budget and begin repaying his loans from the Church. Though the war had damaged Byzantium, it had done even worse harm to the Persians and Avars, and no other strong enemy seemed in prospect.

Yet at just this time a new enemy arose. The prophet Mohammed had nearly finished forging the Arabian peninsula into a single Muslim state before he died in 632. His power passed to new religious and political leaders of the Muslims, titled caliphs, the first of whom started attacking both Byzantium and Persia the next year. When the Arabs defeated the Byzantines in Palestine, Heraclius sent the Army of the East against them under his brother Theodore. They defeated Theodore and swarmed into Syria. The Byzantines counterattacked in 636, when the Arabs met them in battle near the Yarmūk River. The Arabs won a shattering victory by driving most of the Byzantine army over a cliff into the gorge of the Yarmūk.

As he had done with the Persians, Heraclius chose a tactical retreat rather than a desperate defense. Ordering the True Cross to be brought to Constantinople from Jerusalem, he withdrew his troops from most of Syria to make a stand in Egypt. Meanwhile the Arabs overwhelmed the Persians in Mesopotamia and took their capital of Ctesiphon. Less fortunate than the Byzantines in having a capital near the Arab heartland, the Persians had committed so large a share of their resources to a forward defense that they were unable to recover from their defeat. Evidently too much hostility lingered between Byzantium and Persia to let them cooperate against their common enemy.

As Heraclius' armies lost again and again to the Arabs, his compromise doctrine of Monoenergism faltered as well. The Pope and the

Patriarch of Jerusalem rejected it for conceding too much to the Mono-physites, and the Monophysites of Egypt and Syria opposed it for con-ceding too much to the Chalcedonians. As a new compromise, in 638 the emperor and his Patriarch Sergius proposed Monotheletism, the doctrine that Christ had two natures but one will. While somewhat more coherent than Monoenergism, Monotheletism met with the same unwillingness of both sides to make concessions.

The Byzantines prepared to defend Egypt at the Nile Delta, and in a hard-fought battle managed to hold the first Arab invaders there. But in 640 the Arabs regrouped and attacked again, scattering the Byzantines and spreading over the country. Alexandria, though difficult to take by assault, was much easier to starve out once it had been isolated from its hinterland. While Heraclius reinforced Egypt several times, by now he was a sick and broken man of sixty-six. In 641 he died, shortly after abandoning Monotheletism, which the Pope had recently condemned in its turn.

Always praised for his triumph over the Persians and almost always blamed for his defeat by the Arabs, Heraclius had followed much the same strategy against both of them. In each case he offered vigorous but limited resistance, always keeping enough troops in reserve to continue resisting if he lost. He only launched a full-scale counterattack against the Persians some twenty years after they had first invaded the empire, and more than ten years after his accession; the Arab invasion was only in its eighth year when he died. To be sure, by then a successful offensive against the Arabs looked unlikely, though perhaps no more unlikely than total victory over the Persians had seemed at a comparable stage of the Persian war. Yet in both cases Heraclius staved off a com-plete collapse, like the one that was already engulfing the Persian Empire at the time of his death.

Even so, by then Byzantium's survival was in grave doubt. The Arabs' advance showed no signs of slackening, and once they had finished conquering Syria, Egypt, and Persia they were plainly ready to attack Anatolia. The empire still had an army of about 109,000 men, with a payroll that was hard to meet even at its lowered rates; but even the soldiers who were not tied down defending faraway Africa and Italy had fought erratically against the Persians and poorly against the Arabs. Once again, the Byzantines faced a dilemma that had recurred since the first appearance of the plague: their territory produced barely enough revenue to pay their army, but reducing either their army or its pay risked losing still more land.

Constans II the Reformer

Byzantium urgently needed a strong and talented ruler in 641, but Heraclius' arrangements for the succession were irregular and misguided. According to custom, his successor should have been his eldest son by his first wife, Constantine III, aged twenty-nine but tubercular; if Constantine died soon, as he was expected to do, his eleven-year-old son Constans should have been next in line. Yet out of love for his second wife Martina, the companion of his campaigns, Heraclius provided that Constantine III should rule jointly with Martina's eldest surviving son Heraclonas, aged fifteen, who would become sole emperor at Constantine's death. Popular opinion opposed Heraclonas, favoring succession by primogeniture and in any case considering Martina's marriage incestuous because she was Heraclius' niece.

Constantine III ruled only three months before dying of his tuberculosis, leaving Heraclonas to reign with his mother Martina as regent. But as commander of the eastern armies Constantine had appointed his partisan Valentine, who took up the cause of Constantine's son. As Valentine marched on Constantinople, rioters in the city forced Martina to have Constans crowned co-emperor. After Heraclonas had reigned six months, Valentine led his army into the city and deposed the young emperor and his mother. To render them ineligible to rule, Valentine cut off part of Martina's tongue and part of Heraclonas' nose. Installing Constantine's son as Constans II, the general married his daughter to the underage emperor and became the real ruler himself. Two years later Valentine tried to become co-emperor, only to be lynched by a mob loyal to Constans.

Thus Constans became his own master just before he turned fourteen. Though no doubt he consulted advisers, as every sensible emperor did, he was precocious and spirited, and began making decisions for himself. His first major initiative was an attempt to retake Egypt, where the Arabs had just completed their conquest. The year after Valentine's death, the Byzantines sailed into Alexandria to an enthusiastic welcome from the Egyptians. But after the Byzantine army had advanced into the Nile delta, the Arabs defeated it and forced it to abandon the country. In 646 the Exarch of Africa revolted, and two years later the Arabs raided his exarchate. Fortunately for Constans, the Arab raiders killed the rebel exarch, whose successor bought them off and professed his loyalty to the empire.

The Arabs' next target was the Byzantine protectorate in Armenia, the homeland of the Heraclian dynasty. Since most Armenians disliked the Council of Chalcedon but showed some interest in Monotheletism, the emperor issued an edict tolerating that compromise doctrine. The Pope condemned Constans' edict, and the Exarch of Italy took it as an excuse to rebel; but when the exarch died of the plague, Constans had the Pope arrested as a traitor and deposed. The emperor fought fiercely for Armenia, but by 654 the Arabs had taken over the whole Byzantine protectorate. They had also built a large fleet, which in 655 defeated the Byzantine navy under Constans himself.

That same year, a ferocious civil war broke out between the Arabs' Umayyad dynasty and their rival for the Caliphate, Mohammed's son-in-law Ali. These hostilities stopped the almost unbroken Arab advance for the first time since it had begun. As the Arabs spent their energies in fighting each other, Constans restored the Byzantine protectorate over Armenia. In 659 the Umayyad governor of Syria made a formal truce with the empire, even paying the Byzantines tribute so as to free his forces to fight Ali's supporters. This truce lasted three years, until the Umayyads vanquished the partisans of the murdered Ali.

The Byzantines had yet to show that they could stem the Arab onslaught without the help of the Arabs themselves. Whatever the Arabs had made a real effort to take they had taken, including Byzantine Syria, Egypt, and Armenia. Whatever the Arabs had tried to raid they had raided, including Byzantine Anatolia and Africa. The rugged terrain of Armenia and Anatolia had merely slowed them down; in a short time, they had built a fleet that could defeat the seasoned Byzantine navy. Since the death of the last Persian king in 651, the Arabs no longer had organized Persian resistance to distract them. The Caliphate, which when it was much smaller and poorer than Byzantium had already defeated it, was now much larger and richer than the battered empire.

The years of the Arab truce from 659 to 661 were certainly the approximate time, and probably the exact time, of the creation of one of the most important and mysterious Byzantine institutions: the army units known as themes (in Greek, *themata*). When the Arab truce ended in 662, Constans departed for Italy with a large army, leaving his eldest but still barely teenaged son Constantine to rule at Constantinople. At that time Constans was apparently satisfied with his measures for defending the East. The first evidence of specific themes dates from 668, when one theme was in the East and parts of three others from the

East were still in the West with Constans. As the emperor is unlikely to have created eastern themes while he was in the West, all four themes presumably existed before his departure in 662.

The word theme (*thema*) meant something like emplacement, and the themes consisted of armies stationed in specific territories that were also called themes. Their armies were formed from the field armies of earlier times, and most themes kept Hellenized forms of their former Latin names. The old armies of Armenia, the East, and Thrace thus became the Armeniac, Anatolic, and Thracesian themes, though they were now settled in eastern, central, and western Anatolia respectively. The Opsician Theme, with a name derived from a Latin word for the emperor's retinue, consisted of the two former armies in the emperor's presence, now settled in Thrace and northwestern Anatolia. The origin of the Carabisian Theme, a corps of marines with a name derived from a Greek word for ship, is less clear, but it was probably the old Army of Illyricum, now settled in Greece and southern Anatolia. These themes covered the whole empire, except for the exarchates of Africa and Italy and a few isolated outposts. Such a redeployment would have required an interval of peace, which the truce of 559–61 provided.

In later years the soldiers of the themes drew most of their income and supplies from land grants within their theme's territory, but whether this was so from the creation of the themes is disputed by modern historians. The main argument to the contrary is that no source mentions a distribution of land grants at this date; but no source mentions the distribution at any other date either, and in this period of poor sources such an omission is less strange than it would be later. The obvious reason for settling the armies in particular territories is that they received land there; the evident purpose of the grants was to allow their cash pay to be lowered, and at this time, after so many territorial losses, the Byzantine government must have had great trouble raising cash. The grants are most likely to have come from the former imperial estates, which were large in the sixth century and exiguous by the ninth century.

Although the soldiers continued to receive in nomismata half of their already reduced pay, they were apparently expected to purchase their arms and uniforms from the income of their lands, whether in cash or in kind. Beginning about 659, lead seals that survive from vanished documents reveal a network of state warehouses throughout the empire, which seem to have sold the troops their arms and uniforms. Suggesting the warehouses' military function, the seals show that the operator of at least five such warehouses between 659 and 668 also served as the first recorded Military Logothete, the minister in charge of paying the army.

Constans' reforms appear to have included a reorganization of the central bureaucracy. Its principal officials were three new ministers called logothetes: the Military Logothete to pay the army, a General Logothete in charge of tax collection, and a Postal Logothete in charge of diplomacy and internal security. These officials replaced the earlier finance ministers, the Count of the Sacred Largesses and the Count of the Private Estate. The Protoasecretis, another new official, was in charge of government records; the Quaestor remained the chief legal official. The head of each theme was titled a strategus (or for the Opsician Theme a count), and served both as military governor of the theme's territory and commander of its army. The exarchs already had similar powers over Italy and Africa, though their growing independence showed the perils of such an arrangement.

The main purpose of Constans' expedition to the West must have been to strengthen his control over Italy and Africa. The emperor seems to have drawn his expeditionary force from the Carabisian, Opsician, and Anatolic themes. In 663 he reached Italy, where he visited Rome to pay his respects to the current Pope and to collect money. The emperor then moved to Sicily and amassed more cash. When the half-independent Exarch of Africa refused to pay what he was ordered, his own men overthrew him, and Constans appointed a new exarch. Whether Constans introduced land grants for the soldiers of Italy and Africa at this time is uncertain; but quite possibly he did, since seals show that both exarchates soon had warehouses, and parts of both exarchates later became regular themes.

Meanwhile the Arabs had retaken Armenia and resumed raiding Africa and Anatolia, and especially the new Armeniac Theme on the frontier. In 668 the Strategus of the Armeniacs rebelled with the support of the Caliph, but his revolt collapsed when he died in an accident. The same year, however, the Count of the Opsician Theme, who was with the emperor in Sicily, assassinated Constans and proclaimed himself emperor. This revolt also failed when the soldiers of Italy and Africa crushed it, but it showed that Constans had given the themes' commanders a dangerous amount of power.

In other respects, however, the system of themes and military land grants had great advantages for the empire. It cut basic military expenses by almost two-thirds through halving the payroll and shifting spending for uniforms, arms, fodder, and horses from the state to the soldiers themselves. This assured the empire's solvency for the foreseeable future. Moreover, the grants left the soldiers better supplied than before; the process of settlement stationed some of them near any point an enemy might choose to attack, and gave them an incentive to defend their stations, because their own lands were there. Though the soldiers might flee an enemy raid, they had good reason to return after the raiders left. As long as the themes lasted, enemies found it hard to make lasting conquests at Byzantine expense.

In later years Constans II was the least acclaimed of Byzantium's great emperors. He had made no conquests, and won no victories against the enemy; he had pursued an unpopular religious policy, died by assassination, and lived at a time of the worst sources in Byzantine history. Yet his achievements, begun when he was little more than a child, required talent both to plan and to perform, and were vital for the empire's future. Besides creating the themes and rationalizing the bureaucracy, Constans managed his finances carefully, stopped the drift of Byzantine Italy and Africa toward independence, and built many necessary fortifications in Anatolia. He thus readied Byzantium to survive the long struggle with the Arabs that stretched ahead of it.

Raids and Revolutions

Constans' son Constantine IV, though less brilliant than his father and probably under twenty at his accession, was level-headed, decisive, and already experienced. At the news of his father's murder, he mustered an army and sailed for Sicily. Arriving to find order restored, he executed his father's assassin and in spring 669 brought back the troops of the eastern themes from the West. Though that year the Arabs plundered Sicily and invaded Africa and Anatolia, most of Africa remained Byzantine, and Constantine swept the last Arabs from Anatolia in a few months.

The Umayyad Caliph soon formed more ambitious plans for raiding the empire. First seizing some Byzantine islands and border areas, in 674 he sent a large naval expedition that established a base at Cyzicus, not far from Constantinople. There the Arabs settled down for a long stay, reinforced by a land expedition two years later. As long as they raided the whole region and threatened the capital itself, they forced Constantine to neglect other parts of his domain. The Slavs took their chance to besiege Thessalonica, and the Lombards took theirs to conquer Calabria, the heel of the Italian boot. As most of the Calabrians fled, they brought the name of their homeland with them to the boot's still-Byzantine toe, which has been known as Calabria ever since.

After the Arabs had spent three years at Cyzicus, ravaging and paralyzing the empire, Constantine finally counterattacked. The Byzantine navy used a newly invented weapon, later called Greek Fire, which spread over the water, ignited, and burned enemy ships. One battle with Greek Fire was enough to drive the Arabs out. On their way home, they suffered heavy casualties when the remnants of their fleet ran into a storm and their army encountered the troops of the Anatolian themes. After Constantine defeated the Slavs and reoccupied the Aegean islands, the Caliph agreed to a truce.

During this respite, the emperor called an ecumenical council at Constantinople to discuss Monotheletism, which his father had tolerated but few seemed to favor except some Armenians. Now that Armenia was under Arab rule, the council agreed on condemning Monotheletism and affirming that Christ had two wills as he had two natures. Although this finding made compromise with Monophysitism even more distant than before, almost all Monophysites lived in lands that the Arabs had conquered and seemed likely to keep. This sixth ecumenical council, which met from 680 to 681, was to be the last that needed to deal with disputes over Christ himself.

While the council was still in session, the Bulgars, pressed by the Khazars to their east, began to migrate across the Danube into Thrace, where they subjugated the local Slavs. Realizing the Bulgars would make dangerous neighbors, Constantine led an expedition against them. But when he left his camp in mid-campaign to seek treatment for his gout, the army fled after him. The Bulgars settled in northern Thrace, taking a few Byzantine coastal towns along with the Slavic interior. The emperor made a treaty recognizing the Bulgars' new borders, and to bolster his defenses created a separate Theme of Thrace from the European part of the Opsician Theme.

The truce with the Arabs held, because the Umayyads were fighting new civil wars with the descendants of Ali. When the Armenians and Iberians took their chance to rebel against the Caliph and asked for Byzantine protection, the emperor granted them a protectorate, and went on to retake the border areas he had lost to the Arabs earlier. The preoccupied Caliph nonetheless agreed to a new truce in 685, the same year Constantine died of dysentery. At his death, Constantine held nearly all the land that he had inherited from his father. He had ridden out successive enemy attacks, losing only a little of Italy to the Lombards, a bit of Thrace to the Bulgars, and a piece of Africa to the Arabs. Although Constantine was certainly a capable emperor, most of the credit for this successful defense should probably go to the system of themes.

Constantine's son Justinian II began ruling when he was sixteen, slightly older than his father and grandfather had been when they took power. Justinian was more aggressive than his father, and less patient. Seeing that Byzantium seemed stronger and the Arab advance had stopped for the present, he was eager to live up to the name he shared with Justinian I and to work toward restoring imperial greatness. What young Justinian failed quite to grasp was that Byzantium's strengths were mostly defensive, while the Arabs' weaknesses were mostly temporary.

When the Arabs tried to retake Armenia and Iberia, Justinian sent an army that defeated them. Next he made an agreement with the Caliph to share control over Armenia, Iberia, and Cyprus, and to resettle in Byzantium some Christian freebooters called Mardaïtes who had been harrying Arab Syria. Justinian enrolled these Mardaïtes as permanent oarsmen for the fleet of the Carabisian Theme, which had previously hired temporary rowers. He also turned the Balkan part of that theme into a separate Theme of Hellas with its own Mardaïte oarsmen.

While this favorable truce with the Arabs held, in 688 Justinian campaigned against the Slavs in the region between Thrace and Thessalonica. While adding only a little territory to the Byzantine enclave around Thessalonica, he took many Slavic captives, settled them in Anatolia, and enrolled 30,000 of them in the Byzantine army. The next year, before these recruits were ready for service, Justinian broke his treaty by attacking the Caliphate. With the Arab civil war still raging, the Caliph apparently bought Justinian off by giving him full control over Armenia, Iberia, and Cyprus.

For a time the emperor respected this revised treaty. In 692, however, he began minting gold nomismata marked with a bust of Christ, discomfiting the Caliph, who was supposed to pay his tribute in copies of Byzantine coins. When the Caliph paid the same amount of gold in coins without Christ's portrait, Justinian declared war. He prepared to invade the Caliphate with his new Slavic soldiers, but the Arabs invaded the empire first. In the ensuing battle in the Armeniac Theme, most of Justinian's Slavs deserted to the Arabs, who triumphed. While the

Figure 6   Gold nomisma of Justinian II (reigned 685–95 and 705–11) holding a cross, with a bust of Christ on the opposite side of the coin, shown actual size. The minting of this coin in 692 provoked an Arab–Byzantine war when the Caliph refused to pay his tribute to Justinian in coins so explicitly Christian. (*Photo*: Dumbarton Oaks, Washington, D.C., © copyright 1999)

emperor sold the rest of the Slavs into slavery and jailed his general Leontius, the Arabs reoccupied Armenia and began raiding eastern Anatolia again.

Hoping to distract the Byzantines from his defeat, Justinian called a church council at Constantinople to discuss issues of canon law. Meant to complete the work of the preceding fifth and sixth ecumenical councils, this council became known as the "Fifth–Sixth," or Quinisext. Since practically all the bishops who attended were from the East, they codified the practices of the Eastern Church and condemned some of those of the Western Church. The Pope consequently rejected the council. Justinian ordered the army of the Italian Exarchate to arrest the Pope, but it refused to obey.

Next Justinian tried to win glory by building additions to the imperial palace, financing his work by new exactions from the rich of the capital. This exacerbated the emperor's growing unpopularity. In 695, when he tried to placate his enemies by releasing the imprisoned general Leontius, a plot formed to make the general emperor. The conspirators raised a mob in the capital that captured Justinian and proclaimed Leontius. The new emperor had his predecessor's nose and tongue slit, and exiled him to the Crimea.

Leontius thus became only the second eastern emperor since Diocletian to take power without any legal claim, by overthrowing an emperor who had his faults but was far from intolerable. Leontius was personally decent and competent. Yet he found, like Phocas before him, that being a usurper not only sapped his own strength but undermined the stability of the empire itself. Leontius' lack of legitimacy encouraged the Arabs to attack him and his fellow Byzantines to conspire against him.

The year after Leontius' accession, the Arabs invaded Byzantine Africa in force, capturing the exarch's capital at Carthage a year later.

Leontius sent the fleet of the Carabisian Theme with an army that retook Carthage and some of its hinterland. But in 698 the Arabs counterattacked and forced the Byzantine fleet to reembark. On its way back, stopping in Crete and contemplating their failure, the Carabisians rebelled and proclaimed as emperor their second-ranking officer Apsimar, who took the name of Tiberius III. He sailed to Constantinople and besieged the city. When it was betrayed to him, he slit Leontius' nose, made him a monk, and took his place.

Less prudent than Leontius, and in an even less justifiable position, Tiberius tried to prove his fitness to rule by raiding Arab Syria. This raid provoked an Arab assault on the eastern frontier, though it also inspired an Armenian rising against the Arabs that distracted them somewhat. In the West Tiberius gave up on Africa. He however made the remaining islands of the African Exarchate into a feeble Theme of Sardinia and the southern part of the Italian Exarchate into a somewhat stronger Theme of Sicily.

Meanwhile the deposed and mutilated Justinian escaped from his exile in the Crimea to the Khazar Khanate. There he married a daughter of the Khazar Khan, whom he baptized with the significant name of Theodora. When the Khazars seemed about to turn against him, Justinian sailed to the Bulgar Khanate and won over the Bulgar Khan Tervel, who provided him with a Bulgar army to march on Constantinople. In 705 Justinian made his way into the capital through a broken aqueduct and reclaimed power.

Justinian captured Tiberius III, took Leontius from his monastery, and executed both usurpers and a number of their partisans. Nonetheless, though embittered by being deposed and disfigured, Justinian took some pains to avoid making more enemies and to act like the empire's rightful ruler. He invited the Pope to Constantinople to settle their differences over the Quinisext Council. When the Pope arrived in 711, they agreed that the Papacy would accept only those Quinisext canons that were compatible with western practice.

Having finished subduing Armenia, the Arabs were raiding Anatolia more ferociously than ever, and defeating the forces sent against them. What undid Justinian, however, was an apparently minor revolt by the Byzantines of the Crimea, backed by the Khazars but probably provoked by Justinian's measures against those who had offended him during his exile. The rebels proclaimed the exiled Byzantine official Bardanes, an Armenian who took the Greek name of Philippicus. A naval expedition that Justinian sent against Philippicus joined him instead. Sailing back to Constantinople, it seized the city while Justinian was returning from a campaign against the Arabs. After the usurper killed many of Justinian's officials, the emperor's army also deserted him, and Philippicus had Justinian beheaded.

Philippicus proved the least talented usurper to date. Besides overdoing executions of Justinian's partisans, as a Monothelete he insisted on repudiating the Sixth Ecumenical Council and deposing the Patriarch of Constantinople for defending it. Philippicus fought ineptly against the Arabs, who conquered the whole Byzantine border region up to the Taurus Range and made repeated raids beyond it. The Bulgars also raided Thrace. By 713 the Count of the Opsician Theme seized Philippicus and blinded him, intending to take the throne himself.

The Count was outmaneuvered by the Protoasecretis Artemius, who had him blinded for disloyalty and was himself proclaimed emperor as Anastasius II. Having punished a usurper and taken the throne only when it lacked legal claimant, Anastasius had the added advantage of real skill as a ruler. He avoided executions and at once reaffirmed the validity of the Sixth Ecumenical Council. By this time, however, through no fault of his, the Arabs were planning a full land-and-sea attack on Constantinople, with the aim of completing the destruction of an empire that seemed to be destroying itself.

Anastasius began strengthening the sea walls of the capital and stockpiling supplies for a siege. In 715 the emperor sent an expedition to Rhodes to surprise a nearby Arab fleet. But on Rhodes some soldiers from the Opsician Theme, whose former commander Anastasius had blinded, raised a rebellion against him. They landed in Anatolia and proclaimed a local tax official, against his will, as Theodosius III. Anastasius now faced not just an Arab invasion but a civil war with the Opsician Theme. While he led an army to Nicaea in the Opsician, the rebels attacked Constantinople, which received them. Anastasius acknowledged defeat and went into exile as a monk.

The new emperor Theodosius had been right to resist his proclamation, because he was utterly unequal to the task of resisting the vast Arab army and fleet that were massing and advancing against him. Nor did he command the loyalty of much of the Byzantine army in Anatolia, where the Anatolic and Armeniac themes refused to recognize him. After only a year the Strategus of the Anatolics Leo the Syrian proclaimed himself emperor with the support of the Armeniacs. Evading the Arabs, Leo marched on Constantinople, where Theodosius surrendered to him on terms. Leo entered the capital in 717.

Just as the themes had been chiefly responsible for halting the Arab advance under Constans II and Constantine IV, they were largely responsible for the seven revolutions between 695 and 717. Supported by land grants that allowed them to dispense with the pay sent from Constantinople, the themes combined authority over wide stretches of territory with large armies. Any commander of a theme had the power to be a serious contender for the throne. Thus far the Opsician Theme had caused the assassination of Constans II and the overthrow of Philippicus and Anastasius. The Carabisian Theme had deposed Leontius, a fleet probably drawn from the Carabisians had overthrown Justinian II the second time, and the Anatolic Theme had removed Theodosius III. The Armeniac Theme, without making its own emperor, had raised a major revolt under Constans and joined in bringing down Theodosius. Although at first the legitimacy of Constans II, Constantine IV, and Justinian II had helped keep the themes from revolting, the rash of revolutions after 695 had shown how vulnerable emperors were. Now the themes' revolts had almost wrecked the empire.

Three Iconoclast Emperors

Leo III the Syrian, a wily veteran commander aged forty or so, became emperor when Byzantium was in unprecedented peril. The advancing Arabs reportedly had 120,000 men and 1800 ships, surely more than the full strength of the Byzantine army and navy all over the empire. Even the Persians and Avars had threatened Constantinople with much less sea power, and probably a smaller army. Just four months after Leo's coronation, the Arab forces put the city under a close siege on the land side, where their camp stretched from one end of the walls to the other. The main Arab fleet arrived two months later.

Leo was ready for it. He had already concluded an alliance with the Bulgars, who saw that the Arabs would make worse neighbors than the Byzantines. As soon as the Arab fleet tried to sail past the city, Leo attacked it with Greek Fire, so frightening the enemy that they returned to port and stayed there. The Byzantines therefore kept control of the sea, which allowed them to resupply Constantinople whenever they wished. The Arabs found themselves hemmed in between the walls and Byzantine and Bulgar raiders, exhausting their supplies and enduring a snowy winter that was unusually cold for Constantinople and unimaginably frigid for them. Many Arabs died, along with most of the horses and livestock they had brought with them.

In spring 718 the Caliph sent the besiegers a reinforcing army from Syria and supply ships from Egypt and Africa. But the Egyptian and African crews, who were almost all Christians, deserted in large numbers to the emperor, helping him sink their ships and capture their supplies. Leo ambushed, mauled, and drove off the new Arab army before it could join the siege. By late summer the remaining besiegers, afflicted by starvation, disease, and the Bulgars, abandoned the siege. Though most of the army made its way home unopposed, much of the fleet sank in a storm, and most of the rest was burned by a volcanic eruption in the Aegean Sea. After this staggering failure, with immense losses, the Arabs never seriously tried to take Constantinople again.

While the Arabs had been very unlucky, Leo certainly deserved credit for a well-conducted defense. He followed up his success by recapturing some of the land the Arabs had recently taken along the border and advancing into Armenia. When the Bulgars backed an attempt by the former emperor Anastasius II to regain his throne, Leo faced them down and had Anastasius executed. Yet during the Arab siege Byzantium had apparently lost control of its faraway Theme of Sardinia. The Arabs remained so strong and determined that by 720 they returned to the offensive, retaking Leo's reconquests in Armenia and raiding far into Anatolia once more.

Leo, disappointed by the persistence of the empire's troubles, in typical medieval fashion attributed them to God's anger. Exactly why God was angry he took time to decide. In 722 he forced baptism on Byzantine Jews. In 726 he promulgated a brief law code in Greek, which despite being known as the *Ecloga* ("Selection") was not merely selected from the *Justinian Code* but included new provisions to enforce Biblical morality. It further restricted grounds for divorce, outlawed abortion, and reduced the penalty for many crimes from execution to mutilation, though for homosexual acts it increased the penalty from mutilation to execution. Even these measures failed to prevent another volcanic eruption in the Aegean the same year, which unlike that of 718 hurt only Byzantines and not Arabs.

Leo began to settle on the idea that God was angry because the Byzantines prayed before icons of Christ and the saints, which seemed to violate the Mosaic commandment against worshipping images. Muslims had always rejected religious images, and a caliph had recently banned all images in the Caliphate, including Christian ones. A few Byzantines already condemned icons, including two bishops. Yet most Byzantines were accustomed to sacred images and approved of them. When Leo had an icon of Christ removed from the palace gate, he set off a riot. At first he issued an edict against icons without making much effort to implement it. Yet as his troops gained more success against Arab raiders, he became more convinced of the need for outright Iconoclasm, the destruction of icons.

In 730, evidently not trusting a church council to agree with him, Leo called a council of officials that endorsed Iconoclasm. The Patriarch Germanus, who had refused to attend, abdicated and was replaced. The emperor officially banned all icons and ordered those in public places to be removed. Otherwise he mostly left iconophiles alone. His position seems to have been that the veneration of icons was superstitious but not heretical. Yet the Christians under Arab rule rejected Iconoclasm, and the next year the Pope held a council that declared it a heresy.

Leo sent a fleet to Rome in 733, probably to arrest the Pope, but a storm wrecked it before it arrived. Since the emperor had no real control over Rome, he retaliated by confiscating the substantial Papal properties in the Theme of Sicily. He also transferred to the Patriarchate of Constantinople the Papacy's longstanding jurisdiction over Sicily, Calabria, and what remained of Byzantine Greece. Thus the Papacy lost its authority over the Greek-speaking lands of southern Italy, Sicily, and Greece, and almost all Greek-speaking territory was subject to the Patriarchate of Constantinople.

This fitting of the ecclesiastical boundary to the cultural division between Greeks and Latins proved permanent. It became portentous when added to the theological dispute over Iconoclasm and the differences in church practice already revealed by Justinian II's Quinisext Council. By now Byzantine control over the battered remnant of the Italian Exarchate was so weak that Leo did not venture to remove it from Papal authority. Around 738 the Lombards briefly occupied Ravenna, and the Exarch only retook it with Papal help.

The Arabs continued to harry Anatolia, but in 740 Leo defeated one of their raiding parties. Though this made no lasting difference, such victories were rare enough that Leo could claim it showed divine approval of Iconoclasm. Yet Iconophiles could see divine anger at Iconoclasm in an earthquake later that year that damaged Constantinople and the surrounding region, and in Leo's own death from dropsy the next year. The facts remained that the iconoclast emperor had weathered a ferocious Arab siege and died in bed after a fairly long and successful reign.

Nonetheless, the succession of Leo's son Constantine V in 741 was far from uneventful. Aged twenty-two, Constantine had hereditary right, vigor, and intelligence on his side. But the most powerful man in the empire was the much older Artavasdus, Count of the mighty Opsician Theme, who had supported Leo III before his accession and was married to Leo's daughter. As Constantine advanced into the Opsician for a campaign against the Arabs soon after his coronation, Artavasdus attacked him. Constantine fled, and Artavasdus seized Constantinople. After being crowned in the capital, Artavasdus allowed icons to be restored there.

Constantine won the backing of the Anatolic and Thracesian themes and began a civil war to recover his throne. The next year Artavasdus invaded the Thracesian Theme, where Constantine defeated him. After another victory over Artavasdus' son at the head of the Armeniac Theme, Constantine besieged his rival in Constantinople. During a siege of more than a year, Artavasdus failed to drive him off. After reducing the citizens to famine, Constantine carried the walls in a surprise attack. He had Artavasdus and his sons blinded and the war won by the end of 743.

Constantine was perhaps the first emperor to understand that the Opsician, the most rebellious of the themes, was too big and too near to the capital. Not long after Artavasdus' defeat, Constantine reduced both its size and its proximity by transforming part of it into a new branch of the army, the *tagmata* ("regiments"). He established six tagmata, of which three were cavalry units of 4000 men each. The cavalry tagmata of the Scholae, Excubitors, and Watch, taking the names of old guard units that had become insignificant over the years, formed a new mobile army. The other three tagmata were the Numera and Walls, which served as a permanent garrison for Constantinople, and the Optimates, a transport corps of mule drivers to carry the army's baggage on campaigns. The commanders of tagmata were called domestics, except for the Drungary of the Tagma of the Watch and the Count of the Tagma of the Walls. The Domestic of the Scholae became the emperor's chief deputy commander.

The men of the tagmata, while keeping the land grants they had held as soldiers of the Opsician Theme, received their mounts, rations, fodder, arms, and uniforms from the state. Except for the Optimates,

who had a small territory of their own between the remaining part of
the Opsician Theme and the capital, the soldiers of the tagmata were
scattered over the regions of Thrace and Anatolia around Constantinople, so that the emperor could assemble them easily but a rebel or
conspirator could not. By creating the tagmata Constantine not only
broke up the Opsician Theme but provided himself with an especially
mobile and well-equipped force that could campaign either by itself or
with troops from the themes.

Since yet another Arab civil war had pitted the ruling Umayyads
against the rebel family of the Abbasids, Constantine began raiding the
border areas of the Caliphate. Without trying to make conquests from
the Arabs, he rounded up the local Christians and transferred them to
Thrace, where he was pushing the Byzantine frontier forward into land
held by the Slavs. In 747, after a bad outbreak of bubonic plague killed
many of the people of Constantinople, the emperor repopulated the city
with settlers from Greece and the islands. Fortunately for Byzantium,
this was the last of the periodic recurrences of the epidemic that had
begun more than two centuries before.

For ten years after the revolt of Artavasdus, who had shown favor to
iconophiles, Constantine did little to enforce Iconoclasm. Leo's ban on
icons remained the law within the empire, except in central Italy, where
the Pope was practically independent and the exarchs barely held on
until the Lombards conquered Ravenna for good in 751. But Constantine believed in Iconoclasm, and by 753 felt secure enough to call a
church council to affirm it. The council met at the imperial palace of
Hieria near Chalcedon. Its bishops, practically all of them nominees of
Constantine or his father, duly condemned the veneration of icons as a
heresy. They accepted an argument, devised by Constantine himself,
that an icon of Christ must either show him as man in a separate
person, implying Nestorianism, or as both God and man with a single
nature, implying Monophysitism. Even after the Council of Hieria,
however, the emperor scarcely tried to stop those who venerated icons
in private.

With the complete victory of the Abbasids in the Arab civil war, the
Caliphate again became a more unified and formidable adversary. After
some indecisive warfare, Constantine made a truce with the Arabs and
concentrated his military efforts on Thrace. He had conquered enough
Slavic-held land there to threaten the Bulgar Khanate, which he pre-
emptively attacked. Twice he defeated the Bulgars, but without gaining
much to show for his heavy casualties.

By 765 Constantine, exasperated that many if not most of his officials had iconophile sympathies, arrested the iconophile monk Stephen and had the Scholae lynch him. The emperor then demanded all his bishops and officials swear not to venerate icons. The next year he uncovered a major iconophile plot against him that included his Postal Logothete and the commanders of the Tagma of the Excubitors, the Opsician Theme, and the Theme of Thrace. Constantine executed the Logothete and the Domestic of the Excubitors, blinded the rest, and split the Opsician Theme again by creating a new Bucellarian Theme. Noticing that monks were particularly strong iconophiles, he began a general persecution not just of iconophiles but of monks and nuns as such, and confiscated many monasteries and their possessions.

Though the Arabs were raiding Anatolia again, Constantine returned to fighting the Bulgars. He defeated them once more, but on a second campaign against them in 775 he fell ill and died. He left the army strengthened by the creation of the tagmata, the Bulgars somewhat cowed, and the Arabs troublesome as usual. He also left Byzantium divided by Iconoclasm, as his persecution had exacerbated a dispute that most people had previously considered minor. Despite the fear he had spread, the empire's iconophiles seem still to have outnumbered its iconoclasts. Constantine had so antagonized his subjects that some accused him of homosexuality, and gave him the epithet Copronymus, politely translatable as Name of Dung.

Constantine's successor was his son Leo IV, a prudent young man of twenty-five. Without repudiating Iconoclasm, Leo tried to reduce resentment among iconophiles, and ended his father's persecution of monks and nuns. After making a raid on the Caliphate, Leo dealt fairly well with the raids the Arabs sent in retaliation. But he came to grief in 780, when he was shocked to find that his most trusted palace officials had brought icons to his iconophile wife Irene. Feeling betrayed and fearing for his personal safety, he cashiered and punished the officials and stopped sleeping with his wife. A few months later he was dead, allegedly stricken while trying on a crown he had stolen from St Sophia. A more likely cause of death was poisoning by Irene and undetected iconophile officials.

By 780 Byzantium had at last ridden out the great waves of invasions that had begun in 602 with the Persians and Avars and continued with the Arabs and Bulgars. The empire's territorial losses had become steadily smaller and less frequent, until Leo IV became the first emperor since Maurice not to lose any Byzantine territory during his reign. The empire had an army that appeared capable of defending its remaining land. Constantine V seemed to have curbed the themes' tendency to revolt by dividing the Opsician Theme and creating the tagmata. If Iconoclasm remained an unnecessary and troublesome internal problem, it was hardly a fatal one. After many long years of defeats and dangers, Byzantium was no longer struggling for survival, and had attained a modicum of security.

A Retrenched Society

The seventh and eighth centuries changed Byzantium profoundly. By 780 it retained barely a third of the land it had ruled in 602. Accustomed since Roman times to being the greatest power anywhere near, it was now much weaker than the Abbasid Caliphate and not much stronger than the Frankish Kingdom. Once almost immune from attacks except on its periphery, and often at peace with its neighbors even there, now the empire suffered from enemy attacks on every part of its territory. With the loss of Syria, Egypt, Africa, and Armenia, and of most of Italy and the Balkans, Byzantium became a mainly Anatolian power, over-whelmingly Greek-speaking and Chalcedonian Christian. It was much less urbanized than before, with a more primitive economy. Yet while its defeats showed that it had serious weaknesses, its ultimate survival showed that it also had important strengths. As the empire shrank, it grew leaner, tougher, and more cohesive.

In fact, most of the land that the Byzantines lost during the seventh and eighth centuries was already gone by 620, when the Persians held Egypt, Syria, and Armenia and the Avars and Slavs occupied much the largest part of the Balkans. Although Heraclius reclaimed the Persians' conquests, by the end of his reign in 641 he had lost most of them again to the Arabs, who soon took the rest. Meanwhile the empire struggled to maintain its position in distant Africa and Italy, finally losing everything in Africa and about half its seventh-century holdings in Italy. Yet these regions had long been endangered, and were of secondary importance to the central government. From the mid-seventh century, Byzantium successfully defended Anatolia and its remaining islands and Balkan enclaves, with occasional minor losses or minor gains.

Through all these wars, Byzantium kept over half its old field army, though its old frontier troops disappeared along with its former frontiers. As with its territory, the empire suffered most of its losses of soldiers by 641, if not by 620. Thus the army had 150,000 field soldiers in 565, about 109,000 men in 641, and 80,000 men in 780. Only the armies of Africa and Spain were entirely lost, along with Africa and Spain themselves. The other field armies became the themes, with parts of the Opsician Theme eventually becoming the tagmata. By 780 the themes had 62,000 soldiers and the tagmata 18,000.

The themes were less mobile than the old field armies had been, because thematic soldiers expected to return to their military lands after each campaigning season, but they could and did go on campaigns regularly. The tagmata were somewhat more mobile than the themes, though they too had military lands. While the territories of the themes covered practically the whole empire, most of their men were stationed in the interior, leaving relatively few to defend the border regions. Not expecting that they could keep Arab raiders out altogether, the Byzantines contented themselves with holding the main forts during the raids and reoccupying the rest of the land after the Arabs had left.

Under the pressure of enemy attacks, the themes became not only the empire's military divisions but its regular administrative units, replacing the old civil provinces and prefectures. The strategus of a theme was accordingly both a military commander and a territorial governor. Every theme had from two to eighteen territorial and military subdivisions called drungi, each with a thousand soldiers holding military lands within it and responsible for defending it. These drungi were grouped together into turmae, with each drungus commanded and administered by a drungary and each turma by a turmarch.

The strategi and their subordinates had full powers to cope with enemy attacks in their regions. Because the soldiers were essentially self-supporting on their military lands and able to do without their annual pay, the strategi also had the power and independence to mount the many revolts against the central government that began in 668 and became rife between 695 and 717. By breaking up the huge Opsician Theme and creating the tagmata to serve as a counterweight to the themes, Constantine V reduced the danger of such rebellions, but the army retained substantial independence.

The loss of two-thirds of the empire's territory naturally shrank government revenues. By apparently granting almost all the imperial estates to soldiers as military lands, the state reduced its revenues further. Yet the central bureaucracy in Constantinople continued to function, though its numbers decreased, from about 2500 to about

600 officials. The government still kept records of who its soldiers were and what lands they held, and still paid all of them a significant annual wage, with relatively high salaries for the strategi and other senior officers. The empire, though less centralized and more militarized than it had been, remained a bureaucratic state, like the earlier Roman Empire.

The presence of this organized government was the main reason Constantinople stayed a great city, if much reduced in size from its sixth-century peak. After Constantine V brought in settlers to replace the many victims of the plague that ended in 748, the city might have had some 100,000 people. They were numerous enough that Constantine had to restore the aqueducts that the Avars had cut more than a century before. The city's walls, markets, and harbors remained functional, like St Sophia and the Hippodrome, though the number of chariot races diminished and the Blues and Greens ceased to riot.

The need to protect and supply the capital forced the empire to keep its hold on southeastern Thrace, which otherwise it might have abandoned to the Slavs along with most of the rest of the Balkans. The Slavs did occupy much of inland Thrace, probably including the region's old metropolis of Adrianople, which Constantine V seems to have reclaimed when he retook and resettled some formerly Slavic territory during the middle years of his reign. By that time the Theme of Thrace had suffered terribly from the plague and the Avars, Slavs, and Bulgars. Since it lacked a natural frontier, no part of it was truly secure up to the walls of Constantinople itself.

The Anatolian core of the empire had always consisted of two different kinds of land – the coastal plains and the interior plateau. The plains lay in the Thracesian Theme, the remainder of the Carabisian Theme that became known as the Cibyrrhaeot Theme, and the reduced Opsician Theme after Constantine V divided it up. The most populous and fertile land still in Byzantine hands, the plains were also the most secure part of the empire. Because they lay well off the main invasion routes that began at the frontier passes, the Arabs raided the plains only infrequently, and the Persians had scarcely touched them.

The plateau was divided among the Anatolic, Armeniac, and Bucellarian themes. Sparsely populated and mostly pastureland, it was all more or less open to Arab raiders, who appeared from time to time to drive off some of the local livestock. Anatolia's natural frontier was the line of the Taurus and Antitaurus mountains, with several passes that the Arabs could easily cross during most of the year but had trouble negotiating in the cold and snow of winter. Thus the almost annual Arab raids never ended in a sustained Arab occupation of any land on the Byzantine side of the mountains.

Apart from Thrace and Anatolia, Byzantium kept only islands and a few bits of coast in Greece, Dalmatia, Italy, and the Crimea. The Byzantines held their own in seapower, and even forced the Arabs to concede partial Byzantine control over Cyprus, despite its position near the coast of Arab Syria. The empire maintained its Greek, Dalmatian, and Italian outposts against the Slavs and Lombards because those enemies lacked not just ships but the skills to take walled cities. While the Arabs had to fight hard to conquer Byzantine territory up to the Taurus and the Mediterranean, the Lombards, Slavs, Avars, and Bulgars migrated into Italian and Balkan lands that the Byzantines did little to defend. The Byzantines reasonably gave priority to defending Anatolia, and to fighting the much more dangerous Persians and Arabs.

The empire became less urbanized partly because it lost the more urbanized lands of Syria and Africa, but mostly because the cities in what remained of Byzantium shrank. The main evidence for the shrinkage of cities, often uncertain in detail but decisive when taken as a whole, is the archeological excavation of urban sites. Though very few cities were abandoned altogether, and a few military bases seem even to have grown slightly, on average most cities appear to have lost around half their sixth-century population. They also lost almost all their remaining urban monuments, except for some churches. The need to protect them with stronger and more constricted fortifications also made them more crowded, with ever narrower streets and less open space.

Enemy attacks no doubt contributed to the shrinkage of the cities on the Anatolian plateau and in the bits of Europe still under Byzantine control. Many of these cities fell to enemy raiders at one time or another, and nearly all of them had their food supplies reduced from time to time by enemy raids and sieges. Yet the cities in the coastal plains of Anatolia, which only rarely suffered from enemy incursions, seem to have shrunk almost as much as cities in more exposed places. Though the plague always affected cities more than the countryside, natural population increase and refugees from lost lands should approximately have equaled the excess mortality from warfare and the waning outbreaks of the plague. Since any overall demographic decline seems to have been insignificant, it can scarcely have been the main cause of the cities' shrinkage.

The principal reasons for urban decline rather appear to have been economic changes that worked to the disadvantage of cities. Cities of any size depend on trade to supply their food, and these times were bad for business of any sort. After the Arab conquests, trade between the remainder of the empire and Arab-held Syria, Egypt, and Africa fell off dramatically. In particular, the Byzantine government could no longer order and subsidize the large Egyptian and African grain exports that had sustained Constantinople and some other eastern centers. Without the former grain shipments, the capital maintained itself by drawing on the surplus that had formerly supplied the cities of the Anatolian plains. Trade within what remained of Byzantium must also have suffered from Arab raids by land and sea.

Moreover, archeological finds indicate that the amount of money in circulation fell during this time, forcing traders to resort to barter more often than before. A shortage of money was only to be expected once the government had twice halved its soldiers' pay, always the empire's principal means of putting coins into circulation. Yet barter is a cumbersome and inefficient means of exchanging goods. Under such circumstances, subsistence agriculture carried on by peasant villagers must have become even more dominant in the empire's economy than it had been before, severely restricting the economic role left for cities.

Nonetheless, the empire still had cities of some size, probably ten or so with 10,000 people or more, and its government continued to collect monetary taxes from nearly all its subjects and to pay all its soldiers and officials something. Coins, even if rarer than before, were still in general circulation. The seals of the imperial warehouses that become common from the middle of the reign of Constans II seem to be indicators of a kind of economic activity. The warehouses, evidently run by private businessmen on government contracts to sell arms to soldiers in exchange for the produce of military lands, seem also to have served as trading posts for all sorts of goods, including silk and slaves. Their proprietors were presumably ready to buy, sell, or trade anything that offered them a profit, thus putting coins into circulation and facilitating barter.

With the shrinkage of cities and of the central government, and with the various political upheavals that began with the usurpation of Phocas, the old aristocracy of senators and decurions declined to the point where it virtually vanished. Though those who held high government office continued to receive the rank of senator, by the eighth century few if any of them could trace their families back to the senators of the sixth century, and few were men of real wealth. The surviving provincial cities seem also to have had few landholders or traders who would have counted as rich by sixth-century standards. By contrast, poorer men seem to have benefited, as some who had formerly rented their land came to own it and most of the relatively few slaves of the earlier period gained their freedom.

A new aristocracy was however beginning to form on the Anatolian plateau. While the frequent Arab raids could easily ruin those with little land and small herds, a class of large ranchers emerged with the resources to survive the raids, and presumably bought out some of the less fortunate. Most such ranchers aspired not to appointments in the bureaucracy in faraway Constantinople but to commissions as strategi or other high officers in the themes. Given their familiarity with warfare and local conditions, the emperor had good reason to give them the posts they wanted, allowing them, like ordinary soldiers of the themes, to defend their own lands while they defended the empire.

Such magnates seem to have led several of the rebellions of the themes, but rebellion was a hazard of the system as a whole, and Constantine V eventually mitigated it. These aristocrats were in any case only wealthy and powerful by the diminished standards of their own time, since the land of the Anatolian plateau was fairly poor and much of it consisted of the soldiers' military lands and remaining peasant holdings. The new nobles' main strength was their tenacity, which they shared with other inhabitants of the Anatolian plateau who held their own against the Arabs.

The seventh-century invasions and the decline of the empire's cities had effects that ran through all of Byzantine society. Everyone felt the change, even the peasants whose lands were not conquered or raided by the empire's enemies. All farmers paid somewhat less in monetary taxes, but found money harder to raise. Even with the help of barter, they must have had to do without a variety of goods that they had previously been able to buy. Unsettled conditions left the government disrupted, the roads poorly maintained, and brigandage on the increase. Many in the coastal plains who had been renters gained possession of their lands; some on the Anatolian plateau who had been landowners became tenants. Finally, not even the most ignorant and indifferent peasant could remain unaware that his empire was in retreat.

Byzantium had shown signs of decay from the time of the plague in the mid-sixth century. The usurpation of Phocas, the subsequent civil war, and the simultaneous Persian and Avar invasions when the empire was most damaged by its internal troubles all contributed to Byzantine weakness on the eve of the Arab conquests. In view of the extraordinary vigor and enthusiasm of the Arabs, what really needs explaining is not why they defeated the Byzantines but how Byzantium survived at all. The creation of the themes was necessary to that survival, ending an alarming collapse before earlier Arab inroads and beginning a remarkably successful defense of Anatolia. Yet the empire might still have fallen without the defensive barriers of the Taurus and Antitaurus, the respite provided by the Arab civil wars, the abilities of such emperors as Constans II and Leo III, and a spirit of Byzantine resistance that strengthened as the period went on.

A Dark Age

By the most obvious objective measures, the disasters of the seventh and eighth centuries greatly impoverished Byzantine culture. Unless every available indicator is misleading, fewer authors wrote, fewer teachers taught, fewer artists and artisans created, and fewer builders built. The quality of what was written, taught, created, and built also fell off markedly. Most Byzantines recognized that these changes were for the worse, just as they believed that their military and political misfortunes showed God's anger against them. The iconoclast controversy was in large part an argument over how they had angered God. Yet Byzantine civilization survived, and its dark age could have been far darker than it was.

During this time the Byzantine Church reflected both the demoralization and the resilience of Byzantine society as a whole. Although the church leadership could scarcely escape all responsibility for what most Byzantines agreed was divine displeasure, most of the blame for the political and military failures naturally went to the emperors. The Church could take credit for giving moral and financial support to Heraclius' successful wars against the Zoroastrian Persians. The hierarchy also helped rally the Byzantines to resist the worst onslaughts of the Muslim Arabs, especially the siege of Constantinople between 717 and 718.

The emperors, rather than the Church or any widespread popular sentiment, were the prime movers in introducing Monoenergism, Monotheletism, and Iconoclasm, and could be blamed for the failure of the first two doctrines and the long and bitter divisions over the third. The loss of Egypt, Syria, and Armenia left the empire with no significant number of Monophysites, so that Monophysitism ceased to be a major issue for the Byzantines. Then Monoenergism and Monotheletism, which the emperors had tried to use to conciliate Monophysites, lost their main purpose. Most of the clergy never liked Iconoclasm, and accepted the emperors' promotion of it only grudgingly.

In fact, the tribulations of the seventh and eighth centuries were somewhat better for the reputation of the Church than the prosperity of the fifth and sixth centuries had been. The Church was at its best when it had hardships to face, whether from infidel enemies or from heretical emperors, and the comfort Christianity could offer was in more demand in hard times. The Church produced several strong leaders, from the Patriarch Sergius who helped Heraclius fight the Persians to the Patriarch Germanus who opposed Leo III's Iconoclasm. The monk Maximus Confessor won lasting renown for opposing Constans II's toleration of Monotheletism. Later other monks gained similar prestige by resisting the iconoclast emperors when the secular clergy had to conform or lose their posts.

A sign that the Church was gaining in popular regard are contemporary saints' lives of bishops and monks who had died recently, which emphasized not only the saints' spiritual perfection but their benefactions to their fellow Christians. The hagiographers supply much more detail about their subjects' lives and times than their predecessors who had written about saints long dead. Notable seventh-century examples include the lives of the hermit and bishop Theodore of Syceon and the Patriarch of Alexandria John the Almsgiver, as well as the *Spiritual Meadow*, a collection of brief stories about eastern monks by John Moschus, the Patriarch of Jerusalem in exile. Celebration of such recent saints in lives and icons enhanced the reputation of the contemporary Church.

With the Iconoclasm of the eighth century, not just icons but saints' lives became much rarer, probably because most of those likely to be the subjects or authors of hagiography were monks and iconophiles. Leo III and Constantine V seem to have imposed Iconoclasm partly to claim for emperors some of the moral authority of the Church in general and monks in particular. In persecuting iconophiles the emperors confiscated for the treasury much ecclesiastical and especially monastic property, either because it was decorated with images or simply because it belonged to iconophiles.

By 780 Iconoclasm had left the monasteries plundered and the hierarchy dispirited, yet had not won over the majority of Byzantines. Icons
were an important means of making Christ and the saints seem real and
present to many believers. Outside the reach of the iconoclast emperors
but writing in Greek, the Syrian theologian and monk John of Damascus made the obviously correct argument that worshippers intended to
honor not the icons themselves but the persons the icons depicted.

Iconoclasm was always an anomalous doctrine, without strong theological roots or clear theological implications. Since the Church had
used icons for centuries without provoking objections from many
acknowledged saints, Leo III could argue only that icons might lead
to idolatry, not that they always did. Constantine V· revealed Iconoclasm's theological confusion by his muddled arguments that the use
of icons led either to Nestorianism or to Monophysitism. If Leo and
Constantine had expected their Iconoclasm to win them popularity,
they were disappointed. Even with the power of the army and state
behind this hardly radical doctrine, most Byzantines gave it no more
than grudging acquiescence. The only argument for Iconoclasm that
seems to have had much effect was that the relative success of the
iconoclast emperors showed that God favored them.

The iconoclast conflict notwithstanding, the seventh and eighth centuries saw a consolidation of the position of Byzantine Christianity and a
consequent homogenization of Byzantine society. Paganism and the
Christological controversies ceased to be issues. Justinian II's Quinisext
Council standardized many points of canon law. Leo III's *Ecloga* provided a law code so imbued with Christianity that it often enforced
canon law in civil matters. In another work of codification, John of
Damascus composed a comprehensive summary in Greek of the orthodox faith, *The Fountain of Knowledge*, which soon reached iconophiles in
the empire and found favor there.

Although lost to the empire, Armenia, Syria, Egypt, and even northern Africa were not entirely lost to Byzantine civilization. From the late
seventh century Syrian and Egyptian Christians, who remained in the
majority, circulated prophecies that the Byzantine emperor would soon
return to reconquer the East. As late as 718, the Egyptian and African
sailors sent to reinforce the Arab besiegers of Constantinople chose to
desert to the Byzantines. The Caliphs eventually allowed Chalcedonian
patriarchs of Antioch, Alexandria, and Jerusalem to reside in those cities
as heads of the orthodox Christians there, along with a Jacobite
Patriarch of Antioch and a Coptic Patriarch of Alexandria for the

Monophysites. The Chalcedonians under Arab rule were known as Melkites, meaning pro-imperial. They never accepted Iconoclasm, but by arguing against it John of Damascus and other Melkites showed that they still cared about what happened within the empire. The Pope remained nominally a Byzantine subject, and also remained interested in Byzantine affairs. Only in most of the Balkans had the Avars and Slavs driven out so many of the former inhabitants that Christianity and Byzantine influence faded away.

The influence of Christian morality on the Byzantines continued to grow in various ways. Through all the violent revolts and revolutions of these times, the winners seldom executed the losers. The usual penalties for conspiracy were mutilation, relegation to a monastery, or both, although the mutilated Justinian II and the tonsured Anastasius II were executed after they took up arms again. The laws called for stricter standards of sexual chastity, and outlawed whatever superstitious practices seemed to have pagan origins. The decline of urban life drastically limited the theater, though it survived in Constantinople to scandalize some pious spectators.

Social change was most sweeping among city dwellers, because to a great extent these came to be a different group of people. After the decurions disappeared, the new aristocracy of magnates and military officers often lived not in cities or towns but in forts or villages. Family names of the old Roman type, which at least the senatorial class of Byzantines had adopted, disappeared during the course of the seventh century. By the late eighth century, when some new family names began to appear, few if any families could trace their genealogy back more than a hundred years with confidence. The bureaucrats, merchants, and artisans in the capital and other towns, though some must have been descended from those of an earlier time, were scarcely aware of the fact.

While any Byzantine of social consequence still needed to be literate, such people had become fewer, and contented themselves with an education well below earlier standards. As before, the government expected its officials to be educated men, since their duties required them to keep and consult written records with some facility. Yet the small class of professors, the only teachers who had done some research and offered a higher education, gradually dwindled with the withering away of Athens, the loss of Alexandria and Antioch, and the shrinkage of Constantinople. The professorial chairs founded in the capital in the fifth century evidently lapsed after Heraclius' reign. This cannot have been a necessary economy, because the chairs had always been an

insignificant item in the state budget, and Heraclius patronized professors despite his financial distress. After a century of decline, however,
higher education seems simply to have gone out of style.

By the mid-seventh century, professors had died out as a class, and
with them an intellectual community that had begun in Athens in the
fifth century BC. If anyone still had a serious scholarly interest in such
fields as philosophy or science, he was an unusual and isolated figure.
The best available schoolteachers only provided aspiring officials and
the more sophisticated clerics with a secondary education, which meant
reading perhaps a dozen standard Greek authors like Homer and
Demosthenes. The rest of the clergy, lesser bureaucrats, merchants,
and military officers made shift with a primary education, merely learning to read and write the Greek of the Bible.

As the numbers of the literate decreased, very few people could read
classical Greek any longer, and scarcely any could write classical Greek
correctly or read Latin. Therefore no more than a handful could read
the vast bulk of earlier Greek literature, and few would read new
literary works. Some ancient manuscripts were lost or destroyed, and
hardly any were recopied. Few new works were written. Nearly all the
new writing that did appear was religious – hymns, sermons, hagiography, and a little theology – read aloud or sung in churches and
monasteries, or read in private by a handful of clerics or devout civil
servants.

Thus the long succession of histories of the old Classical Greek type
ended with a mediocre account of the reign of Maurice by Theophylact
Simocatta, who wrote under Heraclius. Heraclius' reign also saw a long
line of classicizing poets end with the talented George of Pisidia, whose
secular poems celebrate Heraclius' victories over the Persians. In the
next two generations Maximus Confessor and the Patriarch of Constantinople Germanus were important as theologians, not as literary stylists.
In the generation after Germanus, the only notable Greek author was
John of Damascus, who never visited the empire. After John died
around 750, Byzantine literature seemed almost to have died with
him. Whatever historical records were kept were rudimentary, and
have not survived in their original form.

Although no one seems to have seen much value in higher learning,
which saved no souls, fed no mouths, made no money, and won no
battles, the deterioration of schooling had practical disadvantages. By
726 Leo III was complaining in the preface to his *Ecloga* that his officials
were unable to use older lawbooks competently. Soon afterward

iconoclasts and iconophiles were accusing each other, with reason, of ignorance of theology. Tax receipts also seem to have been falling because government registers were poorly kept. That such things might be connected to poorer education seems not to have occurred to anyone in a position to make improvements.

As usual, art and architecture seem to have followed the same general lines of development as literature, though the surviving evidence suggests that their decline was somewhat less pronounced. Enemy invasions and raids forced the Byzantines to build many new forts and city walls. Yet in most cases the builders threw together these fortifications in haste, often despoiling older buildings and monuments and dispensing with the care and elegance of earlier Roman and Byzantine military engineers. Built by soldiers on active duty with whatever materials were at hand, such structures must have cost the treasury next to nothing.

Even seemingly necessary but costly work like restoring the aqueducts of Constantinople was postponed for over a hundred years. Luxury building practically came to a halt. The exception was the expansion of the imperial palace by Justinian II, paid for by confiscations from the wealthy that helped cause a revolution. The lack of even archeological remains of elaborate buildings from this time obviously reflects the empire's financial embarrassment and the relative poverty of its aristocracy.

By comparison with luxury architecture, other sorts of artwork were inexpensive, and the Byzantines continued to produce them in some quantity. While a good deal less art survives from this period than from the previous one, the main reasons for its scarcity may be its cheaper and more perishable materials and the destruction of religious art by iconoclasts. In the seventh century, to judge from sources for the iconoclast conflict, Byzantine churches and homes had been filled with icons, most painted on the walls or on wood. The few seventh-century wooden icons that have survived in the dry climate of the Monastery of St Catherine on Mount Sinai show considerable artistic skill, though they were presumably well above the average in quality.

The best artists seem still to have been well trained. From 681 to 698 the imperial mint struck some unusually beautiful gold nomismata, showing detailed portraits of the emperors and under Justinian II a majestic bust of Christ, probably copied from an icon. Iconoclasm naturally curbed figural religious art in the eighth century, but the iconoclasts had no objection to secular subjects, whether figural or not, or to crosses or abstract designs. Constantine V commissioned various mosaics of

Figure 7   A seventh-century icon of the Virgin and Child between the warrior saints George (*left*) and Theodore (*right*) with angels behind, from the Monastery of St Catherine on Mt. Sinai. This is perhaps the most beautifully executed wooden icon to survive from the period before Iconoclasm. (*Photo*: courtesy of the Michigan–Princeton–Alexandria Expedition to Mt. Sinai)

these types in the capital. Such evidence as we have suggests that Byzantine artistic traditions maintained themselves better than literary ones.

Continuing the unfavorable trends that had been looming late in the previous period of Byzantine history, the seventh and eighth centuries were a time of military defeat, political instability, economic regression, and cultural decay. In almost every respect, the empire became far poorer and weaker than it had been in the sixth century. In comparison with contemporary Western Europe, however, Byzantium remained an advanced society, with a standing army, a professional bureaucracy, a monetary economy, and a secular educated class, all of which were nothing but remote memories in the Frankish or Lombard kingdoms. The Arab Caliphate, though stronger and richer than Byzantium, was no better organized and little if any more cultured. Moreover, by 780 the Caliphate was past its peak, while Byzantium had passed its nadir.

5

RECOVERY AND VICTORY
(780–1025)

The Revival of the Empire

At Leo IV's death his widow Irene became regent for their nine-year-old son Constantine VI. An empress without the support of a strong emperor was always at a disadvantage at the Byzantine court, and Leo's five younger brothers were all of age and obvious rivals for imperial power. But Irene, in her mid-twenties, was shrewd and iron-willed, with a firm commitment to restoring the icons that had already won her allies in the palace. Not two months after Leo's death, she frustrated a conspiracy to proclaim one of his brothers, and had all five of them ordained priests.

Irene relied most on bureaucrats, who were generally iconophile; on eunuchs, who were ineligible for the throne; and on priests, who were both. As her Postal Logothete and most trusted adviser she chose the eunuch Stauracius. In 781 she sent him against an Arab army raiding northwestern Anatolia. But after cornering the Arabs, Stauracius was betrayed to them by disloyal Byzantine generals. Blaming the generals rather than the Logothete, the empress replaced them and ransomed him, then sent him to begin conquering western Thrace from the Slavs. Without meeting much resistance, Stauracius conquered the land up to the Balkan Mountains, opening the road from the capital to the Byzantine enclave of Thessalonica. Irene soon created a new Theme of Macedonia that included her conquests.

When the incumbent Patriarch of Constantinople died in 784, Irene replaced him with her Protoasecretis Tarasius, who called for an

124

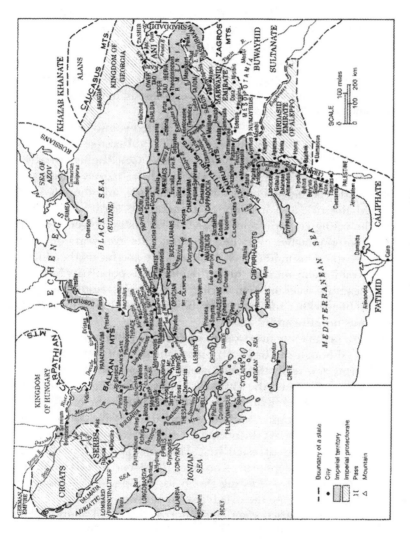

Map 4 The Empire *ca.* 1025

ecumenical council to condemn Iconoclasm. The empress assembled a council two years later, only to be forced to dissolve it after a demonstration by iconoclast soldiers from the tagmata. She responded by ordering the tagmata to campaign against the Arabs, then dismissing their iconoclast ringleaders as soon as they were out of the city. Next she summoned another ecumenical council, with representatives of the Pope and the Melkite eastern patriarchs. Meeting at Nicaea in 787, the council condemned Iconoclasm as a heresy, and declared that venerating an icon was equivalent to venerating the person it depicted. The bishops consecrated under Iconoclasm, who were almost all of them, disowned their former views and remained in office.

The next year, in a competition among selected young noblewomen, Irene chose for her seventeen-year-old son Constantine a beautiful bride he disliked. By now of an age to rule, Constantine loved his mother but resented his subordination, which he naively blamed on Stauracius. In 790 he plotted against the eunuch, and though Irene discovered the plot and imprisoned Constantine, most of the army backed the young emperor and insisted on his taking power. Yet Constantine's responsibilities overwhelmed him. After two years of ruling alone, he restored his mother as his co-ruler. He and his mother shared power uncomfortably until he further damaged his popularity by divorcing his beautiful wife and remarrying. In 797 soldiers loyal to Irene seized and blinded her son, who probably died from his injuries and in any case was never heard of again.

Irene now became the first woman in Roman or Byzantine history to rule alone. Although she had many partisans in the Church, civil service, and army, few really thought that she belonged where she was. In 800 the Pope proclaimed the Frankish king Charlemagne emperor at Rome, on the argument that since a woman could not be emperor the Roman throne was vacant. Charlemagne tried to resolve the matter by offering to marry Irene. As she pondered this extraordinary proposal, a group of her courtiers arrested her. They proclaimed emperor her General Logothete Nicephorus, who relegated Irene to a convent. She had won great credit by restoring the icons, but even by blinding her son never quite overcame the disadvantage of being a woman.

A bit over fifty at his accession, Nicephorus was one of many capable iconophile officials promoted by Irene. He seems to have served as Strategus of the Armeniac Theme before becoming General Logothete, and he combined financial and military expertise with intelligence and unusual energy. Though he had no hereditary claim to the throne, no one else had either, with the dubious exception of Irene. His position seemed fairly secure after Irene died and he put down a rebellion by several Anatolian themes early in his reign.

While Nicephorus fought some skirmishes with the Arabs, his main plans for expansion, like Irene's, were in Slavic-held lands in the Balkans. In 804 his Strategus of Hellas conquered the western Peloponnesus from the local Slavs and began settling it with Byzantines. In 807 and the emperor himself advanced the frontier in Thrace up to Serdica (modern Sofia). The same year Nicephorus ordered a new census of the empire, the first in many years, ending much tax evasion, canceling many tax exemptions, and raising revenues greatly.

In 809 Nicephorus established in what had been Slavic territory in Greece three new themes of the Peloponnesus, Thessalonica, and Cephalonia, where he settled many Byzantines from Anatolia. These themes, and a new tagma he founded called the Hicanati, increased the Byzantine army by 10,000 men. The new themes in Greece, occupied with little trouble, expanded Byzantine farmland and tax revenues, once their settlers became established. The settlements soon changed Greece from a mainly Slavic land back to a mainly Greek one, as it had been before the seventh century.

Not surprisingly, the Byzantine expansion in Thrace and Greece alarmed the Bulgar Khan Krum. When Krum sacked Byzantine Serdica in 809, Nicephorus retaliated by devastating the Bulgar Khanate. Two years later the emperor made another campaign against the Bulgars. After being defeated twice, however, Krum contrived to trap the Byzantine army in a ravine in the Balkan Mountains. The Bulgars killed a large number of Byzantines, including the emperor himself, before the rest made their escape. Krum had Nicephorus' skull turned into a drinking bowl. Despite his substantial achievements, Nicephorus was the first emperor to die in battle since Valens in 378.

Nicephorus' only son Stauracius was paralyzed by a wound he had received in this battle, and though he was proclaimed emperor he was plainly too debilitated to rule. A short time later the chief officials agreed on proclaiming Nicephorus' son-in-law Michael Rhangabe and sending Stauracius to a monastery. Handsome and well-born, the first Byzantine emperor to have a family name, Michael was affable but hopelessly indecisive. He dithered while Krum advanced into Byzantine Thrace, and when Michael finally marched out against the Bulgars the Byzantine army fled. The army then proclaimed the Strategus of the Anatolic Theme Leo the Armenian, who had probably provoked the rout with his own proclamation in mind. Michael retired to a monastery.

However treacherous Leo V had been, he was a wily and vigilant man in his late thirties from a noble Armenian family. At first he actually did little better than Michael in dealing with Krum, who arrived before Constantinople almost at once. After Leo tried to kill him while pretending to negotiate, the angry Khan ravaged the greater part of Thrace for two years, carrying off the population of Adrianople and other cities to Bulgaria. Leo never ventured to take the field against him. Krum was planning an assault on Constantinople when he suddenly died, interrupting the Bulgars' attacks.

Leo's main plan for dealing with the Bulgars was to reinstate Iconoclasm. He argued that all five rulers since the restoration of the icons had come to bad ends, unlike the three iconoclast emperors who had preceded them. In 815 Leo forced the incumbent Patriarch Nicephorus and some other bishops into exile, and chose a new patriarch who recognized Constantine V's Council of Hieria as ecumenical. Once again icons were destroyed on imperial orders, though this time a strong iconophile resistance formed under Abbot Theodore of Studius.

The year after Leo declared his Iconoclasm he marched against the Bulgars, who had resumed raiding Thrace. He pretended to flee from their army, then ambushed and defeated it. Both sides agreed on a peace of thirty years. While Leo renounced his claim to the parts of Thrace gained by Irene and Nicephorus, the Bulgars returned whatever had been Byzantine before that time, kept only part of the rest, and left the remainder to independent Slavs. Leo busied himself with restoring the recovered cities of Thrace. He also created a new Theme of Paphlagonia and a new Ducate of Chaldia along the northern coast of Anatolia, probably to ward off the Rus', Vikings then sending raiding parties south to the Black Sea.

At the end of 820 Leo V was assassinated by conspirators, who proclaimed his imprisoned Domestic of the Excubitors Michael II the Amorian. Michael, sometimes called the Stammerer, was a gruff soldier of about fifty, who cared little about icons one way or the other but kept Iconoclasm in force rather than make a change. He almost immediately faced strong opposition from most of the Anatolian themes, which refused to recognize his seizure of power and proclaimed Thomas the Slav, the second-ranking officer in the Anatolic Theme. Since Michael really had no better claim to the throne than Thomas had, a major civil war developed.

By the time Thomas besieged Constantinople by land and sea in the fall of 821, Michael held only the capital and most of the Opsician and Armeniac themes. But Thomas' assaults on the city walls failed. Michael burned much of Thomas' fleet with Greek Fire, and persuaded the Bulgars to attack Thomas' army from behind. Thomas had to abandon his siege. In 823 Michael defeated his forces, starved him out of a stronghold in Thrace, and executed him. Michael put down Thomas' last adherents the next year.

This three-year civil war damaged the army, and especially the fleet. In 826 rebels took over the Theme of Sicily and called in Arabs from Africa to help. While the Byzantine fleet was sailing to Sicily, a band of Arabs from Spain seized Crete, which since it was not a theme had no proper garrison. With his weakened fleet forced to fight the Arabs on two different islands, Michael lost the western part of Sicily and all of Crete. He died in 829 after a far from glorious reign.

Michael's successor was his sixteen-year-old son Theophilus, one of the more intriguing Byzantine rulers. He chose his charming empress, Theodora, in one of the bride-shows that had become customary since Irene had begun them. His tutor had been John the Grammarian, a cleric known for his learning and his Iconoclasm, both of which he passed on to Theophilus. Precocious, refined, and ambitious, Theophilus cultivated a reputation for justice and accessibility to his subjects.

Theophilus hoped to prove the rightness of Iconoclasm by the success of his reign. He soon defeated an Arab raiding party in the Armeniac Theme, but this simply provoked the Arabs to send larger raiding parties, which defeated the Byzantines. As the Caliph prepared an even bigger expedition, in 833 the emperor issued an edict ordering imprisonment for all his subjects who refused communion with Iconoclasts. Two months later, the Caliph suddenly died on Byzantine territory during his campaign, which his successor abandoned. For Theophilus, the Caliph's death must have seemed an unmistakable sign of God's approval of Iconoclasm.

For the next several years fortune smiled on Theophilus. Thousands of members of a heretical Muslim sect known as Khurramites fled the Caliphate and agreed to turn Christian and serve in the Byzantine army. The emperor sent an expedition that reclaimed the coastal strip between Thrace and Thessalonica, recently surrendered to the Slavs by the treaty with the Bulgars. Next, with the help of the converted Khurramites, Theophilus raided the border region of the Caliphate.

The enraged Caliph readied a great expedition against Byzantium in 838. Before it set out, Theophilus prepared for it by installing his old tutor John the Grammarian as Patriarch of Constantinople and intensifying persecution of iconophiles. These measures proved inadequate. The Caliph led an invasion that swept aside the Byzantine army and sacked Ancyra and Amorium, the headquarters of the Bucellarian and Anatolic themes. Then 30,000 converted Khurramites rebelled and seized part of the Armeniac Theme. The discovery that Iconoclasm did not guarantee military victory shocked Theophilus so profoundly that he fell ill.

On his recovery, the emperor campaigned against the Khurramite rebels and forced them to submit. In 840 he reassigned them to different themes in groups of two thousand, increasing his regular army by a third. In the process he created three new military districts along the Arab frontier called cleisurae ("passes"), and two new themes, Dyrrhachium in today's Albania and the Climata in the Crimea. At the same time Theophilus divided the themes' thousand-man drungi into five two-hundred-man banda, each under a count with authority to call up its men. Moreover, Theophilus ordered the pay of all his soldiers to be almost doubled. With the resulting improvement in morale, in future years the army rebelled much less often and fought much better than before.

Theophilus died of dysentery in 842, after a reign marked by important mistakes and more important accomplishments. Though he spent lavishly on palaces from the beginning of his reign, even after his generous pay increase for the army he left a reserve of seven million nomismata in the treasury, more than twice the annual budget. While Nicephorus I's tax reforms and annexations in Greece must have helped raise revenue, such surpluses must still show increases in population and prosperity since the eighth century, when surpluses were on a more modest scale though expenditures were lower. Scarcely harmed by apparently serious defeats at the hands of the Bulgars and Arabs, Byzantium had clearly grown stronger and more prosperous.

The Revived Empire

Since at Theophilus' death his son Michael III was just two years old, real power passed to Michael's mother Theodora, then in her late twenties. Like Irene before her, Theodora was an active and intelligent woman whose chief adviser was a eunuch, in Theodora's case the Postal Logothete Theoctistus. Yet Theodora, in a stronger position than Irene, neither needed nor employed Irene's ruthlessness. Theodora was an ardent iconophile, but after Theophilus' persecution of iconophiles had failed to deliver military victory, Byzantine opinion, never happy with Iconoclasm, seems to have turned strongly against it. The empress' fabricated story that the dying Theophilus had abjured Iconoclasm won wide acceptance.

Only a year after her husband's death, Theodora and Theoctistus had Irene's Second Council of Nicaea recognized as ecumenical by an assembly of carefully chosen officials, priests, and monks – but not bishops, all of whom had needed to profess Iconoclasm for years. Theodora dismissed the Patriarch John the Grammarian and replaced him with Methodius, an iconophile monk from Sicily imprisoned under Theophilus. Methodius dismissed almost every Byzantine bishop, though nearly all but John the Grammarian repudiated Iconoclasm. The first Sunday in Lent, when the iconophile meeting announced its decision, has been celebrated in the Eastern Church ever since as the Sunday of Orthodoxy. It did in fact mark the end of major theological controversies for centuries to come.

Theoctistus then set off on an expedition to reconquer Crete from the Arabs, hoping to show that iconophilism brought victory where Iconoclasm could not. After an encouraging start, the Logothete returned to fight some Arab raiders on the Bosporus, lost to them, and never returned to Crete, where the Arabs drove the Byzantines out. Despite these setbacks, Theoctistus retained his power, and the Byzantine consensus in favor of the icons held firm. Soon after the treaty with the Bulgars expired in 846, the Byzantine government expelled a Bulgar raiding party and forced a new peace on the Bulgar Khan.

For reasons that had nothing to do with Byzantium, the Arab Caliphate was starting to break up into independent or virtually independent states, like the emirates of Melitene and Tarsus on the Byzantine frontier, which took charge of Arab raids on the empire. The two emirates benefited from an alliance with a ministate founded in the borderlands by the Paulicians, a nominally Christian dualist sect professing the belief that Christ was a good god and the Old Testament God an evil one. Yet this unholy alliance was no substitute for the armies of a unified Caliphate. The Byzantines severely devastated the Emirate of Tarsus in 855.

That year Theodora held the usual competition to marry off her fifteen-year-old son Michael. But Michael already had a mistress, Eudocia Ingerina, and resented the unexceptional wife his mother forced upon him. He found an ally in Theodora's brother Bardas, who had Theoctistus assassinated. Michael asserted himself against his distraught mother and compelled her retirement in early 856. On the whole her regency had been successful, and she was particularly proud of restoring the icons and leaving a slightly increased treasury reserve of 7.8 million nomismata.

Michael III, later known as the Drunkard, was less interested in governing than in heavy drinking, lavish spending, horses, and his mistress Eudocia. He delegated most of his responsibilities to his uncle Bardas, who became Domestic of the Scholae and proved to be a competent ruler. Michael and Bardas soon quarreled with the Patriarch of Constantinople Ignatius, a somber monk chosen by Theodora. In 858 they forced Ignatius to abdicate and replaced him with the Proto-asecretis Photius, the leading scholar of the day. But Photius had been a layman before his hasty consecration, which the Pope eventually ruled invalid.

When the prince of Moravia, a Slavic state northwest of Bulgaria, asked the Byzantines for missionaries to complete the conversion of his country that Frankish missionaries had begun, Photius granted his request in 863. The Byzantine mission, led by the brothers Cyril and Methodius, claimed Moravia for the Eastern Church. Cyril translated the Greek liturgy into Slavonic, devising a means of writing Slavonic in a modified Greek alphabet that later developed into modern Cyrillic.

The same year the Byzantines slaughtered an Arab raiding party in eastern Anatolia and raided Arab Armenia, in the process killing the Emir of Melitene, the former Emir of Tarsus, and the leader of the Paulicians. Next the Byzantines attacked Bulgaria, leading its Khan Boris to conclude an alliance, to accept Byzantine missionaries, and in 865 to receive baptism with the Christian name of Michael, with Michael III as his godfather. Byzantium seemed to be in the ascendant on both its eastern and its western frontiers.

Bardas, recently appointed Caesar, could take much of the credit, but the next year he fell victim to Michael III's fecklessness. When his mistress Eudocia became pregnant, Michael decided to make her the nominal wife of his chamberlain and drinking companion Basil the Macedonian. The emperor let Basil assassinate Bardas, then adopted

Basil, who was almost thirty years his senior, apparently in order to secure the succession for Michael's natural son by Eudocia.

Since Basil never gained as much influence over Michael as Bardas had had, no one was fully in charge. Michael spent wildly, giving vast sums of money to his companions. The Paulicians started raiding Anatolia again, and the Sicilian Arabs raided the remnant of Byzantine Italy. The Pope's rejection of Photius as Patriarch had opened a schism with the Western Church, in which the Bulgarian and Moravian churches sided with the Pope. In 867 a council called by Photius declared the Pope deposed. The supposed grounds were that the Papacy allowed such practices as the use of unleavened bread in the eucharist and altering the Nicene Creed to say that the Holy Spirit proceeded both from the Father "and from the Son" (in Latin, *filioque*). Though such differences had never caused a schism before, they were to trouble relations between the Eastern and Western churches thereafter.

A month after Photius' council, Basil, evidently unsure of his hold over the emperor, had Michael III murdered. Few Byzantines seem to have regretted the passing of their legitimate sovereign, whose rare attempts at ruling had done little more than interfere with the work of Theodora, Theoctistus, Bardas, and Basil. Yet under Michael the empire's gradual progress had gathered speed. Especially through the efforts of Bardas and his generals, Byzantium had grown stronger as the Arabs had grown weaker, until finally the balance of power favored the Byzantines.

Basil, of Armenian blood but called the Macedonian because he was a native of the Theme of Macedonia, became emperor at the age of 55. His origins were humble, but he had shown much skill at intrigue, and by now he had some experience in governing. He had gained power primarily as the husband of the emperor's mistress Eudocia, whose sons Leo and Stephen were both presumably Michael's. But with a real son from an earlier marriage to be his heir, Basil stayed married to Eudocia rather than draw attention to his tangled marital affairs by divorcing her. Although Michael's gifts to various sycophants had emptied the treasury, Basil raised over 4.3 million nomismata by reclaiming half the gifts to everyone but himself and Eudocia.

The new emperor moved to end the schism with the Papacy by replacing the Patriarch Photius with his predecessor Ignatius, disowning Photius' recent anti-papal council, and asking the Pope to send legates for another council. In late 869 this council met and agreed to condemn Photius as the price of unity, but early the next year it

Figure 8 A mosaic of the Virgin and Child in the apse of St Sophia, Constantinople. Note the attendant angel at the right, originally complemented by a similar angel at the left. This elegant mosaic, which replaced a mosaic destroyed by the iconoclasts, dates from 867, when Photius was Patriarch of Constantinople. (*Photo*: Dumbarton Oaks, Washington, D.C., © copyright 1999)

returned the Bulgarian Church to the Patriarchate of Constantinople. The patriarchate also won over the Serbs when they asked for and received Byzantine missionaries, though Moravia remained subject to Rome.

Basil's military efforts were more successful than not. A Byzantine army defeated and killed the current Paulician leader, though when Basil led a force against the Arabs of Melitene he accomplished nothing much. The emperor permanently strengthened the Imperial Fleet by supplying it with professional marines, and it defeated the Sicilian Arabs several times. The Arabs took most of the rest of Byzantine Sicily only when Basil diverted the fleet to haul marble to build a church. Byzantine armies defeated the Arabs of Melitene and Tarsus, and conquered the last of the Paulicians and their stronghold of Tephrice in 879.

That year Photius, whom Basil had brought back to the patriarchate after the death of Ignatius, called a council to settle his differences with the Papacy. When the Pope offered to recognize Photius in return for papal jurisdiction over the Bulgarian Church, Photius deleted this condition from the Greek translation of the papal letter and won recognition anyway. The emperor had come to trust Photius, who tutored his sons and began work on a general recodification of the empire's laws.

Then Basil's son and heir died, making the new heir Leo, actually the son of Michael III. Relations between the emperor and Leo grew openly hostile when Basil forced Leo to leave his mistress Zoë and to marry a chaste young woman he loathed. Basil put Leo under house arrest for three years on a charge of conspiracy. After Basil's advisers persuaded him to release Leo in 886, the emperor died in a hunting accident apparently arranged by Leo's friends. Despite Basil's success in defeating the Arabs and strengthening the hold of the Byzantine Church on the Balkans, the dubious means by which he had become emperor finally undid him.

His successor, the nineteen-year-old Leo VI, shared the general opinion that he was Michael III's son. Leo was cerebral but rather lazy, and at first unsure of himself. He deposed the Patriarch Photius as an ally of Basil's, and adopted as his principal adviser the father of his mistress Zoë, Stylianus Zaützes, who became Postal Logothete. Clever but corrupt, Zaützes took over Photius' project of revising the laws, and in 888 the government promulgated the *Basilica* ("Imperial Code"), a modified Greek version of the *Justinian Code* with many additions.

In 894 Zaützes foolishly provoked the Bulgarians by giving some of his friends a monopoly over Bulgarian trade with Byzantium. The Bulgarian Khan Symeon invaded Byzantine territory and defeated a Byzantine army. Though the emperor incited an attack on the Bulgarians by their neighbors the Magyars, this only temporarily distracted Symeon, who defeated the Byzantines again. The empire had to cede some border territory and agree to pay an annual tribute in order to recover its many prisoners of war and restore the peace. Obviously a Christian Bulgaria could still pose a threat to Byzantium.

Zaützes' influence over the emperor was waning when the empress providentially died the next year, freeing Leo to marry his longtime mistress Zoë, Zautzes' daughter. But this marriage lasted only a year before Zoë and her father also died. Leo exiled the remaining members and cronies of the Zaützes family, and began to rule for himself. Putting an end to the profiteering they had fostered, he grew interested in extending his eastern frontier, though he never took the field in person. At this time Leo seems to have given the themes more mobility by increasing the number of cavalry in most of them.

The emperor went on the offensive in 900, sending an army that raided the Emirate of Tarsus and captured its emir. Byzantine forces began a slow advance into western Armenia, annexing pieces of border territory. The land was so poor and rough that previous rulers had thought it not worth the taking, but its conquest moved the frontier farther from the Byzantine heartland and nearer to more valuable Arab possessions. The Arabs responded with naval attacks, one of which surprised and sacked Thessalonica in 903. Yet devastating and humiliating though the sack of the empire's second city was, it showed poor preparation rather than weakness on the Byzantines' part.

Meanwhile the emperor had been widowed a third time and still had no son, but only his estranged brother Alexander to succeed him. At first, rather than defy the condemnation of fourth marriages in Byzantine canon law, Leo prudently took a mistress, Zoë Carbonopsina. When Zoë bore him a son, however, he decided he had to marry her. Forcing the hostile Patriarch Nicholas Mysticus to abdicate, Leo obtained a dispensation from the Pope, since the Western Church permitted the widowed to remarry as often as they wished. But even the new Patriarch Euthymius regarded Leo's fourth marriage as an abomination, and made Leo declare all future fourth marriages violations of civil as well as canon law.

A Byzantine fleet raided the Syrian coast to retaliate for the sack of Thessalonica, and the Byzantines continued their slow advance in eastern Anatolia. In 911 Leo sent a major expedition to reconquer Crete from the Arabs. But the Arabs still had a strong fleet, and crushed the expeditionary force before it reached the island. Leo died the next year, after a reign of mixed achievement. The defeat in the Bulgarian war, the Arab sack of Thessalonica, and the failure of the campaign against Crete made a bad impression but did little lasting harm. Leo's annexations in the east, completion of the *Basilica*, and strengthening the cavalry in the themes were less striking but more significant.

Rivalries and Progress

The new emperor Alexander, who had never liked his brother Leo, found himself sharing the throne with Leo's six-year-old son

Constantine VII. Childless and suffering from a grave disease that may have been testicular cancer, Alexander reversed some of his brother's policies. He stopped paying the annual tribute to the Bulgarians, and banished Leo's widow Zoë from the palace. He also dismissed the Patriarch Euthymius and restored the deposed Patriarch Nicholas Mysticus. As Alexander lay dying, he named Nicholas the chief regent for his young nephew.

When little Constantine VII became emperor in 913, he was therefore separated from his mother, subject to a regent who considered him a bastard, and threatened by a Bulgarian invasion. Since Nicholas was unready to fight the Bulgarians, he made peace by resuming the tribute, betrothing Constantine to the daughter of the Bulgarian Khan Symeon, and crowning Symeon Emperor of the Bulgarians. Yet the latter two conditions were so humiliating for the empire that they led to a coup that deposed Nicholas from his regency and replaced him with the emperor's mother Zoë.

When Zoë repudiated her son's engagement to Symeon's daughter, the Bulgarian emperor began raiding Byzantine territory. The Byzantines attacked Bulgaria, but Symeon defeated them soundly. After further reverses, Zoë's regency fell victim to a welter of plots and counterplots. The new master of the empire was the commander of the Imperial Fleet, Romanus Lecapenus, who married his own daughter to Constantine VII. In 920 he put Zoë in a monastery and had himself crowned co-emperor with Constantine.

Aged about fifty, the son of an Armenian peasant who had settled in Byzantium, Romanus was crafty and capable, with an affinity for generals from Armenian families and for projects to reclaim Armenian territory. Of course Symeon of Bulgaria was furious that not he but Romanus had become Constantine's father-in-law. But the next year a Byzantine army defeated Symeon outside Constantinople, and after three more years of indecisive warfare Symeon made a truce in return for renewed tribute. In 927 he died, leaving Bulgaria exhausted, and his son and successor Peter married Romanus' granddaughter and became a Byzantine ally.

Peace with the Bulgarians allowed Romanus to turn his attention to his eastern frontier. First he sent his fellow Armenian and Domestic of the Scholae John Curcuas to attack the Emirate of Melitene. After a thorough devastation of his territory, the emir accepted Byzantine suzerainty in desperation. The whole Arab frontier seemed about to collapse before the Byzantines, when a freakishly harsh winter in 927–28 caused a terrible famine in the empire.

The famine reduced much of the peasantry to destitution. Rather than starve, many smallholders sold their farms to wealthy magnates, becoming renters on the lands they had formerly owned. Romanus worried that the new owners, most of whom were civil officials or military officers, would avoid paying some or all of the taxes due on their possessions. That spring he issued a law requiring peasants to sell land only to their fellow villagers. Though this law seems to have been ineffective, in 934 Romanus issued another law requiring that any land purchased illegally since the famine be returned to its sellers without compensation. Even if the wealth and influence of the buyers often made this law unenforceable, some land does seem to have been reclaimed.

Despite the after-effects of the famine, the Byzantines were soon attacking the Arabs again. In 934 John Curcuas conquered the whole Emirate of Melitene and expelled all its Muslims who refused to convert to Christianity. Two years later a large Arab tribe from Mesopotamia deserted to the Byzantines and became Christians, adding 12,000 cavalry to the Byzantine army. These helped conquer and garrison five new themes that extended Byzantine territory well to the east of Melitene.

After the fall of Melitene, the chief Arab power on the frontier was the energetic general Sayf ad-Dawlah, who managed to halt the Byzantine advance and to establish nominal control over most of Armenia. Sayf went on to raid Byzantine Anatolia, but this provoked several retaliatory raids by John Curcuas. The Domestic raided all over southern Armenia and northern Mesopotamia. Curcuas sacked most of the major cities and besieged Edessa, demanding that its citizens surrender the Mandylion, a towel imprinted with a supposedly miraculous image of Christ's face.

Delighted with these victories, Romanus wanted to marry Curcuas' daughter to the young son of his own daughter and Constantine VII, also named Romanus. Yet the old emperor's sons, fearing such a marriage would help Constantine take real power, forced their father to abandon his plans and dismiss Curcuas. In 944, when the Edessenes finally gave up the Mandylion, the sons tried to secure their succession by bundling their father off to a monastery. But this rash act offended old Romanus' supporters and played into the hands of partisans of Constantine VII. A mob in the capital acclaimed Constantine, who assumed power and reunited old Romanus with his sons in shared monastic retirement.

Thus Constantine VII, who had been titular emperor since he was seven, became the real ruler at the age of thirty-nine. His main accomplishment up to then had been to sponsor a series of antiquarian research projects, which included some work so poor that it may even be his own. Shy and bookish, he nonetheless had the basic skills needed to rule, above all that of knowing when to take advice. Though no admirer of Romanus Lecapenus, Constantine made few changes in his policies. He again ordered great landholders to return the lands they had acquired in violation of Romanus' laws, and he resumed the Byzantine offensive on the eastern frontier.

Constantine tried to retake Crete, but the Cretan Arabs overwhelmed his expeditionary force, which he had kept small to avoid risking more men. His excessive caution left so many Byzantine troops in the East that in the year of his campaign they could defeat a major Arab raid and go on to take the Arab stronghold of Theodosiopolis. Sayf ad-Dawlah, now Emir of Aleppo, fought fiercely against the Byzantines, but barely held his own. Two brilliant Byzantine generals, the future emperors Nicephorus Phocas and John Tzimisces, harried him relentlessly, killing his men, destroying his forts, and raiding throughout his domains.

In 959, while preparing another expedition against Crete, Constantine died. During his long reign and shorter rule, Byzantium had overcome internal dissensions and Bulgarian invasions and gained a decisive advantage over the Arabs. If Constantine won no victories in person, neither had Romanus Lecapenus nor most other emperors. While reigning and ruling, Constantine at least avoided making serious errors, and regained power for himself and his dynasty when they seemed to have lost it for good.

Constantine's successor was his fun-loving son Romanus II, aged twenty. Widowed as a child, Romanus had later fallen in love with a tavern keeper's daughter, Theophano, whom his indulgent father allowed him to marry. Romanus was happy to let the empire's excellent generals pursue new triumphs. Probably on their advice, he increased the numbers of the Tagma of the Scholae and divided it into eastern and western branches with separate commanders for Anatolia and the Balkans, the Domestic of the East and the Domestic of the West. As Domestic of the East he chose his best general, Nicephorus Phocas, whose first assignment was to lead the expedition against Crete already planned by Constantine.

A year after Romanus' accession, Phocas sailed for Crete with a huge army and navy, reportedly totaling 77,000 soldiers and oarsmen. Landing safely on the island, he drove the Arabs from the field and penned them up in their stronghold of Chandax. He besieged them through the winter and stormed Chandax in the spring. After well over a century as a nest of Arab pirates, Crete became a Byzantine theme, and Byzantine missionaries began converting its population back to Christianity. Nicephorus returned to Constantinople in triumph. Meanwhile his brother Leo Phocas, the Domestic of the West, fought in the East and had annihilated the army of Sayf ad-Dawlah.

Nicephorus prepared to lead an army east to exploit his brother's victory. He invaded the Emirate of Tarsus in overwhelming force, defeating its emir. Though Sayf ad-Dawlah tried to rally the defenders, he withdrew when Nicephorus and John Tzimisces returned with some 70,000 men. They swept through the hapless Emirate of Tarsus, burst into Syria, and descended upon Sayf's capital of Aleppo. Putting Sayf to flight, they stormed, sacked, and burned the city except for its citadel, then marched back to Byzantine territory at their leisure.

There they learned of the untimely death of young Romanus II, who had overexerted himself while hunting. Though Romanus had presided over only one important conquest, that of Crete, his generals' victories over the eastern Arabs showed that Byzantium could extend its eastern frontier whenever it chose. The Byzantines had already conquered as much land as they needed for a buffer against Arab raids on Anatolia. They now had to decide whether to be satisfied with their present frontiers or to begin reclaiming territory that the Arabs had taken from them more than two and a half centuries before.

Nicephorus II and John I the Conquerors

Romanus left his widow Theophano and two sons, of whom the elder, Basil II, was just five in 962. With few supporters in the government, Theophano invited the empire's leading general, Nicephorus Phocas, to come to the capital and celebrate his victories over the Arabs. On his arrival Nicephorus, who was a widower, evidently agreed to marry the empress. As soon as he left Constantinople, however, Theophano's enemies began to plot against him. He forestalled them by having the Anatolian armies proclaim him emperor, then marched back and seized the capital with the help of enthusiastic crowds. Marrying Theophano, he adopted her two sons, who could expect to inherit the empire in due course because he was fifty-one and had no children of his own.

The devout and dutiful Nicephorus II was hardly an ideal husband for Theophano, who was young enough to be his wayward daughter. But his plan was in any case not to rule peacefully from Constantinople but to return to the Arab front. Most previous emperors had rarely if ever led armies after their accession, and had limited their generals to raiding enemy territory or annexing bases used for attacks on Byzantium, like Crete. Nicephorus, a warrior from a military family in the Cappadocian borderlands, meant to go on fighting in person and to extend Byzantine rule into Syria.

Before departing for the East, Nicephorus appointed some of his friends and relations to high office. He also tried to persuade the Patriarch Polyeuctus to honor as martyrs Byzantine soldiers who died fighting Muslims, but Polyeuctus defended the traditional doctrine that killing in battle was a sin requiring penance. Nicephorus then issued a law prohibiting future gifts of land to the Church, which was accumulating vast estates that paid little in taxes, though he promoted the foundation of monasteries on vacant land.

The emperor set out against the Arabs in 964. He dispatched two naval expeditions, one to rescue the last of Byzantine Sicily, which failed, and the other to capture Cyprus, which succeeded. Nicephorus himself systematically subjected the Emirate of Tarsus, completing the conquest within a year. He established new themes not just in Cilicia, which had been the Emirate, but in the lands immediately to its east. The emperor expelled from his new themes all Muslims who would not convert, and encouraged Christians from Armenia and Syria to settle in the fertile but depopulated country.

Nicephorus returned to the attack in 966, raiding northern Syria and briefly besieging Antioch. Arab resistance was crumbling, especially after Sayf ad-Dawlah died the next year. Then the emperor annexed a large part of western Armenia, most of it voluntarily ceded by its petty princes. He organized these acquisitions into more than a dozen small themes, each with a small garrison that could serve on future campaigns. Nicephorus also created a strong new corps of cavalry in heavy armor to accompany his army.

Having quarreled with the Bulgarian emperor Peter, rather than divert his own energies from the Arab war Nicephorus invited the Russian prince Svyatoslav to invade Bulgaria, pagan though he was. Svyatoslav arrived in 967, swept aside the Bulgarian army, and began incorporating eastern Bulgaria into an enlarged Russian principality. The next year the German emperor Otto I, whom Nicephorus had refused to send a Byzantine princess to marry his son, raided the Byzantine holdings in southern Italy. Meanwhile a famine had broken out in the empire, which together with the mounting costs of the Arab campaigns took a toll on Nicephorus' popularity.

Refusing to be distracted, the emperor attacked the Arabs again. This time he conquered Edessa, which had a sizable Christian population. Though he raided throughout northern Syria, his main objective was the still large and largely Christian city of Antioch. He took the main forts around it and put the city under siege. Since a local famine made supplying his whole army difficult, he left a smaller force to continue the siege through the winter. The next spring the Byzantines took the city by storm. At the same time the Byzantine commander in Italy defeated the forces of Otto of Germany, and the Byzantine commander in Armenia raided what remained of Arab Armenia and sacked its capital.

Yet for all his triumphs on the frontiers, Nicephorus had lost favor with the people and officials at Constantinople, where he only occasionally visited. The famine persisted, and several powerful people felt neglected by the emperor, among them the empress Theophano and the Domestic of the East John Tzimisces. The empress and the general concocted an unusually well-laid plot to kill Nicephorus, marry each other, and rule jointly with her sons. Late in 969 Tzimices and a few supporters murdered the emperor as he slept in the palace.

This was probably the least justifiable murder of an emperor in Byzantine history to date. Nevertheless, once John had cashiered a few of Nicephorus' partisans, scarcely anyone in the capital objected to what had been done. The Patriarch Polyeuctus, who had criticized both Nicephorus' marriage and his legislation on church lands, agreed to crown John on condition that he donate his personal property to the poor, punish his confederates, and exile Theophano. John agreed, executed two of his friends, sent Theophano to a convent, and was crowned.

Although an assassin and a usurper, John ruled as a colleague of the legitimate but underage emperors, and soon allied himself with their dynasty by marrying their aunt. Handsome, charismatic, and well-connected, a nephew of his victim Nicephorus, the forty-four-year-old Armenian was a brilliant general in his own right. Because like Nicephorus he wanted to spend most of his time winning land for the empire, he put most administrative duties into the hands of the Grand Chamberlain Basil Lecapenus, a bastard son of Romanus I.

John's reign began auspiciously with the end of three years of famine and the submission of the Emirate of Aleppo, which became a Byzantine client. To prepare for further advances, John subordinated the thirty-odd small themes created by Nicephorus on the eastern frontier to three ducates: Chaldia in the north, Mesopotamia in the center, and Antioch in the south. To leave himself free to fight the Arabs, Tzimisces made peace with Otto of Germany by sending his niece Theophano as a bride for Otto's son. Prince Svyatoslav, however, remained firmly ensconced in eastern Bulgaria, threatening to march on Constantinople.

When Svyatoslav invaded Byzantine Thrace, even though he was beaten back, John decided on a full-scale campaign against the Russians. At first he had to put down a rebellion by Bardas Phocas, a nephew of Nicephorus II who wanted to avenge his uncle and was exiled. But in 971 John led about 40,000 men against Svyatoslav. With remarkably little trouble, the Byzantines twice defeated the Russians and besieged them with Svyatoslav in the fortress of Dristra on the Danube. Three months later, the Russian prince agreed to evacuate Bulgaria in return for food for his starving army.

John demanded the abdication of the Bulgarian emperor Boris II, whom Svyatoslav had imprisoned, and annexed most of Boris' domains. In eastern Bulgaria John created six new themes, which he made subject to the new ducates of Adrianople and Thessalonica. Although acquired almost by accident, these conquests made a valuable addition to the empire, containing much good farmland and protecting Thrace from attackers from the north. The emperor also wanted to extend Byzantine authority over western Bulgaria, and created two themes there. But the sons of a former Bulgarian governor held the rest of that mountainous territory, and the task of rooting them out at once seemed too much bother for too little profit.

The following year John opened another offensive against the Arabs with a raid on the next Arab power to the east, the Emirate of Mosul. In the emperor's absence, however, an army from Mosul defeated and captured the Byzantine Domestic of the East, who died in his Arab prison. In 974 John returned to the East in person. Making an alliance with the king of the independent part of Armenia, the emperor invaded the Emirate of Mosul again, and, after ravaging it badly, compelled the emir to pay him an annual tribute.

A year later the emperor tackled the strongest of the Muslim states, the Fatimid Caliphate, which was based in Egypt but also held southern Syria. John and his new Domestic of the East Bardas Sclerus advanced into northern Palestine, visited some of the sacred sites of Galilee, and collected tribute from the neighboring towns. Preferring to avoid the Fatimid garrisons in the coastal cities of Palestine, the emperor attacked the places to their north. He entered Berytus (Beirut), took tribute from Sidon, and sacked Byblus. Though Tripoli held out against him, he conquered the whole Syrian coast to its north, organizing several new themes that he added to the Ducate of Antioch.

John was probably exaggerating when he told his Armenian allies that he had hoped to capture Jerusalem on this campaign. Before he could safely have ventured that far south, he would have needed to inflict a decisive defeat on the Fatimids and conquer central Syria. Yet neither task seemed beyond his power, given a little more time. The Fatimids were weaker than the Byzantines, and their hold on their Syrian possessions was insecure. If John had kept up the pace of his first six years of conquests for another six years, he could easily have taken and held all of Palestine.

After the campaigning season the emperor returned to Constantinople, but he fell ill on the way and died soon after his arrival in early 976. A credible report had it that the Grand Chamberlain Basil Lecapenus had poisoned John to prevent him from investigating charges of Basil's corruption. Within seven years Byzantium had lost two great warrior emperors, who had finally harnessed the empire's growing military strength to make major conquests. Between them, Nicephorus Phocas and John Tzimisces had increased Byzantine territory by about a quarter, annexing most of Bulgaria, the Emirate of Tarsus, and much of Armenia. Whether Byzantium could continue to expand under less extraordinary leaders remained to be seen.

Basil II the Triumphant

At the death of Tzimisces the hereditary emperor Basil II was eighteen, and no longer needed a regent. Basil was intelligent enough, but apparently more interested in chasing women than in challenging the Grand Chamberlain Basil Lecapenus, who acted as the real ruler. The junior emperor Constantine VIII was even more frivolous than his brother. Though the chamberlain was a seasoned and clever intriguer, the partisans of both previous emperors resented him, since he had been one of the plotters who killed Nicephorus Phocas and was generally thought to have caused the death of John Tzimisces. When the chamberlain tried to have John's lieutenant Bardas Sclerus dismissed as Domestic of the East, Sclerus declared himself emperor at Melitene.

Tzimisces' friends and admirers rallied to Sclerus, who seems to have meant not to depose Basil II and Constantine VIII but to rule for them as Tzimisces had done. Beginning with strong support in Armenia and Syria, Sclerus defeated loyalist armies first in eastern and then in central Anatolia, capturing nearly the whole Asian part of the empire by 977. The naval theme of the Cibyrrhaeots backed him, but the Imperial Fleet defeated it, leaving Sclerus unable to cross into Europe.

While this civil war raged, the Bulgarians who still held out against the Byzantines retook most of western Bulgaria from them. Romanus, brother of the deposed Bulgarian emperor Boris II, escaped from detention in Byzantium, and the leaders of the Bulgarian resistance hailed him as their emperor. The Byzantine civil war also allowed the Emir of Aleppo to stop paying his tribute to the empire, while the Sultan of Baghdad conquered not only the Byzantine tributary emirate of Mosul but apparently the Byzantine city of Edessa as well.

Despairing of defeating Sclerus by himself, Basil the Chamberlain recalled from exile Bardas Phocas, nephew of Nicephorus II, and had him made Domestic of the East. Phocas was happy to fight Sclerus, a partisan of his uncle's murderer John Tzimisces. With a few men Phocas made his way to eastern Anatolia, where he mustered an army from relatives and friends of the Phocas family. Sclerus turned to meet him, and in two bloody but indecisive battles made him retreat to the east. But Phocas won over some allied troops from Iberia, and in 979 crushed Sclerus' forces. Most of them surrendered, while Sclerus himself escaped to Baghdad.

The war with Sclerus weakened Byzantium only temporarily, though the Byzantines had lost Edessa and their holdings in western Bulgaria. Basil the Chamberlain remained in charge of the government, with Bardas Phocas the chief commander of the army. A short campaign by Phocas was enough to persuade the Emir of Aleppo to resume paying his tribute. When the emir fell behind in his payments, Phocas invaded his emirate in 985, and may well have meant to conquer it.

Then, without warning, the young emperor Basil II had Basil the Grand Chamberlain arrested, and ordered Bardas Phocas to interrupt his campaign against Aleppo. Though the emperor merely demoted

Phocas to Duke of Antioch, he exiled the chamberlain and began ruling
for himself. At age twenty-seven, Basil II certainly had a legal right to
rule, but he also had a reputation as an idle playboy and scarcely any
experience of warfare or administration.

In obvious need of military glory, Basil planned a campaign against
the Bulgarians, who after driving the Byzantines from western Bulgaria
had begun to attack northern Greece. Because they had made their
gains thus far against little opposition, Basil probably assumed that a
large Byzantine force with experienced officers could overcome them
easily. In 986 the emperor led his army to besiege the Bulgarian outpost
of Serdica, not far from Byzantine-held territory. But the siege dragged
on, and Basil ran short of supplies and decided to retreat. As the
Byzantines withdrew, the Bulgarian leader Samuel surprised them in
a mountain pass and put them to flight with heavy losses.

At the news of Basil's humiliation, Bardas Sclerus returned from
Baghdad and raised another revolt. Backed by the Arabs and many
Armenians, Sclerus won control of most of Byzantine Armenia and
Syria. The alarmed emperor reappointed Bardas Phocas Domestic of
the East and sent him against Sclerus. The next year, however, Phocas
proclaimed himself emperor. At first he came to an agreement with
Sclerus, whom he allowed to hold the frontier region in alliance with
him. Then, deciding he could do without Sclerus, Phocas imprisoned
him and took over his forces. Within a year Phocas had secured practically all of Anatolia and the Crimea.

In urgent need of help, the emperor called on the Russian prince
Vladimir, a powerful but pagan ruler. Basil offered to marry his sister
Anna to Vladimir if the prince would convert to Christianity and send
troops to fight Phocas. Vladimir considered a Byzantine princess such a
prize that he accepted at once. He received baptism, married Anna,
adopted Christianity as the official religion of his Russian state, and
dispatched 6000 auxiliaries to Constantinople. These Basil enlisted in
a permanent corps called the Varangian Guard, which was to be replen-
ished with more mercenaries as needed.

The emperor distracted Phocas by landing an army in northwest
Anatolia that marched through Byzantine Armenia recruiting supporters, most probably former supporters of Sclerus. Phocas responded
by obtaining allied troops from Iberia. Early in 989 Basil himself took
his Varangian Guard and landed just across from Constantinople at
Chrysopolis, where he surprised and defeated Phocas' men. The
emperor and his brother then marched against Phocas' main army in

Figure 9 A contemporary miniature of Basil II the Bulgar-Slayer (reigned 963–1025), crowned by Christ, blessed by angels, flanked by saints, and triumphing over his prostrate enemies, from the Venice Psalter. The enemies may be Bulgarians, Arabs, Georgians, Armenians, or Byzantine rebels, or a combination of these; Basil conquered them all. (*Photo*: Biblioteca Marciana, Venice)

the northwest corner of Anatolia at Abydus. When they attacked, Phocas fell dead on the battlefield from a seizure, leaving his army easy prey. Although Bardas' widow released Sclerus, who proclaimed himself emperor again, before the year was out he submitted in return for a pardon.

Mighty though Byzantium was, these three years of a second civil war weakened and impoverished it somewhat. The Bulgarians had taken their chance to regain nearly all their original territory, and the Arabs had failed to profit only because they, like the Byzantines, had been fighting each other. The shock of almost losing his throne had made Basil II dour and vindictive, determined to keep his position unassailable and to disarm or destroy any potential enemies. Now well past the usual Byzantine age for marriage, he decided not to risk taking a wife, who might plot or meddle or have plotting or meddlesome relatives. Instead Basil chose a life of warfare, not so much to expand his state as to defend it aggressively.

The emperor first attacked the Iberians, to retaliate for their aid to Bardas Phocas. He defeated Phocas' main Iberian ally, who placated Basil by naming him heir to his dominions in southern Iberia. Next Basil attacked the Bulgarians. He pushed them out of northern Greece and captured their titular emperor Romanus, though their military commander Samuel remained at large. Basil also sent an army against another former ally of Sclerus, the Marwanid Emirate in southern Armenia, and forced it to accept a Byzantine protectorate. The emperor wanted to pursue his war with the Bulgarians, but for several years he had to keep sending help to the Byzantine client state of Aleppo, which the Fatimids were trying to conquer.

In 996 Basil issued a new law against powerful officials who bought land from peasants. Confirming Romanus I's law of 934, he ordered all land purchased illegally at any time to be returned to its sellers or their heirs without payment. Though as usual many buyers probably held on to their lands despite the law, Basil used it to break up the estates of some of his landholding enemies. At the same time the emperor reclaimed all imperial estates signed away by his former chamberlain Basil Lecapenus, except for grants that the emperor had personally approved.

Meanwhile Samuel of Bulgaria renewed his attacks on northern Greece. The Byzantines repulsed him, and he offered to accept a Byzantine protectorate; but when he heard of the death of the Bulgarian emperor Romanus in captivity, he proclaimed himself emperor in

Romanus' place. The war consequently continued. In 999 the emperor captured Serdica, which he had unsuccessfully besieged in his first campaign. Though he had to interrupt his campaign to fight the Fatimids, in his absence the Byzantine forces fought on, losing Dyrrhachium but retaking most of eastern Bulgaria.

The next year the prince of southern Iberia died, willing his principality to the emperor as he had promised. Basil annexed it as a new Ducate of Iberia. After making a ten-year truce with the Fatimids, he returned to the Bulgarian front, where the garrison of Dyrrhachium had surrendered to the Byzantines. The emperor finished clearing the Bulgarians from northern Greece and advanced into Samuel's remaining lands in western Bulgaria, taking several outposts. Basil used the expense of the Bulgarian war as a pretext for a draconian law making large landholders responsible for the taxes that neighboring smallholders were unable to pay. After some more raiding, however, he suspended operations against the Bulgarians in 1004.

By this time Basil had restored the Byzantine frontiers to more or less their extent at the death of John Tzimisces, and with that he seems to have been content. For several years his main concern was apparently to replenish his treasury, a task made easier by his law forcing the rich to pay the taxes of the poor. He renewed his truce with the Fatimids for another ten years, but never came to an agreement with Samuel of Bulgaria. Finally, probably meaning to persuade Samuel to accept a protectorate, Basil began raiding Bulgaria again.

In 1014 the emperor managed to trap the main Bulgarian army in a mountain pass and to capture 15,000 Bulgarian troops. He might well have accepted terms for their release, if the Bulgarians had not ambushed a Byzantine force a few days later. Irate at their temerity, Basil blinded all his captives, except for one in a hundred left with one eye each to lead the rest back to Samuel. Their appearance so appalled the Bulgarian emperor that he died of a heart attack. Still Basil made no attempt to conquer Bulgaria outright, and went into winter quarters after taking several more forts.

Samuel's son Gabriel inherited a crippled empire confined to part of western Bulgaria. Although he offered to become a Byzantine client, Basil doubted his sincerity and returned to the attack. Gabriel was soon killed and succeeded by his cousin John, who repeated the offer of clientship. This time Basil accepted, only to learn that John was planning an assault on Byzantine Dyrrhachium. Furious at being deceived, the emperor made for the Bulgarian capital of Ochrid, taking and blinding prisoners as he went. He sacked Ochrid, and his generals took several other Bulgarian strongholds.

Bent on pursuing his Bulgarian war to the end, Basil refused to be distracted when King George of Georgia invaded the Byzantine Ducate of Iberia and the Fatimids conquered the Byzantine protectorate of Aleppo. John of Bulgaria reoccupied Ochrid and retained some other fortresses in western Bulgaria, but he lost ground steadily. Early in 1018 John died in a desperate attempt to storm Dyrrhachium. At the news Basil swiftly gathered an army and marched into Bulgaria. The principal Bulgarian generals and John's widow simply capitulated, and the emperor entered Ochrid. Abandoning the idea of a protectorate, he turned his western Bulgarian conquests into a Byzantine Ducate of Bulgaria.

The emperor gave thanks for his victory in the cathedral at Athens, the ancient Parthenon, and celebrated a well-justified triumph in Constantinople. His generals rounded off his Balkan conquests by capturing the last Bulgarian forts on the middle Danube, which became a new Ducate of Sirmium. With the empire's border back at the Danube from Sirmium to the Black Sea, Byzantine holdings in the Balkans were again almost precisely what they had been before the seventh century. Moreover, the Serbs and Croats voluntarily became Byzantine clients.

After the surrender of Bulgaria, Basil shifted his energies to his neglected interests in Iberia and Aleppo. When the Fatimid governor of Aleppo rebelled and asked to become a Byzantine tributary, the emperor naturally agreed. Basil was also ready to grant favorable terms to George of Georgia. But after his attack on Byzantine Iberia George assumed he had gone too far to be forgiven, and allied himself with the Fatimids and the Armenian King of Ani. Basil therefore invaded Georgia, ravaging the land and blinding his captives as had become his custom.

George sued for peace and received rather favorable terms, ceding some border territory that was legally the emperor's and accepting a Byzantine protectorate. The King of Ani not only accepted a protectorate but promised his kingdom to the empire on his death. The Armenian Prince of Kars also became a Byzantine client, while the Armenian King of Vaspurakan simply ceded his kingdom to Basil, who made it a new ducate. Byzantine domination of the Caucasus appeared complete.

Basil's victories notwithstanding, in 1022 Nicephorus Phocas, son of the old rebel Bardas Phocas, proclaimed himself emperor in Anatolia. The kings of Georgia and Ani backed Nicephorus, but he was soon assassinated, and his rebellion collapsed. Basil quickly brought Georgia and Ani back to heel. With ample reserves of gold, aware that his conquests had brought few benefits to his subjects so far, the emperor canceled the empire's land and hearth taxes for two years, though he kept on the books his law holding large landholders liable for any taxes in default.

The triumphant emperor began to plan for one more campaign, to reconquer Sicily from the Arabs. In 1025 he sent an expeditionary force to Byzantine Italy, with instructions to wait for his arrival. Before he could embark, however, he died of a sudden illness at the age of 67. He had reigned for all but five of his years, a span unequaled by any previous emperor, Roman or Byzantine. His overall territorial gains were greater than those of any emperor since Justinian I, and unlike Justinian Basil made most of his conquests in person. Nor did he leave the empire impoverished, as Justinian had done. Even after paying for all his wars and remitting two years of his main taxes, Basil kept in his treasury the huge sum of 14.4 million nomismata.

An Expanding Society

Byzantium was obviously far bigger, stronger, and richer in 1025 than it had been in 780. After acquiring western and northern Greece, most of Armenia, northern Syria, and all of Bulgaria, and losing only Sicily, the empire had almost twice as much land as before. Byzantine political and cultural influence extended well outside its borders to its many client states and the newly converted Principality of Russia. After the conquest of Bulgaria and the breakdown of the Caliphate, for the first time in its history Byzantium was much stronger than all its neighbors. While the Byzantine army had grown roughly threefold and each soldier's pay had nearly doubled, the government was able to meet its expenses easily without raising its tax rates. The economy was thriving, and the population seemed to be as contented as it had ever been, loyal to both the Macedonian Dynasty and the orthodox church hierarchy. In almost every respect, the old empire had regained its vigor, unity, and security.

This recovery began gradually, and when the full development of Byzantine power became evident in the mid-tenth century it seems to have taken the Byzantines themselves by surprise. It was surely not the result of long-term planning by the emperors or anyone else. For most of this period Byzantine acquisitions were few and small, and mostly in depopulated borderlands. Irene, Nicephorus I, and Theophilus, like Constantine V before them, annexed some Balkan lands sparsely inhabited by Slavs, and fought the more formidable Bulgars only when attacked by them. Until the mid-ninth century Byzantine campaigns against the Arabs were retaliatory or defensive, and conquered scarcely any territory. Basil I, Leo VI, and Romanus I attacked the Arabs and their allies more aggressively, but made permanent conquests only in the virtual wasteland between the Antitaurus and Taurus mountains. The empire fought hardest to capture Tephrice, Melitene, and Crete, not because these had much value in themselves but because they had served as bases for enemy raids on Byzantine territory.

Byzantium's defensive posture changed dramatically in 963 with the accession of Nicephorus Phocas, the conqueror of Crete two years before. Not only was Nicephorus II a brilliant general, but he displayed more enthusiasm for conquest than any emperor since Justinian I. Meanwhile the Arabs, who had been fighting the Byzantines fiercely despite their own internal divisions, showed signs of impending collapse; and the Bulgarians, who had recently been defeating the Byzantines, were exhausted and temporarily impotent. Breaking with precedent, Nicephorus began a rapid expansion into Arab territory beyond the Taurus. Though his reign was short, his successor John Tzimisces was if anything a more skillful and aggressive conqueror than Nicephorus. Between them they conquered much of Syria and northern Mesopotamia, and most of Armenia and Bulgaria. Basil II, a less avid conqueror, did little more than recover and round off the parts of their conquests that had been lost during the civil wars of the early years of his rule.

Although Basil could almost certainly have conquered more than he did if he had been more ambitious, in some ways at his death the empire had approached its natural limits. Its northern frontier was almost precisely that of the Eastern Roman Empire in 395, and with the Byzantines' Serbian and Croatian clients the border lay near to that of the eastern empire under Diocletian. Though to the west Italy had been Byzantine under Justinian, it lay outside the region of Greek culture, except for the south of the peninsula, which Byzantium held, and Sicily, which Basil planned to retake. The Italian ports of Venice, Gaeta, Naples, and Amalfi were nominally Byzantine anyway, though they were in practice independent city-states. To the northeast, Basil's frontier differed from Diocletian's mainly because Basil had annexed more of Armenia, leaving less of the Caucasus region to Armenian and Iberian protectorates than Diocletian had done. The emperors understandably saw no point in attacking Hungary, the Papal States, or Georgia, none of which was necessarily an enemy or seemed nearly worth the trouble of conquering it.

Only to the south did Basil's frontier fall far short of the old Eastern Roman Empire's, because neither Basil nor his predecessors reclaimed inland Syria, Palestine, or Egypt, though Aleppo had become a Byzantine client. Nicephorus captured Edessa, which Basil lost during the civil wars and never retook, and John passed through northern Palestine without trying to keep it. Had Basil wanted to annex Edessa, Aleppo, or Palestine, he could probably have done so. He might even have been able to conquer Fatimid Egypt, which was not much stronger than Samuel's Bulgarian Empire, though more distant and better guarded by natural defenses.

However, once in Byzantine hands these Arab lands would been much more troublesome possessions for the empire than the conquests it actually made. The Byzantines had never ruled any large Muslim minorities, and were unused to ruling any religious minorities but Jews. Everything else that the Byzantines took had either been Christian already, like Bulgaria and Armenia, or like Crete and northern Syria had enough Christians that they could be made the majority by expelling or converting local Muslims and bringing in Christian settlers. Although Egypt, inland Syria, and Palestine still had many Christians in the tenth century, as they do today, their Muslim majorities were too large to be converted or expelled quickly or easily. Basil was certainly not eager to undertake any such task of assimilation. Probably not even John Tzimisces would have attempted it beyond Palestine, which had a special attraction as the Christian Holy Land that might have compensated for the difficulties of holding it. So the Byzantines had good reasons not to advance beyond their frontiers of 1025, except perhaps into Edessa and Sicily.

Within those borders the Byzantines had already conquered some sparsely populated and economically backward territory. The empire's western Bulgarian conquests were overwhelmingly rural and still paid their taxes in kind. Their main value to Byzantium was to provide a defensive buffer for Greece and Thrace. Greece enjoyed an unwonted peace and prosperity after Nicephorus I recovered and resettled the parts occupied by the Slavs, and Thrace too seems generally to have prospered, despite some Bulgarian raids. Towns throughout the

Balkans grew, though they had been so small at first that they still remained of modest size. Constantinople grew continuously, and like other cities and towns in Byzantine Europe should at least have doubled its population between the eighth and eleventh centuries. In the tenth century the city occasionally suffered from famines, but its problems of supply seem to have been overcome through increased agricultural production in Thrace and Anatolia.

The coastal plains of Anatolia remained the richest parts of the empire, for the most part a region of small farmers who owned the land they worked. The imperial land legislation of the tenth century seems to have succeeded in protecting these smallholders, to judge from the almost complete absence of great landholding families in the Opsician, Thracesian, and Cibyrrhaeot themes. The Phocas, Sclerus, and other families of magnates lived on the Anatolian plateau, with ranches that had already been extensive before the land legislation. No doubt these magnates became richer and more powerful, but much of the reason must have been a boom in agriculture with the end of Arab raids on their livestock. Since people usually want land only if they can profit from it, the land hunger attested by the laws seems to be a sign of growing population and rising production. Tenth-century Arab travelers to Anatolia found flourishing farms and lively overland trade.

The Byzantine acquisitions beyond the Taurus and Antitaurus consisted largely of marginal land, and years of wars between Byzantines and Arabs had depopulated even the fairly fertile plains of Cilicia and northern Syria. Yet the Byzantine conquest finally brought most of the border region peace, which together with resettlement and the distribution of pay to local troops should have helped revive both trade and agriculture. The Armenian lands, always poor and usually open to raiders and invaders, had long been a source of soldiers and settlers for the empire, and the Armenian themes continued to provide many of its best officers and soldiers. The emperors Leo V, Basil I, Romanus I, Nicephorus II, and John Tzimisces were all from Armenian families, and all of them but Basil had served as military officers.

The tenth-century land legislation and civil wars notwithstanding, the emperors and the army were allies more often than they were rivals. Military revolts became much rarer after Theophilus raised the army's pay in 840. The latest emperor that the army actually deposed was the incapable Michael I in 813. The army respected the Amorian and Macedonian dynasties, but it also wanted vigorous and talented emperors. When it intervened in politics, its aim was usually to give a weak young emperor an older and stronger colleague, as Romanus Lecapenus was for Constantine VII or Bardas Sclerus would presumably have been for Basil II. For the emperors' part, the main purpose of their land laws seems to have been to keep newly rich civil officials from becoming large landholders, not to break up the existing holdings of established magnates.

The emperors, who could appoint any generals they liked, almost always chose members of the great aristocratic families from the Anatolian plateau, simply because by tradition and experience such men were best qualified to command. Even Basil II chose Anatolian aristocrats as his generals, despite having fought almost the whole Anatolian aristocracy at one time or another. Basil knew that the magnates distrusted each other more than they distrusted him. The Phocas and Sclerus families had headed rival clans for generations, and dissension between Bardas Phocas and Bardas Sclerus repeatedly helped Basil during the civil wars. Besides, all aristocrats shared the emperor's interest in the empire's military strength, which defended their own estates and won them glory and plunder on campaign. The strong emperors of the tenth century wisely diverted most of the energies of their magnates from buying the land of Byzantine peasants to conquering the land of Arabs and Bulgarians.

During this period the army made a successful transition from being a mainly defensive force to acting as a mainly offensive one. The emperors' earliest military reforms were merely meant to improve the army's defensive capabilities. Such was the case when Nicephorus I recruited new garrisons for his acquisitions in Greece, and Theophilus used his converted Khurramites to reinforce the existing themes and his new cleisurae on the eastern frontier. But by raising the soldiers' pay and tightening their organization, Theophilus also improved their loyalty and professionalism. The importance of the change became clear after his reign, when for the first time the military balance shifted from the Arabs to the Byzantines. In later years Basil I provided the Imperial Fleet with professional marines, Leo VI increased the number of cavalry in the themes, and both Leo and Romanus I created and garrisoned new themes on the eastern frontier. All these military improvements made possible the victories of Nicephorus II, John Tzimisces, and Basil II.

Since each Byzantine conquest resulted in more themes and new garrisons for them, the expansion of the empire caused a great expansion of the army, at least on paper. Late in Basil II's reign it had about a quarter million soldiers. Yet the number of men on the muster-rolls was deceptive. By 1025, the empire had far more soldiers than it needed, and scarcely any use for the garrisons of the older themes that lay far from the new frontiers. The part of the army actually used in campaigns consisted of the tagmata and the themes nearest the frontiers, which John Tzimisces had grouped under dukes. The other soldiers fought only in civil wars, got out of training, and drew pay for doing practically nothing. Though the government occasionally asked them for cash contributions in place of the service they did not do, and may sometimes have paid them in underweight nomismata, it generally preferred to avoid trouble by paying its surplus troops with its surplus cash.

The civil service grew more slowly than the army in both numbers and influence. While the Postal Logothete continued to serve as foreign and security minister, the General Logothete as the chief tax official, and the Military Logothete as the army's paymaster, these three positions gradually became less important. The emperors began to retain much of their conquests as crown lands under separate officials, and rents from these became a major source of state income alongside taxation. Often the most important civil servant was the Grand Chamberlain, simply because he was closest to the emperor. Yet as a rule even the highest civil officials had less power than the chief military commander, the Domestic of the Scholae or, after that command was divided, the domestics of the East and West.

The bureaucracy failed to expand as quickly as the empire because the new themes were mainly administered by military officers. Though leading civil servants tried to enter the real aristocracy of magnates by buying themselves estates, and some did buy lands in the Balkans, the emperors' land legislation seems to have restrained their ambitions. From the time of Nicephorus I, the emperors were evidently on their guard against official corruption. The explosive growth in government revenues from the eighth to the eleventh century is a sign that the bureaucracy was performing its duties with reasonable efficiency and without much corruption.

The basis for the Byzantines' many conquests was evidently a strong economic expansion, and the basis for that economic expansion was apparently strong demographic growth. Though territorial annexations accounted for some of the added population, most of the lands conquered in Bulgaria, Greece, and the Arab borderlands must have been much less densely populated than the lands the Byzantines held all along. Thus most of the Byzantines' demographic expansion must have represented natural increases in Anatolia and Thrace after the plague ended and conditions became more peaceful. As the Byzantines settled previously vacant land, both around existing settlements and on the frontiers, the amount of land under cultivation and the number of livestock must also have grown. Breeding more oxen for plowing would also have increased agricultural productivity.

The demographic increase must however have begun first. To a great extent, the empire simply participated in a general recovery of population throughout Eurasia after the bubonic plague had ended. Similar demographic and economic trends should also have been benefiting the Arab world and Bulgaria, which nonetheless fell behind Byzantium. To be sure, the Arabs and Bulgarians inflicted some damage on themselves. With the breakup of the Abbasid Caliphate, the Arabs wasted their strength in fighting each other. Though Bulgaria evidently grew stronger between the eighth century and the tenth, the wars of Symeon and Samuel with Byzantium proved ruinous to Bulgaria. Yet if the wars of Nicephorus II, John Tzimisces, and Basil II invigorated Byzantium, presumably Byzantium was stronger than Bulgaria from the start. Its ability to weather its own civil wars without lasting harm also showed strength that the Caliphate could not match.

The Byzantines' advantages over the Bulgarians were fairly clear. Byzantium was bigger, richer, more populous, more urbanized, and better organized than Bulgaria, and consequently better able to survive setbacks and to exploit victories. Although Byzantium was smaller, poorer, less populous, and somewhat less urbanized than the Caliphate, on the whole it was better organized and more unified. Many if not most of the Caliphs' subjects still spoke no Arabic and were not orthodox Muslims, while the great majority of Byzantines spoke Greek and were orthodox Christians. With neither their army nor their bureaucracy as well trained or disciplined as those of Byzantium, the Caliphs eventually lost control of their provinces and became dominated by their own soldiers and officials. These Byzantine advantages proved crucial, because without them the Arabs found their Caliphate too big, rich, and populous to hold together.

Meanwhile the Byzantines made the best of their economic recovery. Nicephorus I overhauled their bureaucracy and system of taxation. Theophilus greatly increased the supply of both gold and copper coins to raise the army's pay, and the money quickly found its way into general circulation. As barter became less necessary, and Arab raiding and piracy were suppressed, internal and external trade became easier.

As customers became more numerous and more prosperous, trading became more profitable. Although Byzantine trade with western Europe was mostly in the hands of the Italian city-states nominally subject to the empire, native Byzantine traders still largely controlled the silk trade from China by way of Trebizond, the fur trade from Russia through the Crimea, and the spice trade from India by way of Antioch and Attalia. Constantinople remained the largest city and trading center of the Mediterranean world.

The cities of Anatolia seem not quite to have kept pace with the general growth of the Byzantine population, and the cities of the Balkans grew faster only because they had started so small, in some cases from practically nothing. Now that the urbanized provincial aristocracy of the early Byzantine period had disappeared, most of the great Anatolian magnates lived in villages and had little use for cities. Walled towns were no longer needed as places of refuge from invaders. The headquarters of themes were often not in major cities, and attracted only a few people, since most of their soldiers were spread throughout the themes' territories. In central Anatolia pigs, sheep, and cattle all probably outnumbered people by a wide margin. Such an economy required only middle-sized market towns and a few seaports. Most of the population growth surely came in the villages in which most Byzantines lived.

By 1025 the Byzantines had become rich and won victories without acquiring particularly luxurious tastes. The government spent most of its money on the army, and saved most of the rest in the treasury. The emperors kept busy by conquering more land and humiliating the empire's steadily weakening enemies. The empire's aristocracy consisted of austere ranchers who liked to fight. The bureaucracy remained relatively small and efficient. The military and administrative organizations that had allowed Byzantium to hold off the Arabs and Bulgarians had been converted into an effective means of subduing them. Now that Byzantium had conquered the Bulgarians and as many Arabs as it could conveniently absorb, the Byzantines' most vexing problem was to decide what to do next with all their wealth and power.

A Cultural Revival

While the empire expanded its borders and acquired client states, the conversion of the Slavs spread Byzantine cultural influence over a far wider area. As with the political expansion, the Byzantine cultural expansion was mostly unplanned. The Moravians, Serbs, and Bulgarians had requested Byzantine missionaries on their own initiative, while the conversion of Russia was the almost accidental result of Basil II's appeal for military help to the Russian prince Vladimir. The eagerness of the Slavs to accept Byzantine Christianity showed their admiration for all of Byzantine civilization, much of which they adopted along with its religion. The development of Byzantine civilization during this period was in fact remarkable, as the Byzantines emerged from their dark age to recover earlier Greek culture.

Toward the end of the eighth century the Byzantines finally found a use for education that almost all of them understood: to settle the dispute over Iconoclasm. In preparation for the Second Council of Nicaea in 787, the scholarly Patriarch Tarasius commissioned various clerics to search the writings of the Greek Fathers for passages that favored icons or refuted iconoclast arguments. This required a good deal of careful reading, because the Fathers had seldom referred to religious images, but the results made a good impression on the council.

Patristic research was continued by a new generation of iconophile monks, led by Theodore, Abbot of the Monastery of Studius in Constantinople. As the idea took hold that monks should not just pray but copy, read, and write theology, monks at Studius and elsewhere began copying theological manuscripts in the cursive minuscule hand, which made copying quicker and manuscripts consequently easier to produce. The secular church and the state bureaucracy also developed more interest in education under the emperor Nicephorus I and his Patriarch Nicephorus, both former civil servants.

When Leo V reintroduced Iconoclasm, he sponsored his own research to show that some of the Fathers really disapproved of icons, entrusting the task to the learned future Patriarch John the Grammarian. The emperor Theophilus, who had studied with John and made him patriarch, was an active patron of scholars, even if he kept superstitiously pressing them to predict the future for him. In 838 he chose John's relative Leo the Mathematician to open the first public school known at Byzantium for two centuries, which seems primarily to have offered a higher education to aspiring bureaucrats and clergy. Though Theophilus then appointed Leo Archbishop of Thessalonica, after the end of Iconoclasm Leo returned to his school to head a faculty of three professors. By this time the Byzantine revival of learning was well under

way, and the future Patriarch Photius, who had been exiled under
Iconoclasm, began making a name for himself as a scholar.

The condemnation of Iconoclasm, while resolving Byzantium's last
major theological dispute, began a time of some turmoil for the Byzantine Church. After the wholesale dismissal of the bishops who had
collaborated with the iconoclast emperors, at first iconophile monks
dominated the hierarchy. For many years to come, monks, often living
a little apart from cities in places like Mount Olympus in the Opsician
Theme and Mount Athos near Thessalonica, continued to enjoy more
prestige than bishops or other secular clergy.

One of the iconophile monks elevated to the hierarchy was the Patriarch Ignatius, who lost his office to Photius for reasons of court politics.
The Byzantine Church soon split between Photians and Ignatians, with
the Ignatians, backed by the Pope, refusing to recognize Photius as
patriarch. Ignatius' restoration, Photius' reinstatement after Ignatius'
death, and Photius' later deposition resolved the Photian Schism with
the Papacy, but caused lingering disputes about the validity of Photius'
ordinations of clergy.

The Byzantine Church split again over Leo VI's fourth marriage.
Most Photians joined the Patriarch Nicholas Mysticus in rejecting the
marriage, while most Ignatians sided with the Pope and Leo's Patriarch
Euthymius, another holy monk, in condoning it. Nicholas' partisans
disputed Euthymius' ordinations until a compromise finally restored
church unity in 920. Thereafter emperors avoided challenging the
Church and the Church avoided challenging emperors. Thus the
Church submitted to Nicephorus II's laws curtailing donations to monasteries, and Nicephorus accepted the Church's rejection of his idea that
soldiers killed fighting Muslims should be considered martyrs. The
Byzantines also remained in communion with the Western Church,
despite the differences over the *filioque* and unleavened eucharistic
bread that Photius had emphasized during the brief Photian Schism.

Meanwhile Byzantine scholarship continued its advance under the
patronage of the Caesar Bardas and the emperors Basil I, Leo VI, and
Constantine VII. For the first time in three hundred years, the *Basilica*
of Basil and Leo, and the *Novels* that Leo added to bring it up to date,
allowed Byzantine jurists to make full use of the *Justinian Code*. Yet like
Leo's *Tactica* on the organization of the army, the *Basilica* and *Novels*
included a good deal of obviously outdated or unenforceable provisions,
showing a love of learning for its own sake that was typical of Byzantine
culture at the time and often at odds with practical needs. During the

dark age Byzantine judges, generals, and officials had learned to rely on experience and custom rather than books, and most of them went on doing so.

After the revival of learning had begun by rediscovering the works of the Greek Fathers, it turned to rediscovering secular Greek literature. Photius' early studies are recorded in an enormous and untidy account of his private reading, later called the *Bibliotheca* ("Library"). The four hundred or so books described in it are about half Christian and half secular, and about half of what he read is lost today, making the *Bibliotheca* a source of great interest to us. Several dictionaries of classical Greek also came to be compiled in the ninth century, making the earlier language more accessible.

An uncritical antiquarianism disfigures most of the compilations sponsored by Constantine VII, such as *On Administering the Empire* and *On Ceremonies*, which jumble together current and useful information with obsolete curiosities. Among the finer scholarly compilations of the tenth century are a massive encyclopedia called the *Suda* ("Moat"), which records a great deal of classical lore, and the priceless *Palatine Anthology*, which preserves a selection of Greek verse from the earliest times to its own. Moreover, most of Classical Greek literature that survives today survived through manuscripts copied by Byzantines in the ninth and tenth centuries.

The effect of this newfound knowledge of the ancients on Byzantine scholars was not so much to inspire them to rival their brilliant predecessors as to make them despair of writing anything comparable. The best-educated Byzantines were particularly solicitous to copy the style and grammar of ancient Greek, and however well or badly they succeeded the result was almost always stilted and artificial prose. Naturally the early iconophiles wrote a good deal of theology. Various treatises, sermons, and letters survive by Theodore of Studius, the Patriarch Nicephorus, Photius, and others, many of them interesting as historical sources. Hagiographers recorded the sufferings of the principal iconophile saints under Iconoclasm. In the late tenth century Symeon Metaphrastes ("the Paraphraser") collected and rewrote many earlier lives to transform their originally simple and colloquial Greek into the more rhetorical language favored by educated Byzantines.

Enthusiasm for scholarship at least led the Byzantines to resume writing history, though chronicles compiled from books were more in fashion than contemporary accounts by participants. In the early ninth century George Syncellus chronicled the period from the creation of the world to Diocletian. Theophanes Confessor, using material left by George at his death, continued the story up to the accession of Leo V, including an iconophile account of the first phase of Iconoclasm. Neither work has literary pretensions, but the chronicle of Theophanes, arranged in separate entries for each year, performed the important service of preserving most of what was still known about the period after Heraclius. The Patriarch Nicephorus also wrote a brief history of the seventh and eighth centuries, adding little not in Theophanes but reviving the old classicizing style.

Except for some fragments relating to the reign of Leo V and one very skeletal monastic chronicle, the next surviving histories date from the scholarly activity of the tenth century, beginning where Theophanes had ended. The most elaborate, an anonymous compilation known simply as Theophanes Continuatus ("Theophanes Continued") was commissioned by Constantine VII as an official history, and is accordingly reticent about the embarrassing origins of the Macedonian Dynasty. A more reliable source is the chronicle of Symeon the Logothete, though Symeon did little more than copy his own sources faithfully.

Late in the tenth century Leo the Deacon wrote an account of the reigns of Romanus II, Nicephorus II, and John Tzimisces on the pattern of earlier classicizing contemporary histories. Interestingly, though Leo brings out some of the drama of the great conquests, he avoids glorifying either his emperors or their glorious age. Strangely, the eventful and victorious reign of Basil II, which would seem an ideal subject for history, attracted no contemporary Greek historian at all.

The only notable creative work that may belong to the end of this period is the original redaction of the epic poem *Digenes Acrites* ("The Double-blooded Frontiersman"). It celebrates the legendary exploits of a half-Arab Byzantine noble on the Anatolian border in what seems to be the late ninth or early tenth century. Since the poem survives only in later versions, and its compiler apparently drew upon ballads from before his own time, its original date and form are hard to conjecture. Yet it seems to have been composed for an audience of Anatolian magnates and their retainers. It has a heroic spirit that fits the period of the Byzantine conquests, but is missing from the contemporary literature penned by sedentary antiquarians in the capital.

Art and architecture naturally benefited from the Byzantines' returning prosperity. At first architects were unfamiliar with the techniques of constructing large monuments, but they gained experience by building a palace and some churches and fortifications for Irene and her successors. Theophilus was able to do more luxury building than any emperor since Justinian I. He was best known for making lavish additions to the Great Palace and decorating the throne room with mechanical golden lions that roared and golden birds that sang, to the astonishment of visitors. Most later emperors also made their mark by building, from the imperial stables of Michael III to the churches and monasteries of Basil I, Leo VI, and Romanus I. Such buildings were usually small but elegant, like a monastery church built in Constantinople by Romanus that is almost the only one remaining today. By the tenth century, some magnates began to follow the imperial fashion for building, commissioning churches and monasteries in the provinces.

Since even iconoclasts like Theophilus had put up secular mosaics and paintings, Byzantine artists had the expertise to make new religious images after the repudiation of Iconoclasm. The finest of these still extant are some mosaics on the walls of St Sophia, which like portable icons are magnificent in themselves but tend to be overshadowed by the architecture of the church. In the tenth century the Byzantines began to favor a more naturalistic and classicizing style in manuscript illumination, probably because the ancient manuscripts then being copied included illustrations that painters were asked to reproduce. No doubt they simply copied some images, like those from manuscripts of the Bible; but in other cases they must have adapted the classicizing style to new subjects, like the portraits of recent Byzantine saints in a manuscript prepared for Basil II. A similar style appears in ivory plaques of the period that depict emperors.

The revival of culture, though in part a symptom of growing Byzantine wealth and confidence, also made a contribution to the empire's economic and political recovery. The main producers and patrons of Byzantine education and art were government officials and churchmen. As the bureaucracy became better educated in reading, writing, and calculating, it functioned better in running the elaborate machinery of government at maximal efficiency and minimal cost. Byzantine officials collected more taxes, prepared and supplied more military expeditions, set up new military districts, and conducted diplomacy more successfully. The Slavs who sought Byzantine missionaries did so in large part because their envoys were impressed by Byzantine wealth, art, and imperial and ecclesiastical rituals. The advanced education of the missionaries to the Slavs, which allowed them to devise a Slavonic alphabet, contributed to their success in spreading Byzantine Christianity.

Although the demographic recovery had been the natural result of impersonal forces, Byzantine political, military, economic, and cultural advances were not. For all its advantages, Byzantium could have disintegrated like the Abbasid Caliphate, the Frankish Kingdom, or the Bulgar Khanate. A further decline of Byzantine education after the eighth century would probably have caused a breakdown of the administration and a loss of central control over the provinces. Longer reigns by the incompetent Michael I or Michael III could have bankrupted the empire and led to castastrophic military rebellions. At any of several times, rivals for the Byzantine throne could have fought their civil wars more recklessly, dividing the empire among them or betraying parts of it to the Bulgarians or Arabs. Less astute rulers could also have ignored the empire's opportunities to convert the Slavs or to defeat the Arabs and Bulgarians. Byzantium prospered in large part because from Irene to Basil II it was blessed with unusually capable rulers, clergy, officials, and generals.

6

WEALTH AND WEAKNESS
(1025–1204)

Thirteen Minor Emperors

Nothing reveals Basil II's narrow conception of his responsibilities so starkly as his lack of interest in the succession. Though he could hardly have disinherited his old and feeble brother Constantine VIII, Basil should at least have married one of Constantine's daughters to a man fit to be emperor while she was young enough to bear children. Yet after a short and undistinguished reign even Constantine waited until he was on his deathbed to see his daughter Zoë married. The forty-nine-year-old Zoë cared mostly for cosmetics, and Constantine's officials recommended her new husband Romanus Argyrus chiefly because they thought they could control him. Worse yet, similar bureaucrats were to run the government for most of the next half-century, always favoring malleable candidates for the throne.

Aged about sixty when he took power in 1028, Romanus III was a bureaucrat from a family of Anatolian landowners. With the treasury still full, he spent freely on building churches, and canceled Basil II's edict making the rich pay the unpaid taxes of the poor. His main military project was to annex the Emirate of Aleppo, a harmless imperial client. After an unsuccessful attempt to buy out the emir, Romanus attacked the emirate in the midsummer of 1030, leading his sweltering troops into two ambushes that ended in ignominious flight. But the next year the gifted young general George Maniaces undid the defeat by raiding the emirate, which became a Byzantine client again, and retaking Edessa, lost during the civil wars of Basil II's reign. Romanus' only

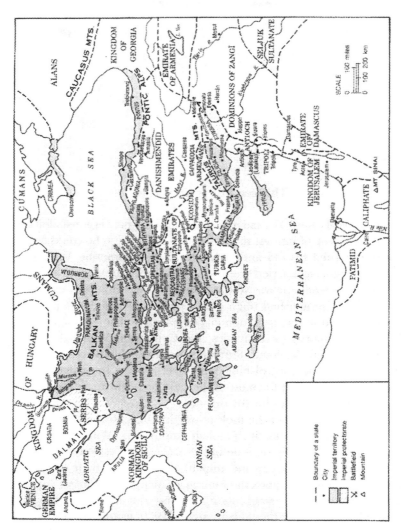

Map 5 The Empire *ca.* 1143

fatal mistake was to neglect his wife Zoë, who had him murdered in 1034 with the help of her lover, Michael the Paphlagonian.

Zoë married Michael and made him emperor the day after the murder. The first emperor from the commercial class, not out of his twenties but already ill with epilepsy, Michael IV was a barely adequate ruler. His main adviser was his brother John the Orphanotrophus, a eunuch and head of the state orphanage, who had Zoë adopt his nephew as a successor. The supine government's main initiative was to send George Maniaces to reconquer Sicily. Yet after Maniaces had taken Syracuse, John imprisoned him on suspicion of disloyalty, letting the Arabs retake the city and rebellious Norman mercenaries begin conquering southern Italy. John also ordered the Bulgarians to pay in cash the taxes they had always paid in kind, provoking a Bulgarian revolt that would have been grave had the Bulgarians not fallen out among themselves and surrendered.

In 1041 Michael IV died of his disease, and his nephew Michael V, though far from brilliant, tried to escape from the mediocrity around him. He exiled his uncle John the Orphanotrophus, released George Maniaces and sent him against the Normans in southern Italy, and in 1042 even exiled his adopted mother Zoë. Nonetheless, however incapable, she was the hereditary ruler, and the people of Constantinople rose up in her favor. Forcing the emperor to recall Zoë, a mob acclaimed her along with her sister Theodora and deposed and blinded Michael V. Uninterested either in ruling or in cooperating with her sister, Zoë soon married a third husband, Constantine Monomachus.

About forty, affable and aristocratic, Constantine IX only looked more competent than his four predecessors. Unlike them, with a longer reign, he did lasting harm to the empire's finances and security. While he probably spent about as lavishly as they had on buildings and largesse, under him the immense treasury reserve left by Basil II seems finally to have run out. Only under Constantine IX did neglect of the army cause severe discontent and decay. When he ordered George Maniaces back from Italy, the great general rebelled, crossed the Adriatic, and would probably have seized the throne if he had not suffered a fatal wound in a battle he was winning against the emperor's forces.

Around 1050, when the elderly empress Zoë died, Constantine began to mint nomismata that were only three-quarters gold, the first time since the third century that an emperor had adulterated the gold coinage. While Constantine seems to have raised the salaries of his courtiers and bureaucrats in proportion, the debasement lowered the value of

Figure 10 Mosaic of Constantine IX Monomachus (reigned 1042–55) and his empress Zoë (reigned 1042), presenting offerings to Christ, from the Church of St Sophia, Constantinople. In this mosaic Constantine's head and inscription have been substituted for those of Zoë's first husband, Romanus III Argyrus (reigned 1028–34). (*Photo*: Dumbarton Oaks, Washington, D.C., © copyright 1999)

most military pay. Much of the army had long been inactive and superfluous; but Constantine, who preferred hiring temporary mercenaries, allowed even his best thematic troops to become ineffective. In 1053, in return for annual payments, he decommissioned the 50,000 troops manning the Armenian themes on the northeastern frontier. Within two years the most aggressive Muslims to the East, the Seljuk Turks, were raiding unopposed through those very themes.

When Constantine tried to halt the Normans' conquest of southern Italy through an alliance with the Papacy, the Normans defeated the allies and captured the Pope. Then a Papal embassy sent to Constantinople in 1054 quarreled with the Patriarch Michael Cerularius, who objected to the Western and Armenian practice of using unleavened bread in the Eucharist. In spite of the ailing emperor's efforts to defuse the issue, the Papal legates and the patriarch excommunicated each other. The excommunications began an estrangement between the Eastern and Western churches that was the harder to end because it depended more on vague antipathies than on concrete issues.

At Constantine's death the next year, Zoë's sister Theodora, the last survivor of the Macedonian Dynasty, took power in her mid-seventies. She lived only a year longer, then adopted as her heir another nonentity, Michael Bringas, the Military Logothete. Just elevated from the office that had been paying the army in debased nomismata, the sixtyish Michael VI had trouble with his Anatolian generals almost at once. In 1057 they proclaimed one of themselves, Isaac Comnenus, who marched on Constantinople. Unable to rely on the dynastic loyalties that had bolstered his predecessors, Michael VI lost a battle to Isaac and abdicated.

Isaac Comnenus, an Anatolian aristocrat about fifty years old, was the most capable emperor since Basil II. But Isaac had to deal with a decaying army and a bankrupt treasury, rampant corruption and inflation, Seljuk raids on Anatolia, and Norman victories in Italy. Unable to rely on any of his bureaucrats or even on many of his generals, Isaac decided to tackle financial problems before military ones. His attempts to curb tax exemptions, cut salaries, and reclaim imperial lands naturally made him unpopular, and in 1059 an illness so disheartened him that he abdicated. Having no son, he named as his successor a fellow Anatolian general, Constantine Ducas.

The fifty-three-year-old Constantine X was a milder man than Isaac, and much less inclined to do things that could make him enemies. By now, however, the Normans had practically finished conquering southern Italy, the Seljuk Turks were taking forts in the Armenian themes, and the Balkans were under attack by other groups of Turks, the Pechenegs and the Uzes. When Constantine died in 1067, leaving his widow Eudocia as regent for their young son Michael VII, the gravity of the crisis was obvious to anyone who was sensible and responsible. Since Eudocia was both, in 1068 she married the general Romanus Diogenes, even though he had recently conspired against her husband.

An energetic Anatolian magnate in his thirties, Romanus IV was the first emperor since Basil II to give priority to the empire's military needs. Though Romanus despaired of saving Byzantine Italy from the

Normans, he was determined to save Anatolia and the almost defense-less Armenian themes that were supposed to shield it. Finding the tagmata and mercenaries too few to drive out the Seljuks, he called up many of the men on the rolls of the Anatolian themes, long inactive though they had been. Training them as best he could, Romanus hastily led them against the Turks.

Though this makeshift Byzantine army failed to catch any Seljuk raiders who fled from it, it defeated most of those who would fight. The Turks sacked many poorly defended Byzantine cities, but held scarcely any of them but the Armenian border town of Manzikert. In 1071, hoping to force a Turkish withdrawal by winning a major battle, Romanus led a large force to Manzikert and retook it. Then he attacked the main Turkish army under the Seljuk Sultan Alp Arslan. The emperor had the better of the fighting until an officer from the Ducas family, which resented his rule, spread the rumor that Romanus had fled. His inexperienced soldiers panicked, leaving Romanus to be cap-tured by Alp Arslan.

The emperor kept his head in captivity and made a treaty with the sultan. To gain both peace and his freedom, Romanus agreed to pay the Seljuks tribute and to cede them a strip of border territory including Manzikert, Antioch, and Edessa. Although under the circumstances the treaty was generous, the news of Romanus' release was unwelcome to the Ducas family. They declared him deposed, relegating his wife Eudo-cia to a convent and proclaiming Michael VII the only emperor. Their supporters in the army forced Romanus to surrender by 1072, then blinded him so savagely that he died.

Michael VII Ducas had turned twenty, but he was passive and stupid, with relatives only a little more competent than he. The main talent of their chief adviser, the Postal Logothete Nicephoritzes, was for palace intrigue. Michael's government did manage to suppress some Bulgarian rebels, but it never won over or subdued Romanus' general Philaretus Brachamius, who kept control over most of the eastern tagmata and much of the southeastern frontier region. Bypassing Philaretus, Anti-och, and Edessa, bands of Turks began to advance through the Arme-nian themes into Anatolia.

When they met no resistance, the Turks advanced farther and farther, and began to think not just of plundering but of outright conquest. Without Romanus to steady them, the remaining soldiers of the themes abandoned their arms in despair. The government, plagued by plum-meting revenues, famine, and a rash of military rebellions, debased the coinage further and even called on the Turks to fight its rebels. With the mercenaries and the eastern and western tagmata in revolt, the Turks found hardly anything to stop them once they arrived in force on the broad Anatolian plain. Military talent was so scarce that the government turned to a commander in his late teens, Alexius Comnenus. In 1078 Alexius declared for the leader of the truncated eastern army, Nicephorus Botaniates, and Michael VII entered a monastery.

An enfeebled seventy-six, Nicephorus III leaned on his courtiers and generals, especially Alexius Comnenus. The new government, like the old, gave subduing rebels priority over fighting invaders. The Pechenegs had taken over northern Thrace, and the Normans of southern Italy were preparing to invade the Balkans. While Alexius put down various rebels, the emperor Nicephorus won nominal recognition from Philaretus, whose fiefdom around Antioch and Edessa was now surrounded by Turks. The emperor tried to legitimize his rule by marrying the wife of Michael VII, who as a monk could no longer live with her. But the marriage still caused a scandal, and when Nicephorus announced that his heir would not be Michael's son the Ducas family turned against him. In 1081 Alexius, whose wife was a Ducas, marched on the capital and forced the old emperor to abdicate.

The two generations of Byzantine history after the death of Basil II are a classic case of the effects of prolonged misgovernment. Beginning with an overwhelmingly rich and powerful state, myopic bureaucrats and the unfit emperors they promoted gradually squandered the empire's treasury, ruined its coinage, wrecked its army, and lost half its land to disorganized Turkish and Norman freebooters. No economic, demographic, or strategic weaknesses caused this debacle. It resulted from a fateful combination of the indifference of Basil II to the succession, the untimely death of George Maniaces, the idiocy of Constantine IX in disbanding the Armenian themes, Isaac Comnenus' failure of nerve, and the Ducas family's betrayal of Romanus IV. After all these had done their work, the Byzantine heartland of Anatolia was as good as lost, and the empire's survival was in doubt again for the first time since the eighth century.

Two Managing Emperors

In these dire straits, Alexius Comnenus was crowned emperor at the age of twenty-four. Despite his youth, he already had six years' experience as a general, during which he had performed great feats of improvisation. He had never known military security or political stability in his lifetime, and had seen his elders fail dismally at running the empire. Neither tired nor set in his ways, the shrewd and devious Alexius was in some ways well suited to handling the crisis. If he could stave off immediate collapse and stay on the throne, Byzantium still had the land and wealth to recover much of what it had lost. The empire suffered above all from anarchy, and its opportunistic opponents were none too strong themselves.

The most acute threat came from the Normans of southern Italy, who were preparing to cross the Adriatic. Alexius resorted to various expedients. He relied to an unusual degree on his relatives, and gave his mother Anna Dalassena extraordinary administrative powers while he was on campaign. Lacking the money to make gifts in cash, he gave some other relatives and rivals special powers to collect and keep the taxes from designated districts. Finding that the scattered Byzantine outposts in Anatolia were practically indefensible against the Turks, he withdrew his men from most of the peninsula and mustered them against the Normans. The emperor collected some money by debasing the coinage even further, hired Turkish mercenaries, and appealed to the Venetians.

A few months after Alexius' accession, the Norman duke Robert Guiscard landed an army near Dyrrhachium and besieged the town. The emperor marched against him with almost all his forces. When Alexius attacked, Robert won a crushing victory, destroying the western tagmata, the last of the old Byzantine army except for the isolated eastern tagmata under Philaretus Brachamius. The emperor was lucky to escape with his life as the Normans captured Dyrrachium and spread over northwestern Greece. By appropriating gold and silver from the Church Alexius hired a new force of mercenaries, but the Normans routed it twice.

In desperation Alexius hired even more Turks and made a pact with the Venetians, granting them exemption from tariffs and a commercial quarter at Constantinople in return for their help against the Normans. The next year, backed by a Venetian navy and leading his Turkish mercenaries, Alexius expelled the Normans from the empire. Though Robert returned to the attack a year later, with some success, in 1085 he died, and his sons withdrew his army to Italy. Alexius' persistence had saved the damaged empire from outright conquest by the Normans.

The emperor then turned to fight the Pechenegs, who held northern Thrace and were raiding to the south. They made short work of his army of mercenaries, and while Alexius strove to replace it they continued their raids. Meanwhile some renegade Turks took to the sea and began seizing islands in the Aegean, and the Byzantine governors of Cyprus and Crete revolted. Only in 1091, with the aid of another group of Turks, the Cumans, did Alexius overwhelm the Pechenegs and retake northern Thrace. Next he rebuilt the Byzantine navy, and used it to reconquer the Aegean islands from the Turks and Cyprus and Crete from the rebels.

During ten years of careful management, Alexius had amassed a modest reserve in the treasury and begun repaying his forced loans from the Church. He started issuing a relatively pure gold coin, the hyperpyron, worth seven-eighths of the old pure gold nomisma. What the emperor had utterly failed to do was reclaim any part of Anatolia, where the Turks held everything but the refuge in the Taurus Mountains of a few former troops of the late Philaretus Brachamius. Having laboriously cleared Byzantine territory in Europe, Alexius seemed content that Byzantium should remain a European power.

The emperor was however surprised to learn in 1095 that an appeal of his for mercenaries from Pope Urban II had inspired the Pope to call a Crusade to free Eastern Christians from the Turks. The soldiers of this First Crusade, drawn from all over Western Europe and evidently outnumbering the whole Byzantine army, were to assemble at Constantinople before marching on to Jerusalem. Although the Pope intended for the Crusaders to help the Byzantines, to Alexius their army looked less likely to reclaim Jerusalem than to conquer Byzantium. Notwithstanding his suspicions, the emperor was too astute to antagonize the formidable Crusaders while he was so weak.

In 1097, as a force of some 35,000 Crusaders descended on Constantinople, Alexius negotiated warily with their commanders. They obligingly swore that they would hand over to him anything they captured that had recently been Byzantine, and would hold as his vassals anything else they won. Then the Crusaders and Byzantines joined in besieging Turkish-held Nicaea, which surrendered to the Byzantines to avoid being sacked. The Crusaders actually had little interest in Anatolia, but as they marched across it on their way to Antioch they terrorized the local Turks, allowing the Byzantines to make further reconquests.

Alexius acted cautiously. He waited the better part of a year before advancing beyond Nicaea. In 1098 he sent an army under his brother-in-law John Ducas that retook the coast and valleys of western Anatolia without much trouble. Yet as soon as Alexius reached the edge of the Anatolian plateau he began razing towns rather than holding them, resettling their Christian inhabitants in the territory he already held. In the meantime the Crusaders had taken Antioch only to be besieged there by a Turkish army, and were appealing to Alexius for help. Instead of hurrying to their aid, the emperor turned back to Constantinople.

Thus Alexius made only limited use of an excellent opportunity to recapture most or even all of Anatolia from the Turks. Even if he lacked the troops to reconquer the whole peninsula at once, he could quickly have hired more mercenaries if he had wished. Evidently Alexius did not want to reclaim the interior of Anatolia, just as he did not want to rescue the Crusaders, whom he regarded as a threat. If he had enlarged his army and regained all of Anatolia, the magnates who served him as military officers would have recovered their estates on the Anatolian plateau and become stronger. Rather than seeing magnates or Crusaders as potential allies, Alexius apparently saw all of them as rivals.

To Alexius' surprise, the Crusaders drove the Turks from Antioch in 1099 and extended their conquests all the way south to Jerusalem. Since the emperor had done nothing to help them, instead of ceding Antioch to him they allowed the Norman noble Bohemund, a son of Robert Guiscard, to make it the capital of his own principality. The news that his old enemies the Normans had taken a former Byzantine possession roused Alexius to action. He sent an army that seized much of the southern Anatolian coast from Bohemund, though not Antioch itself. Soon afterward Bohemund fell into the hands of the Turks, who were reestablishing themselves in the interior of Anatolia between the Byzantines and Crusaders.

During the next few years distrust between Byzantines and Crusaders increased. Bohemund made an alliance with the Turks who had captured him, and prepared another Norman invasion of Byzantium from Italy. In 1107 it landed near Dyrrhachium, like the Norman expedition of 26 years before. But by now the empire was stronger, and Alexius was more experienced. Without hazarding a battle with the Normans, within a year the emperor had Bohemund so hemmed in that in order to escape he promised to make Antioch a Byzantine vassal. Though Bohemund never fulfilled his promise, the immediate Norman danger to the empire had passed.

Byzantium now held most of the coasts and valleys of Anatolia, which made up the richer and more populous part of the peninsula, though not the larger. The Turks of the plateau often raided the Byzantine valleys, and the Byzantines regularly counterattacked, without either side's gaining much advantage. By the time Alexius died in 1118, Byzantium had enjoyed twenty years of prosperity and comparative stability, a vast improvement over the chaos that had prevailed when Alexius took power. Yet by failing to rebuild a large army, to drive the Turks from Anatolia, or to make a firm alliance with the Crusaders, Alexius had left the Byzantines weaker, the Turks stronger, and the Crusaders more anti-Byzantine than they might otherwise have been.

Alexius' successor was his eldest son John II Comnenus, aged 30 at his accession, and active and intelligent. John faced some problems that his father had neglected or created. Alexius had concentrated power in the hands of his relatives, who had mostly been loyal to him but were less loyal to his son. John soon had to suppress a conspiracy led by his mother, his brother-in-law, and especially his sister, the future historian Anna Comnena. Alexius had granted the Venetians overly generous trading privileges, which John revoked. John also tried to extend Byzantine power in Anatolia, a task that had become much harder after his father had let the Turks entrench themselves for forty years.

John's limited plans seemed not to be beyond the empire's strength. He wanted to gain real control over Antioch, and to secure the land routes between the main Byzantine holdings in northwestern Anatolia and those on the northern and southern coasts, then cut off by Turkish-held territory. John managed to open up a tenuous route to the south by 1120. But he was soon interrupted by Pecheneg and Cuman raids on Thrace, Venetian plundering of the Byzantine islands, rebellions by the Byzantine governors of the northern Anatolian coast, a war with Hungary, and a Serbian revolt.

After dextrously defeating the Pechenegs, Cumans, Hungarians, and Serbs, and placating the Venetians by restoring their trading privileges, the emperor returned to Anatolia. The main obstacles to his reconquering the northern coast were not the rebellious Byzantine governors but his scheming brother Isaac, the Turks, and the mountainous terrain that extended right up to the Black Sea. In six years of fighting John retook only the western part of the seaboard, until in 1137 he found a pretext to march against Antioch.

The emperor quickly forced his way through to the city. He extracted a promise from its prince to surrender it if the emperor helped him conquer a new principality around Aleppo from the Turks. When this proved too difficult, John gave up, and went back to fight the Turks who had retaken his reconquests in northern Anatolia. He reconciled with his brother Isaac, and after three more years of fighting recovered the whole northern coast. In 1142 John again opened the land route to the south, which the local Turks had overrun, and made for Antioch. But a year later the emperor died not far from the city, after a somewhat suspicious hunting accident.

Although John won many battles, his actual gains were rather small, and his overall strategy unrealistic. Even if he had conquered or reconquered everything he sought, the result would still have been a collection of narrow strips of Anatolian territory with indefensibly long frontiers. Shortly before his death, John contemplated giving his youngest son Manuel a sort of appanage consisting of the southern Anatolian coast, Antioch, and Cyprus. The idea shows that even John had begun to see that Antioch could not be governed from Constantinople without secure control over Anatolia.

Yet John seems never to have seriously considered abandoning his designs on Antioch in favor of a general offensive against the scattered and divided Anatolian Turks. Like his father before him, John liked to save money, managed the empire's problems a few years at a time, and seems to have feared that he might be unable to manage too large an army and too much territory. Also like Alexius, John distrusted powerful foreigners, including Western Europeans, and even powerful Byzantines apart from his none too trustworthy relatives. Although Alexius and John seemed successful, over the long term their strategy of limiting Byzantine strength and enlisting no allies posed grave risks.

Ambition and Disintegration

Since the first and second of John II's four sons died shortly before the emperor himself, most Byzantines expected his heir to be his third son Isaac, then at Constantinople. Instead, on his deathbed John allegedly chose his youngest son Manuel, who was in the camp and cannot be confidently cleared of complicity in his father's death. Though just twenty-four, Manuel was already a dashing figure, as energetic and crafty as his father and grandfather. He was somewhat more sure of the empire's power, which now seemed well established, and correspondingly less distrustful of Westerners. Without pursuing a strategy basically different from the one he had inherited, he was more adventurous and flamboyant, not to say reckless.

Although Manuel liked to consort with Westerners, he shared his predecessors' hostility to both the Norman state in Italy and the Principality of Antioch. Soon after his coronation at Constantinople, he rebuffed the Normans' offer of a marriage alliance, married a relative of the German emperor to win support against the Normans, and attacked Antioch. Manuel's attack gained a nominal submission from the city's prince, but also kept the prince from helping the neighboring Crusader state of Edessa, which fell to the Turks. The fall of Edessa led to a Second Crusade, which failed amid squabbling between the Crusaders and Byzantines.

Then Manuel prepared to attack the Norman Kingdom, which had just raided Greece. The Norman king responded by fomenting attacks on Byzantium by its Serbian vassals, the Hungarians, the Armenians of southwest Anatolia, and the Turks of both Anatolia and Syria. When Manuel fought off all of these with only the loss of southwest Anatolia, the next Norman king incited another Hungarian invasion and a conspiracy by Manuel's cousin Andronicus. After frustrating both of these, Manuel landed an army in southern Italy in 1155, but the Normans crushed it the following year. Two years later Manuel accepted the peace that the Normans had offered all along, before he had wasted large sums of money and fought all his neighbors.

The restless emperor then shifted his attention from Italy to the East. He enlarged his army, not by paying mercenaries from the depleted treasury but by granting soldiers and officers the power to collect taxes in various districts, a privilege previously limited to a few relatives and associates of the imperial family. Manuel used his expanded army to regain southwestern Anatolia from the Armenians, to extract another nominal submission from the prince of Antioch, and to humble the Anatolian Turks. When his German empress died, Manuel married a Norman princess from Antioch, but gained nothing by the marriage but a more attractive wife.

In 1162 the emperor became interested in Hungary. After failing to install his own candidate as its king, Manuel engaged his daughter to the Hungarian prince Béla, who was to rule a slice of Hungary along the Byzantine border as a Byzantine client. The emperor put this arrangement into effect by fighting a war with the Hungarian king and naming Béla heir to the empire, since Manuel still had no legitimate son. The emperor also tried to negotiate an end to the schism with the Western Church, making an impractical offer to appoint the Pope as Patriarch of Constantinople in return for the Pope's denying recognition to the

German emperor. Manuel also agreed to join the Crusader king of Jerusalem in conquering Egypt, with no success.

When Manuel's second wife bore him a son in 1169, he broke off his daughter's engagement to Béla and lost some of his interest in the West. The emperor ended the trading concessions his father and grandfather had granted the Venetians, simultaneously arresting all Venetians in the empire and confiscating their property. Venice retaliated by raiding the Greek islands and arranging a Serbian revolt, but Manuel persisted. After he married his sister-in-law to Béla, who had become king of Hungary in the meantime, the emperor was able to annex Béla's old fiefdom on the frontier and to force the Serbs back into submission.

In 1175 the emperor declared war on the Anatolian Turks. He began seizing borderlands, rebuffed an attempt by the Turkish sultan to negotiate, and the next year led an army against the sultan's capital at Iconium. On his way Manuel fell into a Turkish ambush at Myriocephalum, and to disengage himself and his army agreed to surrender his recent conquests. Yet the following year the Byzantines defeated the sultan's army, and the division of Anatolia between Byzantines and Turks remained approximately as before.

By this time in declining health, Manuel tried to arrange a smooth succession by improving relations with his neighbors. First he married his ten-year-old son Alexius to an eight-year-old French princess. He made an uneasy peace with Venice, releasing the Venetians whom he had imprisoned. He reconciled with his rebellious cousin Andronicus, who had followed the earlier example of his rebellious father Isaac and fled to the Turks. If at his death in 1180 Manuel had failed to gain very much by his costly and ambitious schemes, he had also lost very little. Byzantium seemed about as secure as it had been anytime in the previous century, except that for the first time in that century the empire lacked a mature and skillful ruler.

Still just eleven, Manuel's son Alexius II fell under the influence of his mother, Maria of Antioch. Though she took vows as a nun, she also took a nephew of her husband's as a lover. Because she was a Norman many Byzantines disliked her, and some members of the Comnenus family soon tried to overthrow her. Maria remained passive as the Serbs revolted again, Béla of Hungary reclaimed his border territories, and the Turks and Armenians captured Byzantine outposts in Anatolia. Andronicus Comnenus, though he had sworn to be loyal to Alexius II, started a rebellion. The fragility of the Comnenian system, disguised for so long by the efforts of Alexius I, John II, and Manuel, began to show.

In 1182 Andronicus marched on Constantinople, ostensibly to rule for Alexius II in place of the incapable and foreign Maria. The people of the capital rioted in behalf of Andronicus, had Maria's lover blinded, and massacred most of the Italian merchants in the capital. As soon as the rioting ended, Andronicus entered the city, sent Maria to the convent where she belonged, and assumed control over the empire as regent for young Alexius. The following year he put down a conspiracy against his regency and executed Maria, whom he blamed for inciting an invasion by King Béla of Hungary. Next Andronicus took a revolt in Anatolia as an excuse to have himself crowned co-emperor.

Though before being crowned at age sixty-five Andronicus had stayed on his good behavior, his rashness and cruelty soon overcame his judgement. He acted not like a hereditary emperor, which he had at least a dubious claim to be, but as a usurper and outsider. He murdered his colleague Alexius and married the boy's pubescent widow, and he suppressed the Anatolian rebellion with such savagery that he discredited himself further. Andronicus offended some powerful interests by curbing the official corruption that had spread under Manuel, and by reaching an agreement with the Venetians to compensate them for the property that Manuel had expropriated.

An emperor with little real or apparent legitimacy made an obvious target for rebels. Manuel's grandnephew Isaac Comnenus declared himself emperor on Cyprus, and Andronicus lashed out by killing Isaac's relatives. The emperor also blinded a bastard son of Manuel's for conspiracy, executing some co-conspirators. The Normans claimed to have the legitimate but dead Alexius II in Italy, and in his interest they invaded northern Greece in 1185 and advanced on Thessalonica by land and sea. As a suspicious Andronicus quarreled with his generals, the Normans took Byzantium's second city by surrender and sacked it.

Instead of defending his empire against the invaders, the emperor hunted down real or imagined enemies in Constantinople. One of these, the former rebel Isaac Angelus, took sanctuary in St Sophia. A crowd rallied to Isaac, and the patriarch crowned him emperor. Isaac let the enraged rabble plunder the treasury, mutilate Andronicus and his sons, and finally tear the old emperor to pieces. Andronicus deserved most of the blame for destroying his own dynasty and setting a precedent of lawlessness and violence. Worst of all, he had shown foreign enemies and potential rebels how vulnerable Byzantium was.

After this inauspicious start, the amiable Isaac II Angelus became emperor at twenty-nine, with no claim to the throne but as the

subjugator of a usurper. Though not an outstanding ruler, Isaac took his
heavy responsibilities seriously. He gave the command against the Normans to a good general, Alexius Branas, who took them by surprise,
routed them, and drove them from Thessalonica. Isaac himself finished
expelling the Normans from Byzantine territory. He made peace with
Hungary by marrying King Béla's daughter, and made an alliance with
the Venetians by beginning to pay installments on the compensation
promised to them. He sent a fleet to reclaim Cyprus from its self-styled
emperor, though the Normans thwarted the expedition.

Meanwhile a major revolt of Bulgarians and Vlachs along the Danube
proclaimed a new Bulgarian Empire. Isaac fought hard to suppress it, at
first with some success. But when he sent Alexius Branas against the
Bulgarians, Branas declared himself emperor, and Isaac lost valuable
time and money eliminating him. When the emperor began making
headway against the Bulgarians once more, he had to rush to Anatolia
to fight a rebel magnate. Isaac had just begun to suppress this rebellion
in 1189 when the German emperor Frederick Barbarossa arrived on
the Third Crusade, pillaging Thrace as he went. Other Crusaders took
Cyprus from its rebel emperor.

After negotiating a peace with Frederick, Isaac fought the Bulgarians
and Serbs who had followed the Crusaders into Thrace. As rebel after
rebel appeared in Byzantine Anatolia, the emperor's forces barely held
their own. Isaac sent an army against the Bulgarians under his cousin,
who also proclaimed himself emperor. Though the cousin was betrayed
to Isaac, the Bulgarians advanced farther into Thrace. The emperor led
another army against them in 1195, only to be overthrown and blinded
by his older brother Alexius. Isaac had won no decisive victories, but he
had fought doggedly against a mass of rebels, and he finally fell by a
hand he should have been able to trust.

Alexius III Angelus, in his early forties, was unpleasant, improvident,
and indolent, though he had a rudimentary talent for personal survival.
His seizure of power could only encourage more plots and revolts at a
time when they were already rife. While the Bulgarians and Turks
raided Byzantine territory, Alexius sent armies against an Anatolian
rebel claiming to be Alexius II, the last hereditary emperor. The
emperor gained nothing from a Bulgarian civil war, because his own
army mutinied and the Vlachs who joined him kept deserting him.

Alexius stopped paying the Venetians the indemnity promised by his
brother, though barely a quarter of it was still due. Meanwhile the
Norman Kingdom passed to the German emperor Henry VI, who

demanded blackmail not to invade Byzantium. Alexius agreed to pay four times the sum he had refused the Venetians, but Henry died before collecting the money. Henry's brother Philip, heir to Germany though not to Norman Italy, was an even bitterer enemy of Alexius, because his wife was the daughter of Isaac II, whom Alexius had deposed, blinded, and imprisoned.

By 1200 Byzantium seemed to be falling to pieces. Alexius' cousin Michael Ducas seized part of Anatolia, while a local magnate took another part. Provincial commanders raised revolts in central Thrace and northern and southern Greece. All these rebels apparently aimed not to seize Constantinople but to carve out domains of their own. Alexius quickly put down a rebellion in Constantinople itself, but in the confusion Isaac II's son Alexius escaped from the city to Germany. There he appealed to his brother-in-law Philip for help.

Late in 1202 Philip conveyed an offer from prince Alexius to the army of the Fourth Crusade, then unable to pay its passage to Egypt under a contract with the Venetians. Prince Alexius offered almost six times the Crusaders' debt if they and the Venetians would restore his father Isaac to the Byzantine throne. The Venetians, eager to be paid and to gain influence at Constantinople, convinced the Crusaders, despite protests by a papal legate that the Crusade was forbidden to attack Christians. The next spring, joined by young Alexius, the Crusaders began conquering Greek ports and islands. By summer they were before Constantinople.

Although Alexius III evidently had a bigger army than that of the Crusaders, he never adopted an effective strategy to fight them, and his fleet was far worse than the Venetians'. When the Venetians made a daring attack on the sea walls, the emperor panicked and absconded, leaving the Constantinopolitans to put the blinded Isaac II on the throne. Against his better judgement, Isaac had to agree to pay the sum promised the Crusaders by his son Alexius, whom he crowned as his colleague.

Since his father was a blind and broken man, Alexius IV became the real ruler, but he was barely twenty, and quite inexperienced. With most of the empire in the hands of earlier rebels or Alexius III, who had moreover left with much of the treasury, the new emperor found the amount he had promised his Western allies well beyond his means. After heavy exactions from the Constantinopolitans, the most he could pay was just over half. By this time he had alienated not only the Crusaders and Venetians but his subjects, who deposed him at the beginning of 1204.

The new emperor, Alexius V Ducas Murtzuphlus, was in his mid-sixties but game enough to tackle the empire's nearly hopeless situation. He executed Alexius IV so that the Crusaders could not demand his restoration; the enfeebled Isaac II also died, perhaps without assistance. Alexius V refused to pay anything more to the Crusaders and Venetians. Indignant at his execution of their ally and repudiation of their agreement, they again attacked Constantinople, concentrating as before on the sea walls. When they broke through and set much of the city on fire, the Byzantine defenders fled, joined by their emperor and patriarch. The Crusaders and Venetians entered the city in triumph, claiming the empire for themselves by right of conquest.

Thus, almost nine hundred years after its foundation, Constantinople fell for the first time to a foreign army, a modest force of about 20,000 Crusaders. Alexius III, Alexius V, and various Byzantine governors and rebels still held much of Thrace, Greece, and Anatolia, but the Byzantine central administration, directly descended from the government of the ancient Roman Empire, was destroyed. This catastrophe had occurred just a century and a half after one of the peaks of Byzantine power, and not even a quarter century after Byzantium had seemed to be, under Manuel Comnenus, still the richest and strongest state in the Western world. The result astonished the Byzantines and Crusaders themselves.

A Restive Society

The decline of Byzantium between the death of Basil II and the Fourth Crusade was political and military, not economic or cultural. While the empire's political and military reverses must have done some harm to the economy, it remained buoyant through the whole period. The land Byzantium lost on the Anatolian plateau had always been fairly poor and sparsely populated. Except for a few brief intervals, the empire kept all its most fertile and populous territory in western Anatolia and the Balkans, where agriculture and trade continued to thrive. Growth was so strong that the population and state revenue seem to have been considerably higher in the twelfth century than they had been in the tenth, when Byzantine territory had been almost a third larger. The Crusaders of 1204, who had embarked at Venice, found Constantinople by far the biggest and richest city they had ever seen. Like the Seljuk

Turks, the Crusaders and Venetians were much poorer than the Byzantines they defeated.

Byzantine strategy and diplomacy were greatly at fault. The dithering eleventh-century emperors, relying on the military superiority they had inherited, scarcely bothered with foreign affairs. The emperors before and after Romanus IV never saw the gravity of the Seljuk invasion until it had advanced too far to stop. Alexius I kept his army small, gave most attention to the Balkans, nursed a grudge against the Normans, and distrusted all Crusaders. His successors by and large followed the same policies. A more promising course would have been to build up the Byzantine army, give priority to retaking inland Anatolia from the Turks, accept Norman rule over Italy and Antioch, and ally with the main body of Crusaders, who desperately needed help. Instead the Byzantine government concentrated its efforts in Anatolia on futile attempts to keep open the road through Turkish territory to Antioch. The empire fought the Normans in Antioch and even Italy long after they were ready to make peace, and so antagonized the Venetians and members of the first three Crusades as almost to provoke the diversion of the fourth.

In spite of all their failings, the Byzantines suffered no crippling losses until the very end of this period. Except during one brief uprising, they held onto their recent conquest of Bulgaria until 1185. They turned back two great Norman invasions of the Balkans and within a few years regained everything the Normans had taken. With some help from the Crusaders, the Byzantines recovered western Anatolia after a Turkish occupation of about fifteen years. Except for the Anatolian plateau, their main losses were in Armenia and northern Syria, which they had conquered only recently, and in southern Italy, which they had never held securely. Even the Anatolian plateau had been vulnerable to Arab raids until the middle of the tenth century. Since what the empire had gained from the Bulgarians was about as valuable as what it had lost to the Turks, the land it held in the twelfth century was hardly worse than what it had held before its great conquests.

These years were particularly good ones for the Byzantine Balkans, which for the first time became the most important part of the empire. Alexius I resettled many of the dispossessed Anatolian magnates there, where they joined an already developing local aristocracy. The occasional inroads of the Normans, Pechenegs, Hungarians, and Serbs seem to have been less destructive than the earlier wars between the Bulgarians and Byzantines. The few and small towns of the northern Balkans continued to grow. In Greece both agriculture and manufacturing, and with them cities, seem to have recovered to a level not seen since antiquity. Greece began exporting food to Italy for the first time on record. Thessalonica, the empire's second city, became a great trading center by handling the region's exports and imports, and Thebes had a flourishing textile industry. Foreign travelers commented on the size and prosperity of the empire's European ports.

Byzantine Anatolia, though less vital than before, was still nearly as important to the empire as the Balkans. When Alexius I had his chance to campaign in Anatolia after the Crusaders had left, he retook the coastal plains and left the plateau to the Turks. Thereafter, though the Byzantines held only about a quarter of the land in Anatolia, they probably ruled at least half the population, including the settlers Alexius brought in from Turkish territory. The plains also had the peninsula's best farmland, most of its cities, and nearly all its ports. Since transport remained much cheaper and safer by sea than by land, the straits and the Aegean Sea united western Anatolia with Thrace, Greece, and the Greek islands as a natural economic unit.

What Byzantine Anatolia lacked was defensible frontiers. The Pontic Alps and the Taurus Mountains helped keep the Turks away from the northern and southern coasts, but also isolated the Pontus and Cilicia from the rest of the empire, which had to fight over them with Pontic magnates and Cilician Armenians. The main part of western Anatolia had no proper frontier at all, and nomadic Turks raided it periodically, as the Arabs had once raided the Anatolian plateau. Like the plateau in the preceding period, western Anatolia became a land of magnates, who bought out smallholders and kept them on as tenants. With the resources to survive the Turkish raids, these aristocrats were also strong enough to rebel against the central government, as they did in the years before the Fourth Crusade. Their estates, now raising crops more often than livestock, evidently produced a healthy surplus to sell through merchants in the local ports.

During these years, while Byzantine merchants and large landowners became richer and more numerous, peasant smallholders seem to have become a minority of the population for the first time in Byzantine history. This development was a natural result of continuing demographic growth without territorial expansion. Land became scarcer and more valuable, and labor became more abundant and less valuable. In the competition for land, the land went to those with the most money, including established magnates, newly rich officials, and even monasteries. As these groups bid for land, the feeble emperors of the eleventh century gave up the increasingly hopeless task of trying to enforce the tenth-century land legislation.

The rise of magnates remained worrisome for the emperors, giving them another reason to neglect the army for which the aristocracy had long provided officers. Several eleventh-century emperors, especially Michael IV and Michael V with their origins in the commercial class, preferred merchants to magnates when they appointed officials, and assembled armies of mercenaries without loyalties to the traditional officer corps. Even emperors from aristocratic families, like Constantine X Ducas and Alexius I Comnenus, distrusted other aristocrats as possible rivals. Alexius also distrusted Byzantine merchants, and put them at a disadvantage by exempting the Venetians from trade duties that Byzantines still had to pay. While he did gain valuable help from the Venetians in return, he might have done the same thing by direct payments from the treasury.

Beginning with Michael IV, the emperors gradually concentrated high ranks and military commands in their own families, hoping that they could at least trust their relatives. The emperors beginning with Alexius I also developed the practice of rewarding their relatives with the right to collect and keep the tax revenues from specified regions. Such concessions let Alexius display munificence when he had no more imperial estates or money to give away, but carried the danger that undependable recipients might become almost independent of the government. Although some imperial relatives were capable and loyal, many were not. Several with such grants of tax revenue conspired or rebelled, including the usurpers Andronicus Comnenus and Alexius III Angelus, who brought about the ruin of their own dynasties and horribly damaged the empire itself.

Manuel Comnenus extended to many regular officers and soldiers Alexius I's practice of granting tax revenues in the place of land or salaries. A grant of this type, usually quite small, was called a *pronoia* ("provision"), and its recipient can be termed a pronoiar. Probably Manuel's intention was to give these soldiers revenues like those of the old military lands, at a time when he lacked the actual land to distribute. Yet pronoiars, unlike earlier soldiers with military lands, paid no taxes and received no salaries, and were therefore more likely to rebel. Independent farmers who paid taxes to a pronoiar found themselves much like tenants who paid rent to a landowner, and subject to additional duties and various abuses. Though the system seems temporarily to have strengthened the army under Manuel, it inevitably reduced the revenue that went to the central government, and may well have contributed to the rash of regional revolts in the years between Manuel's death and the Fourth Crusade.

The overriding cause of the empire's defensive troubles during the eleventh and twelfth centuries was the near dissolution of its army. Constantine IX disbanded the newer Armenian themes, whose army of 50,000 experienced soldiers guarded the weakest spot in the eastern frontier. Most of the nominal soldiers of the older themes had never seen service in their lives until their mustering by Romanus IV, and after the Battle of Manzikert they melted away. The last of the western tagmata fell during Alexius I's wars with the Normans. The Turkish conquest of Anatolia apparently cut off the last of the eastern tagmata under Philaretus Brachamius in Cilicia, where any who survived were lost to the empire. By the year 1100 every unit of the old army of the themes and tagmata seems to have vanished. What remained were mercenaries fighting on contracts, most of them foreign but some Byzantine, who were later supplemented by pronoiars, most of them Byzantine but a few foreign.

This new army of mercenaries and pronoiars could often win battles. Its soldiers were professionals and, man for man, most of them fought better than the part-time soldiers of the old themes had done. Byzantium could however put fewer soldiers into the field than before, and had particular trouble fighting on more than one front at the same time. Above all, the new army was far inferior to the former themes in defending territory. Before the eleventh century thematic soldiers had fought stubbornly, and usually successfully, to hold even the remotest outposts. But without the bond of military lands to keep them where they were, garrisons of mercenaries readily surrendered, rebelled, or fled. After Manzikert the former bulwarks of Byzantine Armenia and Anatolia fell in a heap at the approach of the Turks. During the twelfth century outlying provinces like Cilicia and the Pontus fell to rebels or invaders again and again. John II could lead his army from one end of Anatolia to the other, but his conquests would not stay conquered. By the time of the Fourth Crusade, the Byzantine government had already lost control over most of its frontier regions in both Europe and Asia.

The principal commanders of the army continued to be titled domestics of the East and West for the Asian and European parts of the empire, commands that were sometimes combined under a Grand Domestic. The mercenaries that the domestics commanded were organized into corps called tagmata, with varying numbers and names. The chief regional commanders, commanding both mercenaries and local pronoiars, were still the dukes whom John Tzimisces had given responsibility for groups of themes. The themes themselves ceased to have military significance, and became purely administrative provinces with civil governors subordinate to the dukes. Alexius I created an additional commander, the Grand Duke, to oversee the navy along with the islands and some coasts that the navy defended. Even if foreigners were the majority of the empire's soldiers, nearly all the chief military commanders were still Byzantines, and often relatives of the emperor.

After Basil II's death the civil service recovered the influence it had lost to the army, as bureaucrats promoted the candidacies of inferior emperors who would rely heavily on bureaucrats. Under Constantine IX a powerful new official, the *Mesazon*, emerged as the head of the central bureaucracy. Sometimes the most powerful position in the government fell to a civil servant like John the Orphanotrophus, the Military Logothete Michael Bringas who became the emperor Michael VI, or the Postal Logothete Nicephoritzes. Administrative posts were prestigious enough that many wealthy merchants paid the emperors high prices to join the bureaucracy, though what they received was usually a salary and an honorary title without duties. Under the Comneni, however, the central bureaucracy became much less influential, and the only honorary officials of consequence were members of the imperial dynasty.

The end result of the power struggle was really not a victory for either the bureaucracy, the army, the merchants, the magnates, the emperor, or the emperor's relatives. There were too many rich and strong contestants to allow any one group, let alone any individual, to defeat the others decisively. Growing Byzantine wealth, which might under prudent management have made the empire stronger, instead caused social unrest, factionalism, and regional rebellions, which in the end harmed all Byzantines and helped only foreigners. The empire had done far better at managing the tensions resulting from prosperity before, in the late fifth and early sixth centuries and again in the earlier stages of its current economic expansion, which had been more or less continuous since the late eighth century.

Nevertheless, the additional growth of the eleventh and twelfth centuries appears to have brought Byzantium to the highest level of economic development that it had yet seen. According to the astonished Crusaders, by 1203 Constantinople had a population of 400,000, which would have matched or even exceeded its zenith before the plague arrived in 541. Since other Byzantine cities seem to have grown at something approaching this rate, and the empire was only about a third as large and populous in the twelfth century as it had been just before the plague, Byzantium must have been much more urbanized around 1200 than in Late Antiquity. The estimates that can be made for government revenue, speculative though they must be, also suggest that the empire's economy was more monetarized in the twelfth century than in the sixth. That is likely anyway, because urbanization and monetarization usually go together, along with growth in the trade needed to supply the cities from the countryside.

Byzantine farmers expanded their production enough not only to feed their own greater numbers and the greater numbers of Byzantine city dwellers, but to export food abroad, as they had seldom done before. This accomplishment was the more remarkable after the loss of the Anatolian plateau. Most of the agricultural expansion must have occurred in the Byzantine Balkans, whose herds largely replaced the pork and mutton lost from Anatolia, though the Turks still exported some animals to Byzantine territory. Along with meat, exports from Greece to Italy included grain and wine. Yet most of the surplus of all of these, and of fruit, vegetables, and olive oil, would of course have been consumed by Byzantine townsmen.

Since the government no longer subsidized the food of any Byzantine cities, the townsmen had somehow to earn enough to pay for their own provisions. The leading urban industry was probably weaving wool, cotton, and silk into cloth, which everyone needed; but the cities also produced finished clothing, pottery, glassware, bricks, metalwork, furniture, and tools and artworks of various kinds. Of these, most would have gone to the Byzantine countryside, but some were exported to the West and East. Finally, as before, the Byzantines imported spices by the Spice Route from India, silks by the Silk Route from China, and furs and slaves from Russia. While rich Byzantines bought the larger part of these luxury imports, many were re-exported to Italy and Western Europe.

Most of the trade between Byzantium and the West had passed into the hands of Venetian and other Italian merchants, especially after Alexius I exempted them from the trade duties levied on everyone else. On the other hand, most of the internal trade of the empire, and a good deal of Byzantine trade with the East, surely remained in the hands of the growing Byzantine mercantile class. Most Italians limited their activities within the empire to the main ports, above all

Constantinople. The value of Italian trade can be measured with some precision from the amounts confiscated by the Byzantines from Venetian, Genoese, and Pisan merchants. Although these sums were very large ones for the Italians, they were small in comparison with the fortunes of Byzantine magnates, and smaller still when compared with the budget of the Byzantine state. What is particularly interesting is that the expropriations and expulsions of Italian traders in the twelfth century caused no known problems for the Byzantines. Evidently the Italians' business formed an insignificant part of the internal system of distribution, and a quite small portion of the Byzantine economy.

That economy still remained primarily agricultural, and most Byzantines still lived in villages rather than towns or cities. Yet Byzantine trade, manufacturing, cities, towns, and indeed villages were all bigger than they had been for centuries, and in proportion to the empire's smaller size they were bigger than ever before. The Byzantines were consequently richer than they had been earlier. They were also richer than the richest Italians, who were themselves richer than any other people in an increasingly prosperous Western Europe. The Byzantine economic expansion was by no means unique to Byzantium, since at the same time Western Europe, and to some extent the whole of Eurasia, was enjoying a similar expansion as the result of similar population growth. Byzantium however remained in advance, partly because it had been richer and more developed at the start, and partly because the Byzantine government, for all its defects, by and large provided better security and order than its Western and Muslim competitors.

An Invigorated Culture

Byzantium in the eleventh and twelfth centuries bears a certain resemblance to Classical Greece or Renaissance Italy. Those two societies also underwent explosive demographic, urban, and economic growth, which led to competition and discord among their members, and finally to military defeat at the hands of outsiders. The changes and tensions at Byzantium were less violent, largely because the Classical Greeks and Renaissance Italians each belonged to many states, and in spite of various invasions and rebellions most Byzantines continued to live under only one state until 1204. Yet the comparison illustrates that cultural ferment and creative advances can accompany even apparently disastrous political upheavals. Although the Byzantine culture of this time never developed quite the brilliance of earlier Greece or later Italy, some Byzantines did show unprecedented intellectual vitality and artistic inspiration.

In cultural as in political history, the loss of most of Anatolia and the rise of the Comneni in 1081 marked a new stage. The different political regimes before and after that date fostered somewhat different cultural elites. Under the weak rulers before Alexius I, the church hierarchy and civil bureaucracy, which had similar backgrounds and outlooks, enjoyed unusual influence and the independence to set educational and cultural standards. These groups lost much of their power under the Comneni, who were more favorable to their own relatives and to lower-ranking clergy. Moreover, the political decline of Byzantium from an unrivaled superpower to merely the strongest of several strong states subtly changed the cultural mood. The unquestioned self-assurance of the period of Byzantine dominance gave way to a more defensive sense of superiority. The change left Byzantines feeling less similar to Western Europeans than before, though still intellectually superior to them.

During the eleventh century the Byzantine Church had some notably powerful patriarchs, above all Michael Cerularius. A civil servant forced to become a monk after a failed conspiracy, he was appointed patriarch by his friend Constantine IX. Cerularius enjoyed popular support in Constantinople, and asserted himself against all four of the emperors under whom he served. He provoked the schism of 1054 with the Papacy against Constantine's wishes, challenged the empress Theodora's right to select bishops, pressed Michael VI to abdicate, and opposed Isaac I for taking imperial lands back from the Church. Although the next three patriarchs were less aggressive, they too felt able to thwart imperial desires in some circumstances. One, the legal scholar John Xiphilinus, defied the Ducas dynasty by releasing Constantine X's widow Eudocia from her promise not to remarry. Cosmas, Xiphilinus' successor as patriarch, refused to condone the marriage of the wife of the deposed Michael VII to either Nicephorus III or Alexius I.

Michael Cerularius tried to subject the Church of recently conquered Armenia to the Patriarchate of Constantinople, and in particular to forbid the Armenian practice of using unleavened bread for communion. Because the Western Church followed the same practice, the patriarch's ban on unleavened eucharistic bread also affected churches used by Westerners in Constantinople. The Pope objected, and after further exchanges a papal legation exchanged excommunications with the patriarch in 1054. These excommunications, which invoked no differences between the Eastern and Western churches except those that had been compatible with generations of unity, frustrated the emperor's proposals for a military alliance with the Papacy against the Norman rebels in southern Italy. Since the Papacy then allied itself with the Normans, who after taking Byzantine Italy invaded the Balkans, political differences blocked attempts to end the schism for more than thirty years.

Meanwhile Constantinople became at least as hospitable to scholars as it had been in the fifth and sixth centuries. Constantine IX founded an imperial law school under John Xiphilinus and an imperial school of philosophy under Constantine (later Michael) Psellus, both of them meant to train civil servants but also to do original academic research. Perhaps the greatest Byzantine scholar of any time, Psellus combined orthodox Christian beliefs with a willingness, inspired by Plato and Aristotle, to analyze the created world on its own terms. Though under the irresolute Constantine IX the prominence of Psellus and Xiphilinus eventually aroused such envy that they were forced to resign their posts and become monks, they regained influence later. Psellus was an important if not always wise adviser to every emperor from Michael VI to Michael VII. He helped Isaac I depose Michael Cerularius from the patriarchate, and persuaded Constantine X to name Xiphilinus patriarch.

Just as strong patriarchs had been the rule under the weak emperors of the eleventh century, so under the strong emperors beginning with Alexius I weaker patriarchs predominated. The Church as a whole was not necessarily weaker, because the emperors were pious, or at any rate wanted reputations for piety. Alexius presided over the beginning of a reform of the empire's monasteries, many of which had become virtual possessions of wealthy patrons. The reform movement favored monastic independence and attached more importance to the monks' spiritual life. Most of the most prestigious monasteries were on secluded islands or mountains, especially on Mount Athos, and both reformed and unreformed monks tended to stay out of politics. At the same time the patriarchs exercised less control over their bishops and other clergy, who in a series of synods conducted some celebrated heresy trials.

Their first victim was John Italus, Psellus' best student and successor as head of the imperial school of philosophy. Italus ("the Italian") had an abrasive personality and the added disadvantage of coming from southern Italy, then ruled by the Byzantines' Norman enemies. Put on

trial in 1082, Italus was convicted of propounding various pagan philosophical propositions and, absurdly, of Iconoclasm. Although eager to
condemn the unorthodox tenets that he was accused of believing, Italus
was confined to a monastery and forbidden to teach. The school of
philosophy remained open, but in the future Byzantine philosophers
had to be much more careful of what they taught. Later synods conducted further trials for heresy, some on very dubious grounds and
against the emperor's will. They did however condemn some genuine
heretics, like the Bulgarian Bogomils, dualists who believed in separate
good and evil gods.

The Crusades further complicated Byzantine relations with the West.
Pope Urban II, who officially lifted his predecessor's excommunication
of Alexius I as a usurper, wanted the Crusaders to assist the empire, and
they did help it retake much of Anatolia. Once established in Syria,
however, they ruled many orthodox and Monophysite Christians
belonging to the old patriarchates of Antioch and Jerusalem. The Crusaders appointed Latin patriarchs and bishops, displacing the Melkite
hierarchy in communion with Constantinople. The Crusading rulers
also found some favor with the Monophysites. Eventually the crusaders
negotiated an ephemeral church union with the Armenians, whom the
Byzantines had alienated, and a lasting union with the Maronite Christians of Mount Lebanon.

Despite Byzantine distrust of the Crusaders, Alexius I, John II, and
Manuel all negotiated with the Papacy in the hope of restoring church
unity. They set up discussions between Latin and Byzantine theologians
at Constantinople, which treated the main issues in a civil and thought-
ful manner. While most westerners would have been content to restore
unity on the same terms as before, many Byzantines now objected to
practices long established in the western church and to the long-
acknowledged right of the Pope to decide appeals from Eastern Christians on doctrinal and disciplinary matters. The Byzantines would now
admit only the Pope's right to a primacy of honor and representation at
ecumenical councils.

Given that the Papacy was not about to change Western practices
because of Byzantine criticism, or to abandon Papal privileges that the
Byzantines had once accepted, any feasible settlement would have
required Byzantine concessions and left many Byzantines in opposition.
The emperors came to realize that such a settlement might well cause
more discord than the schism did, at least among Byzantines. Although
at the time of the schism of 1054 the Byzantines had taken the

superiority of their customs for granted, by the twelfth century some felt obliged to insist that they alone were right, perhaps especially because they found some of the arguments of Western theologians hard to dismiss.

The margin of Byzantine superiority over the West was eroding, not only in political and military power but in education and scholarship. The Byzantines' foundation of new schools, reexamination of Classical philosophy, and innovations in literature all had their contemporary counterparts in Western Europe. In sheer breadth and depth of knowledge, certainly of philosophy and science, Western scholars had started far behind and stayed behind. For example, they began with a mere smattering of ancient philosophy, then discovered Aristotle through translations from the Arabic without learning much about Plato or other philosophers. Yet the multiple divisions of the Western Church and Western states put fewer constraints on Western scholars than the authoritative synods that condemned John Italus and some other Byzantine intellectuals. Although Byzantine learning and literature continued developing, by the twelfth century they were not so far in advance of the West as to be absolutely immune to Western cultural influence and fashions. The emperor Manuel in particular was sometimes criticized as a Westernizer.

In the eleventh century Byzantine scholars were still peerless. Michael Psellus and his contemporaries, unlike their predecessors, were so familiar with ancient Greek literature that they no longer felt intimidated by it. Psellus' style is often convoluted and bizarre, but he was in control of its intricacies and obscurities, and could use them as he wished to express original ideas. Perhaps his most original work is his memoirs, written in the form of a political history but showing an interest in human character almost unparalleled in earlier Greek literature. Relying mainly on personal experience, he describes each of the emperors from Basil II to Michael VII, and except for the last, whom as the reigning emperor he had to eulogize, he weighs their faults and virtues with discernment and relative objectivity. Though he shows only partial awareness of the causes of Byzantine political and military decline, his chosen subjects were people rather than events.

Among several other fine histories of a more traditional type, two classics stand out. The first is the *Alexiad*, a history of the reign of Alexius I by his daughter, Anna Comnena. Anna skillfully exploits her stirring subject, her father's restoration of the empire's lost glory, with a sure narrative sense and due attention to character and detail. Her account succeeds in being both approving and truthful, since Alexius was brilliant at managing the day-to-day events that she treats and only deficient in a wider vision that she also lacked. Anna's continuer Nicetas Choniates chose a similarly dramatic but this time tragic subject, the twelfth-century decline of the empire until its fall to the Fourth Crusade. Agonizingly aware of the impending catastrophe, and free from any need or desire to spare the emperors he blamed for it, Nicetas combines the human understanding of Psellus and the elegant composition of Anna with more historical perspective than either of them.

The eleventh and especially the twelfth century produced dozens of accomplished Byzantine writers of other sorts. These included epistolographers, court poets, and commentators on Classical Greek literature. Among particularly original works are the satiric dialogue *Timarion*, which depicts a trip to Hades where the hero meets some of his contemporaries, and the satiric poems of Theodore Prodromus in everyday Greek, which describe scenes of daily life in Constantinople. Also notable are four love stories set in Classical Greece, three of them in verse. These romances revived a genre not practiced since the third century, except to some extent in the epic of *Digenes Acrites*, which during the twelfth century found its final form. Such works' celebration of love and marriage reflects an increase in family feeling among Byzantine aristocrats and others, evident in the politics of the time. Though family loyalties may also have caused somewhat more favorable attitudes toward women, Byzantine views on women had always been such a complex mixture of positive and negative that any change was of degree rather than kind.

Not since the sixth century, if ever, had Byzantium produced so much and such exquisite art as in this period. During the eleventh century several emperors built enormously expensive monasteries in the capital, all lost today but described with awe by contemporaries. The most lavish of these was the work of Constantine IX, who also constructed an opulent monastery on the island of Chios, the Nea Monē ("New Monastery"), that still stands with most of its impressive mosaics and marble inlays. Aristocrats, following the example of the emperors as usual, built elaborately decorated churches and monasteries all over the provinces, of which those hewn from the rock formations of Cappadocia have survived best. The mosaics and manuscript illuminations from the period show that Byzantine artists, while following mainly traditional styles, had reached a peak of proficiency.

Figure 11   Exterior of the Monastery of Christ Pantocrator ("Ruler of All"), Constantinople, showing its three connected churches. John II Comnenus (reigned 1118–43) dedicated the monastery in 1136 as a thank-offering for his victories over the Turks and Byzantine conspirators. (*Photo*: Dumbarton Oaks, Washington, D.C., © copyright 1999)

Although the Turkish invasion of Anatolia temporarily impoverished the treasury and aristocracy enough to reduce the most expensive kinds of architecture and art, by the early twelfth century artistic productions show no traces of lingering poverty. Alexius I and Manuel greatly expanded the Blachernae Palace in northwestern Constantinople, making it the main imperial residence. The imperial ecclesiastical foundations in Constantinople culminated in John II Comnenus' hilltop Monastery of Christ Pantocrator ("Ruler of All"), a monumental pile still visible from much of the modern city of Istanbul.

The remaining twelfth-century monasteries in the provinces, all evidently financed by aristocratic patrons, include Daphne near Athens and Hosius Lucas near Thebes, both of them magnificently decorated with marble and mosaics. Recognizing Byzantine art as the highest standard for the Western world, the Norman kings and the Venetian Republic hired Byzantine mosaicists to decorate the most sumptuous of their own churches in this period, most of which retain their decoration almost complete up to the present. Twelfth-century Byzantine mosaics, icons, ivories, and illuminated manuscripts reached an almost excessive level of artistry, some of which borders on preciosity.

That such an affluent and resourceful society eventually fell prey to its enemies is no real mystery. The emperors of the time, like the Classical Greeks confronted by the Romans, misused their advantages by misjudging their adversaries. The Byzantines expected the Turks to resemble Arabs, whom they had learned how to defeat, and the Venetians and Crusaders to be like themselves, only stupider and more ignorant. When not idly enjoying their seemingly boundless riches, most Byzantine rulers worried less about foreigners than about their own unruly subjects. To most emperors, the old army of conquest and the Anatolian plateau looked like nests of overmighty and rebellious aristocrats, which when lost made the empire easier to rule. Eventually, since the Byzantines made little use of their resources to defend themselves, their wealth actually made them less secure, because it lured foreigners to plunder them.

7

RESTORATION AND FALL (1204–1461)

The Successors

The best proof of Byzantium's underlying strength is that Byzantine states survived for more than two and a half centuries after the seemingly fatal Fourth Crusade. Strong and unified leadership was certainly not the reason. When the Crusaders stormed Constantinople, the deposed Alexius III Angelus still held the region of Thessalonica, while his son-in-law Theodore Lascaris held the northwest part of Byzantine Anatolia, supposedly in Alexius' interest. The fugitive Alexius V held most of eastern Thrace. Alexius Comnenus, a grandson of the late emperor Andronicus, had seized the northern coast of Anatolia and declared himself emperor at Trebizond. Yet though he claimed to be the Byzantine emperor, Alexius, whom today we call the Emperor of Trebizond, was merely a local potentate. The rebels in southern Greece and southwest Anatolia had purely local ambitions.

Many Byzantines might have accepted their conquerors if the Crusaders and Venetians had been less shortsighted. But the victors looted and burned their new capital, and had already arranged to divide their new empire into almost independent fiefs, leaving only eastern Thrace and northwestern Anatolia for the emperor they were to elect. Moreover, instead of choosing their energetic leader Boniface of Montferrat, who was related by marriage to the Angeli and Comneni and now betrothed to the widow of Isaac II, some Crusaders joined the Venetians

197

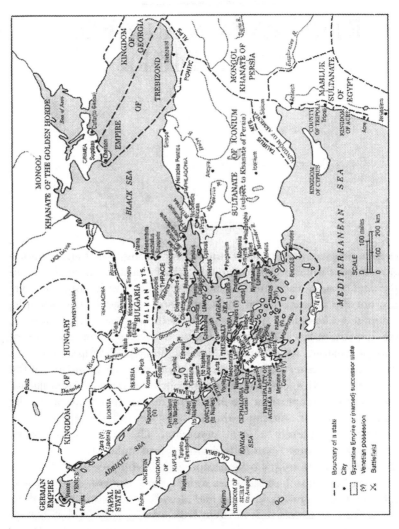

Map 6 The Empire *ca.* 1282

in electing Baldwin of Flanders, a weaker candidate whom they hoped to manipulate. Baldwin, called the Latin emperor by the Byzantines, promised the disgruntled Boniface his own vassal kingdom around Thessalonica. The Venetians took many of the ports and most of the islands, and a Venetian became Latin Patriarch of Constantinople.

The Latins first campaigned against the two former Byzantine emperors. Alexius V sensibly tried to ally himself with Alexius III and married his daughter, only to be blinded by his myopic new father-in-law and captured and killed by the Latins. When Boniface claimed Thessalonica as its king, Alexius III fled into central Greece, where Boniface took him prisoner. Meanwhile Michael Ducas, a cousin of Alexius III and a former rebel against him, made himself master of Epirus in northwest Greece, without venturing to declare himself emperor. King Boniface marched into the Peloponnesus, but Epirus seemed too poor and rugged to be worth his while for the moment.

The forces of the Latin emperor Baldwin were pushing back Theodore Lascaris and other Byzantines in Anatolia when the Bulgarian emperor Kaloyan invaded Thrace. Kaloyan not only overwhelmed the Latin army but captured Baldwin himself. Though the Bulgarian emperor gained little from his victory, it crippled the Latin Empire and allowed Theodore Lascaris to strengthen his hold on most of Byzantine Anatolia. In 1205, after routing an army that had advanced to attack him from Trebizond, Theodore proclaimed himself the Byzantine emperor at Nicaea.

Although Theodore was just one of several pretenders to the Byzantine throne, and is best called Emperor of Nicaea, he was at least as plausible an emperor as any other in the Byzantine world. He had defeated the forces of Emperor Alexius of Trebizond. His father-in-law Alexius III was imprisoned in Italy, and the Latin emperor Baldwin soon died in captivity in Bulgaria. Then the Bulgarian emperor Kaloyan died, after killing King Boniface of Thessalonica. Michael of Epirus claimed no title at all. Theodore's most inspired gesture was to name a Byzantine Patriarch at Nicaea in 1208, once the exiled Patriarch of Constantinople had died in Thrace. By crowning Theodore, the new Patriarch made him the natural leader of all Eastern Christians who rejected the Western Church.

Most of what had been Byzantium before the Fourth Crusade was now divided among Theodore of Nicaea, Alexius of Trebizond, the Latin emperor Baldwin's brother and successor Henry, and Michael of Epirus. Michael, the only one not to call himself emperor, seemed the weakest of the four; but he was a born troublemaker, and stirred up dissension among his rivals. First, allying with the Latin Empire, Michael ransomed his cousin Alexius III, who joined the Seljuks in invading the Empire of Nicaea. Alexius' adventure, which ended when the Nicene army captured him, led to a war between Nicaea and the Latins, in which the Latins won some territory. Meanwhile Michael expanded at the expense of both the Venetians and the Latin Empire, taking Dyrrhachium and western Thessaly.

After Michael of Epirus' murder in 1215, his enlarged realm fell into the hands of his even more ambitious half-brother, Theodore Ducas. From Epirus Theodore seized the adjacent part of the Bulgarian Empire and, after the emperor Henry died, advanced on Thessalonica. The new Latin emperor, Henry's brother-in-law Peter, invaded Epirus from the west, but died in an Epirote ambush, or at any rate in captivity afterward. Theodore then took eastern Thessaly, surrounded Thessalonica, and in 1224 captured it, making it his capital. This conquest of the second city of the Byzantine world both extinguished the Latin Kingdom of Thessalonica and turned Theodore's state into a major power.

Theodore of Nicaea had died in 1221 and was succeeded by his able son-in-law John Ducas Vatatzes, who conquered the Latin holdings in Anatolia. Both John of Nicaea and Theodore, now of Thessalonica, descended upon the prostrate Latin Empire. John landed a small force in Thrace, but Theodore pushed it out and advanced almost to Constantinople. Yet Theodore feared that if he attacked the city John and the Bulgarian emperor Asen would join against him. After having the Archbishop of Ochrid crown him Byzantine emperor, Theodore attacked Asen in 1230, but lost disastrously. Asen captured and blinded Theodore, and conquered the inland part of his fledgling Empire of Thessalonica. While one of Theodore's brothers took over the land around Thessalonica itself, Epirus went to Michael II Ducas, son of Theodore's late brother Michael.

The ruin of the Empire of Thessalonica left the Empire of Nicaea the principal Byzantine successor state. Its emperor John Vatatzes minted traditional Byzantine hyperpyra as a sign of his increasingly convincing claim to be Byzantine emperor. John married his son to the daughter of Asen of Bulgaria, promising Asen some of Latin Thrace in return for help in taking Constantinople. The allies advanced up to the city walls, but failed to capture the city. Asen, never happy about helping John take such a prize, broke off his alliance and released his blinded prisoner

Theodore Ducas. Theodore returned to Thessalonica, naming his son its emperor.

John Vatatzes invaded western Thrace and forced Theodore's son to give up his imperial title and accept the supremacy of John's Empire of Nicaea. After Asen died, the regents for his underage son ruled Bulgaria badly, and when Asen's son also died in 1246 Vatatzes decided to attack Bulgaria's southern frontier. The Greeks under Bulgarian rule received him so warmly that he soon overran the whole southern half of the Bulgarian Empire, which stretched to the northwest of Thessalonica. John's feat so impressed the Greeks of Thessalonica that they too welcomed him into their city. The next year John conquered whatever was left of Latin Thrace outside the walls of Constantinople.

Although Michael II of Epirus had also accepted the nominal authority of the Empire of Nicaea with the title of despot, he soon attacked the new Nicene territories from the west. John returned from Thrace and chased Michael back into Epirus. In the end Michael had to cede the western and northern parts of his territory, extending John's empire to the Adriatic. Pope Innocent IV actually seemed ready to broker a surrender of Constantinople to John in return for a reunion of the eastern and western churches, but both he and John died in 1254.

Through a combination of skill, daring, and luck, John Vatatzes had won as much land in the Balkans as he had inherited in Anatolia. After humbling the Latin Empire, the Empire of Thessalonica, the Bulgarian Empire, and Epirus, John had made the Empire of Nicaea the dominant power in the lands that had formerly been Byzantine. The Empire of Trebizond had become insignificant, a vassal first of the Seljuks and then of the Mongols, cut off from the Empire of Nicaea by Seljuk territory. Yet as long as Constantinople remained a Latin enclave, the Nicene state that John had built up was a geographical and historical anomaly, and could not truly be considered a restored Byzantine Empire.

The heir to the Empire of Nicaea was John's son, who by taking the family name of his mother and imperial grandfather became Theodore II Lascaris. Although epilepsy kept Theodore in fragile health, he had an active mind and spirit. The year after John's death, when the young Bulgarian emperor invaded the territory that John had taken from him, Theodore marched against him, drove him out, and forced a peace that confirmed John's conquests. Next Theodore negotiated a marriage between his daughter and the son of Michael II of Epirus, but only after forcing Michael to cede more territory on their shared border, including Dyrrhachium.

Once the wedding had taken place, Michael instigated a rebellion against Nicene rule among the Albanians in the hinterland of Dyrrhachium. Joining the Albanians, Michael defeated and captured the local Nicene forces. Michael made further alliances with the Latin prince of the Peloponnesus and the German regent of southern Italy, who was following the old Norman custom of invading Greece. With such support, Epirus seemed a match for Nicaea, even after Theodore made his own alliance with the new Bulgarian emperor Constantine Tich. But before the two alliances could clash, Theodore died in 1258, leaving a regent to rule for his underage son John Lascaris.

Thus far the Byzantine successor states had shown more enthusiasm for fighting each other than for conquering the Latin Empire. This remained true even when the Latin state consisted of little more than the city of Constantinople, with a few fiefs in southern Greece that contributed scarcely anything to the city's defense. Yet only John Vatatzes had made even a brief attempt to besiege Constantinople, without trying to take it by storm. John preferred to attack Bulgaria, as Theodore II chose to provoke Epirus, though neither Bulgaria nor Epirus was as weak as the Latins. Even so, the Nicene emperors had made their state the only one with any real prospect of restoring Byzantium.

Michael VIII's Restoration

The courtiers of the young emperor John Lascaris speedily assassinated his designated regent and gave the regency to a talented general, Michael Palaeologus. Palaeologus had himself crowned co-emperor in 1259, and sent an army under his brother John against Michael of Epirus and Epirus' Albanian, German, and Latin allies. John Palaeologus met them at Pelagonia, midway between Thessalonica and Dyrrhachium, and won a smashing victory. He captured many Latin lords, including the Peloponnesian prince William of Villehardouin, took Thessaly, and occupied all of Epirus except for two strongholds that he besieged. Though after John's departure Michael II retook most of Epirus and Thessaly, his failure to win the war that he had started weakened him greatly, while the capture of the Latin lords left their Greek fiefs almost helpless.

Michael Palaeologus evidently recalled his brother in order to attack the Latins in Constantinople. His first attempts on the strongly fortified city failed, and he made a truce with the Latins. To gain naval support for a renewed assault, in 1261 Michael granted extensive trading privileges to Genoa, the only Italian seapower that rivaled Venice. Before the Genoese could give any aid, however, a small Nicene contingent passing near Constantinople learned that the city's garrison was away. Seizing the chance, the Nicene commander broke into the city by night and took possession, forcing the Latin emperor Baldwin II and the Venetians to flee. Shortly afterward, the emperor Michael made his ceremonial entrance into the capital of his restored Byzantine Empire, where he was crowned in St Sophia.

In this way, in his mid-thirties, Michael Palaeologus of Nicaea became Michael VIII of Byzantium, tracing the Byzantine succession retrospectively through the Nicene emperors, who became the Byzantine emperors Theodore I, John III, Theodore II, and John IV. In fact, in 1204 Theodore Lascaris had been just one of several Greek dynasts,

Figure 12   Exterior of the Palace of the Porphyrogenitus (now known as Tekfur Seray), Constantinople, probably built by Michael VIII Palaeologus (reigned 1261–82) for his younger son Constantine after the recovery of the city from the Latin Empire. (*Photo*: Irina Andreescu-Treadgold)

and originally had not even claimed the title of emperor, as the deposed Alexius III or the self-proclaimed Alexius Comnenus of Trebizond had done. The Nicene empire's actual conquest of Constantinople came by a stroke of luck. Yet Michael VIII's vigor and resolution made his luck deserved. Before long, given his determination and the Latins' weakness, he would probably have taken the city in any case.

The new Byzantium and its emperor still had many foreign and Byzantine enemies, each individually weaker than the empire but formidable if they could stay together long enough. Without waiting for the Latins to recover from their shock, Michael dictated his terms to the lords he still held captive. William of Villehardouin gained his freedom only by ceding the southeastern quarter of the Peloponnesus to the emperor. Michael feverishly recruited new troops and built new ships to defend his winnings. While his prestige was still high after his recapture of Constantinople and coronation there, he deposed and blinded young John IV and became senior emperor, though the Patriarch Arsenius excommunicated him for the blinding.

In 1262 William of Villehardouin and the Venetians allied with the dispossessed Latin emperor Baldwin II against Byzantium. Michael II of Epirus returned to the attack. The Turks raided Byzantine Anatolia, and Constantine Tich of Bulgaria invaded Byzantine Thrace. Michael VIII sent armies against them all. During the next two years his forces defeated Villehardouin and the Venetians, Epirotes, Turks, and Bulgarians, conquering a strip of Bulgarian borderland and some Venetian islands and Peloponnesian forts. The defeated Venetians, Epirotes, and Bulgarians made peace with the empire. Though by that time Michael seems temporarily to have run out of money, he had already shown that he could defend what he held. The emperor also deposed the Patriarch Arsenius, who refused to lift his excommunication on any tolerable terms, and at length found a new patriarch, Joseph, who received him back into the Church.

Meanwhile the Pope had put southern Italy under the ambitious French prince Charles of Anjou, who joined with the deposed Latin emperor Baldwin to organize a crusade against the Byzantines on the ground that they were schismatics. Charles captured much of Byzantine Albania and made alliances with the Hungarians, Serbs, and Bulgarians. To head off Charles' crusade, Michael VIII came to an agreement with Pope Gregory IX to reunite the Byzantine Church with Rome. At the Council of Lyons of 1274, the Pope and a Byzantine delegation proclaimed a reunion based on mutual toleration of Eastern and

Western usages. With the end of the schism, Charles of Anjou could no longer call his war a crusade, and Michael drove back Charles' forces in Albania.

Yet Michael, despite some determined persecution, failed to reconcile most Byzantines to the Union of Lyons. The Patriarch Joseph abdicated rather than accept the union, leaving the Byzantine Church split between Josephites who supported him, Arsenites who recognized his predecessor Arsenius, and a minority of unionists. The union found scarcely any adherents among the Eastern christians outside Michael's control. Soon Michael was fighting the Bulgarians, the Serbs, and the two separatist states of Epirus and Thessaly, now ruled by sons of the late Michael II Ducas.

In the name of continuing the schism, Nicephorus of Epirus actually joined Charles of Anjou, lately a crusader against schismatics, in attacking Byzantine Albania. Though the Byzantines defeated this unholy alliance in 1281, Charles persuaded a new Pope that the Byzantines had not truly accepted the Union of Lyons. Resuming his plans for a crusade, Charles enlisted the Pope, the Venetians, and the heir to the Latin Empire. But a year later Michael helped foment a rebellion in Sicily known as the Sicilian Vespers, which cost Charles half his kingdom and forced him to give up crusading.

A few months later, Michael VIII died of disease after a reign of agile improvisation and sound achievement. While he had gained relatively little land, his gains included Constantinople, and despite frantic opposition from a host of enemies his losses were negligible. He had strengthened the Byzantine army and fleet and put them to good use, and had somehow paid for everything with only minimal debasement of the coinage. His diplomacy had executed such difficult maneuvers as the Union of Lyons and the Sicilian Vespers. Soon before his death, he even won the formal submission of John II of Trebizond, who began calling himself Emperor of the East rather than Emperor of the Romans. Disliked at home, Michael had nonetheless kept the Byzantine throne and overcome excommunication. If he had not quite restored Byzantium as it had been in the twelfth century, he had made good progress toward its recovery.

Michael's eldest son Andronicus II Palaeologus, who was twenty-four when he became emperor in 1282, saw the reasons for his father's unpopularity without understanding those for his father's success. Pious and eager to please, Andronicus immediately repudiated the Union of Lyons. He returned the antiunionist Joseph to the patriarchate and allowed the unionists to be condemned and persecuted, though the Church remained divided between Arsenites and Josephites. The end of the stillborn union won the emperor the nominal submission of Nicephorus of Epirus without much offending the Latins. The widowed Andronicus married the heiress of the long-vanished Latin Kingdom of Thessalonica, and on the death of Charles of Anjou the Venetians made a truce with the empire.

After what seemed a promising start to his reign, Andronicus decided to save money by reducing the size of the regular Byzantine army and almost eliminating the Byzantine fleet. Instead he relied on Western mercenaries and the ships of the empire's Genoese allies. At first Byzantium seemed to suffer no ill-effects. It gained the nominal submission of Thessaly and made modest additions to its holdings in Albania and the Peloponnesus. The main sign of danger was that the Turks were intensifying their raids on Byzantine Anatolia, and capturing some border outposts. The Byzantine general sent against the Turkish raiders rebelled and had to be blinded.

Then Charles II of Naples, son and heir of Charles of Anjou, made an alliance with Nicephorus of Epirus. While the Serbs captured several Byzantine outposts on their border, Nicephorus repudiated Byzantine sovereignty and defeated a Byzantine army before he died in 1296. Worst of all, that year the Venetians, though supposedly at peace with the empire, burned the Genoese trading quarter in the suburbs of Constantinople. The infuriated emperor declared war on Venice, which took advantage of the empire's impotence on the seas to conquer Byzantine islands in the Aegean. Andronicus was unable to stop the Venetian advance in the islands or the Turkish advance in Anatolia, though he made peace with the Serbs by marrying his underage daughter to their king.

By 1303 Byzantium was in grave distress. Andronicus' attempt to stop the Turks with a band of Alan mercenaries miscarried after the Alans, with only a few regular soldiers to steady them, deserted. The increasingly menacing Turkish emir Osmān took much of the Anatolian countryside for his new Ottoman Emirate. Andronicus' Latin wife Yolanda-Irene claimed her inheritance of Thessalonica for her sons, and seized the city as a practically independent possession. The emperor made a hasty truce with Venice, promising heavy reparations and recognizing the Venetians' conquest of his islands.

Late in this disastrous year, the desperate Andronicus promised enormous wages to 6500 Aragonese mercenaries, known as the Catalan

Grand Company, to fight the Ottoman Turks in Anatolia. This move proved catastrophic, because the empire had neither the regular troops to control the Catalans nor the resources to pay them for any length of time. While handily defeating the Turks, the Catalans mercilessly plundered the local Byzantines, and had to be recalled to Thrace. Andronicus failed to pay the Catalans in full, even after raising taxes and debasing the hyperpyron until it was only half gold. As tensions rose, Andronicus' son Michael had the Catalans' commanders assassinated early in 1305.

The outraged Catalans elected new commanders and began to rampage through Thrace. They repeatedly defeated Michael and a Byzantine army of Alan and Turkish mercenaries, most of whom deserted and joined the Catalans in pillaging the countryside. The Bulgarians overran the Byzantine ports near their border, and a Neapolitan army captured Byzantine Dyrrhachium. The Turks swarmed back into Byzantine Anatolia almost unopposed, and some crossed over to Thrace as well. The empire's Genoese allies seized the main Byzantine ports in Anatolia and the offshore islands, claiming to be saving them from the Turks. With peasants in Thrace and Anatolia afraid to tend their farms, a famine broke out. To escape the famine, the Catalans moved on to plundering the region of Thessalonica. Andronicus appeared catatonic.

Seeing Byzantium falling to pieces, the French prince Charles of Valois, heir by marriage to the defunct Latin Empire, prepared a crusade against Constantinople. Charles won the backing of the Pope, Venice, Serbia, and the Catalan Company, but never actually came to the point of setting sail. The Catalans attacked the separatist empress Yolanda-Irene in Thessalonica, but failed to take the city. They then turned south, looted Thessaly for a year, took service with the Latin Duke of Athens, and in 1311 conquered Athens and settled there as its rulers. After Andronicus made peace with the Venetians, Bulgarians, and Serbs, Charles of Valois gave up his plans for a crusade.

Thus Byzantium survived, maimed by the loss of the best part of Anatolia, shorn of the lands along its Balkan borders, and ravaged throughout. The Serbs sent a small force that cleared Byzantine Thrace of its last Turkish looters. The emperor finally reconciled the Arsenite schismatics, and regained control of Thessalonica when his estranged empress Yolanda-Irene died. Andronicus slowly collected some money and brought himself to spend some of it on native Byzantine troops. In

1318 he took advantage of the extinction of the Ducas dynasties of Epirus and Thessaly to conquer the northern part of each of them from their new rulers. He raised taxes and made further plans to expand his small army and tiny navy.

In the midst of this recovery, in 1320, a scandal tore the imperial family apart. Andronicus' eldest grandson, also named Andronicus, having plotted to kill a former lover of his mistress, by mistaken identity had his own brother murdered instead. The incident hastened the death of the emperor's son Michael, father of both the murderer and the victim, and deeply affected the emperor himself. Old Andronicus refused to confirm the right to succession of young Andronicus, who the next year proclaimed himself emperor as Andronicus III. He had little trouble rallying support against his discredited grandfather, or in forcing a settlement that gave him control over most of Thrace.

This arrangement, which weakened the empire and pleased neither side, soon led to open civil war. Andronicus III had the better of the fighting, and obtained recognition as co-emperor throughout the empire. He managed to repel a Bulgarian invasion of Byzantine Thrace, but his grandfather refused to let him march to the relief of the Anatolian city of Prusa, which fell to the Ottoman Turks in 1326. As each emperor prepared for war, Andronicus II allied with the Serbs and Andronicus III with the Bulgarians. In 1328 young Andronicus took first Thessalonica and then Constantinople, and old Andronicus abdicated.

The reign of Andronicus II saw damage to Byzantine power that was never repaired and was perhaps irreparable. The disaster was the direct result of the emperor's failure to maintain the small but effective army and navy that had been holding their own, and usually better than their own, since the time of Theodore I of Nicaea. Even after the Byzantine forces were cut, contemporaries took several years to realize how weak the empire had become. In the absence of enough native soldiers and sailors, foreign mercenaries and the empire's Genoese allies proved to be more destructive than avowed enemies. They left Byzantium with less than half its former land and resources, and barely stronger than Serbia, Bulgaria, or the Ottoman Emirate that had grown at the empire's expense. Andronicus II salvaged even this much only because, late in his reign, he realized what had happened and partly rebuilt his army and navy.

Missed Opportunities

Andronicus III, aged thirty-one when he assumed full imperial powers, was lively and charming, but his greatest asset was his Grand Domestic John Cantacuzenus, a more responsible and intelligent man whose help and advice had been vital to winning the civil war. Andronicus and Cantacuzenus hoped that some of the empire's recent losses could be retrieved, and they prepared an offensive to rescue the endangered remnants of Byzantine Anatolia. The campaign failed when the emperor was slightly wounded and his army fled before the Ottoman Turks. Yet the Byzantines did retake the island of Chios from the occupying Genoese, and negotiated alliances with two Turkish emirs who were rivals of the Ottomans. Cantacuzenus became particularly friendly with the Emir of Aydin, whose base was in Smyrna. For the time being, the emperor and his Grand Domestic abandoned Anatolia and concentrated their energies on Europe.

In 1333 the separatist ruler of Thessaly died, and Andronicus promptly added the whole province to the empire. Though during the next few years Serbian and Genoese attacks and an Albanian rebellion occupied the emperor and Cantacuzenus, they held off the invaders and subdued the rebels. When the separatist Despot of Epirus was murdered, the Byzantines made a determined effort to annex his state. Their initial occupation met with an uprising backed by the heiress to the Latin Empire, but Cantacuzenus persuaded the Epirotes to surrender in 1339. With the conquest of Epirus, Byzantium secured Greece as far south as the Catalan Duchy of Athens. Impressed by the empire's advance, the Latin lords of the Peloponnesus offered to abandon their nominal loyalty to the phantom Latin Empire and accept Andronicus III as their suzerain. Byzantium seemed about to claim mastery over all of Greece when Andronicus III suddenly died in 1341.

Since the Grand Domestic John Cantacuzenus had taken a more active role in Andronicus' government than the emperor himself, he was the obvious regent for Andronicus' nine-year-old son John V Palaeologus. Ruling the convalescent empire called for all of Cantacuzenus' great talents. The Latin lords had not yet made their submission. At the news of Andronicus' death, the Serbs and Bulgarians encroached on Byzantine territory, and Turkish pirates raided Thrace. A theological dispute was raging over the orthodoxy of Hesychasm, a belief among monks on Mount Athos that by particular techniques of prayer they could see a light emanating directly from God. Yet Andronicus had died

without making any official provisions for the regency, and Cantacuzenus had ambitious and envious enemies.

Showing his usual energy, the Grand Domestic called a council while
he prepared to march against the invaders. With Cantacuzenus'
approval, the council endorsed Hesychasm, condemning some intellectuals who found it heretical. Then Cantacuzenus made his expedition,
expelling the Turks, persuading the Serbs and Bulgarians to withdraw,
and receiving the submission of the Latin lords. After returning briefly
to Constantinople, Cantacuzenus set out for the Peloponnesus.

He had reached Didymotichus in Thrace when his enemies struck.
The empress mother Anna of Savoy, the Patriarch of Constantinople
John Calecas, and the Grand Duke Alexius Apocaucus declared them-
selves regents for little John V and cashiered Cantacuzenus as Grand
Domestic. Mobs in Constantinople looted the houses and property of
Cantacuzenus and his friends. Unable to take possession of Latin
Greece, Cantacuzenus had his army proclaim him emperor as John
VI, promising to rule jointly with John V.

The ensuing civil war stirred up old and new resentments and split
Byzantine society down the middle. The regents began with the hereditary emperor and the capital, while Cantacuzenus had the army. Most
magnates and generals backed Cantacuzenus as one of their own, and
most monks backed him as a supporter of Hesychasm. With little love
for magnates, most merchants backed the regents, who held the cities
and had better relations with the Latins with whom business was done.
As for ordinary Byzantines, many urban workers were loyalists like the
merchants; many peasants were Cantacuzenists like their landlords.
Most of the empire's military governors were Cantacuzenists, but most
of their headquarters were in cities dominated by loyalists, who particularly liked plundering the property of Cantacuzenists.

Thus the governor of Thessalonica, aware that most of his city's
people were loyalists, made a secret offer to surrender if Cantacuzenus
could come with an army. Leaving a force at Didymotichus with his wife
Irene, John marched to Thessalonica, only to find that a band of
loyalists known as Zealots had thrown out the governor. Cantacuzenus'
cause seemed hopeless until he opened negotiations with King Stephen
Dushan of Serbia, who admired him and was happy to keep the Byzantine civil war going. Dushan gave Cantacuzenus some Serbian troops
and invaded the empire himself, almost reaching Thessaly before it
declared for the Cantacuzenists. From Thessaly the Cantacuzenists
took Epirus. John gained additional support from the Bulgarians, who

helped his wife hold Didymotichus. By 1343 Cantacuzenus was besieging the Zealots in Thessalonica.

Stephen Dushan, having conquered everything to the north of Cantacuzenus' holdings in Epirus, Thessaly, and the region of Thessalonica, now changed sides and attacked the Cantacuzenists. Cantacuzenus called on his old friend the Emir of Aydin, who helped him fight his way through to his wife in Didymotichus. With yet more troops gained by allying with the Ottoman emir, Cantacuzenus slowly took over almost all of Thrace, including Adrianople. The regents steadily lost support, especially after their most vigorous leader, Alexius Apocaucus, was lynched by some Cantacuzenist prisoners he was inspecting. The regency gained nothing from ceding Philippopolis to the Bulgarians, and lost Chios to the Genoese. Dushan of Serbia gained most, conquering the hinterland of Thessalonica and cutting the city off from Byzantine Thrace and Thessaly. In 1346 Dushan had himself crowned emperor of the Serbs and the Romans.

The next year, when the empress Anna deposed the Patriarch John Calecas, the other remaining regent, Cantacuzenus took his chance to break into Constantinople with his men. He and Anna reached an agreement that he would rule for ten years as the senior colleague of John V, and thereafter as his equal, while the fourteen-year-old John V married Cantacuzenus' daughter Helena. All houses and land seized since the beginning of the civil war were returned to their owners, though no attempt was made to return other loot. The only Byzantines who rejected this settlement were the Zealots of Thessalonica, surrounded on land by the forces of Dushan of Serbia.

So, after six years of ruinous civil war, John VI Cantacuzenus finally became senior emperor in his early fifties. Splendidly qualified for the throne in everything but hereditary right, he could reasonably claim that his enemies had forced the civil war upon him, and that he was the one best able to repair its ravages. He demanded that Dushan return the conquests he had made from the empire since breaking his alliance with the Cantacuzenists. This arrangement would leave the Serbs with the former Byzantine holdings in Albania but not the lands connecting Byzantine Thrace, Thessalonica, and Thessaly with each other. The Serbian emperor delayed his answer, realizing Cantacuzenus was a much more formidable adversary than before.

Then, barely four months after John VI had taken power, the bubonic plague returned to Byzantium after an absence of almost six hundred years. Virulent as ever, this time known as the Black Death, it arrived along the Silk Route from China by way of rats on ships from the Crimea. As always, the plague hit hardest at ports and coastlands, which were about all that the Byzantines still held, and had less effect on the country away from the sea, which was held by the Turks, Bulgarians, and Serbs. By killing urban officials and taxpayers, it also did more harm to centralized and monetarized Byzantium than to its more primitive rivals.

When the Black Death killed the Byzantine governor of Thessaly, Dushan invaded both Thessaly and Epirus. John VI appealed to his ally the Ottoman emir for help against the Serbs, but the Ottoman soldiers who came simply plundered Byzantine Thrace. The emperor drove out the Ottomans and built a new fleet, only to have Genoese raiders burn it in the docks at Constantinople. The Serbs conquered Epirus and Thessaly, and advanced on Thessalonica. The Zealots at last decided that the Serbs would be worse than John VI, and received him into the city with his army and rebuilt navy. He secured Thessalonica, and temporarily drove back the Serbs, but after he left they reclaimed the little he had retaken.

Resigned to the fragmentation of the empire for the present, in 1350 John VI divided its administration into parts. Having already given his elder son Matthew authority over western Thrace and his younger son Manuel responsibility for the Byzantine Peloponnesus, Cantacuzenus assigned Thessalonica to John V. This arrangement worked well enough among the members of the Cantacuzenus family, who trusted each other, but young John V began plotting with his neighbor Stephen Dushan. To prevent another civil war, John's mother Anna sailed to Thessalonica, where she persuaded her son to leave the city to her and take over Matthew Cantacuzenus' territory in western Thrace. Matthew reluctantly moved to eastern Thrace.

Within months John V attacked Matthew, and civil warfare began once more in 1352. The Serbs, Bulgarians, and Venetians backed John V. John VI supported his son with the help of the Ottoman Turks. He and his Turkish allies prevailed in a battle in Thrace, sending John V fleeing to his mother at Thessalonica. Deposing John V as a rebel, John VI proclaimed his son Matthew his co-emperor. When the sitting patriarch refused to crown Matthew and fled to John V, John VI chose a new patriarch. His Ottoman allies remained in Thrace.

In 1354 an earthquake damaged the walls of the Thracian port of Callipolis (Gallipoli), allowing the Turks allied to John VI to seize it. When the emperor was unable to get them out again, many Byzantines realized that the Ottomans intended to stay in Europe, posing a mortal threat to what remained of Byzantium. Coming as the latest of many terrible setbacks, the Ottoman occupation of Callipolis discredited any claim John VI could make that he had helped the empire. When John V landed secretly in Constantinople, mobs of partisans acclaimed him and rioted. Within two weeks, John VI abdicated and entered a monastery as the monk Joasaph.

Two civil wars, the Black Death, and the earthquake at Callipolis, all of them exploited by the empire's Turkish, Serbian, and Bulgarian enemies as allies of one Byzantine claimaint or another, had reduced the empire to ruins. John Cantacuzenus cannot fairly be blamed for resisting his enemies, who were far less competent than he, or for the earthquake or plague. As before in Byzantine history, the plague had more serious effects than contemporaries recognized, and frustrated attempts by John VI to restore the empire that might well have succeeded otherwise. By the time John V became senior emperor at age twenty-three, Byzantium's situation was truly wretched.

If John VI Cantacuzenus was capable but unpopular, John V Palaeologus was popular but incapable. Obsessed with Matthew and Manuel Cantacuzenus, he asked the Pope for aid to fight them, not the advancing Ottoman Turks. When Stephen Dushan died in 1355 and his empire began to disintegrate, John V did nothing to exploit Serbian weakness, which allowed an heir to the Despotate of Epirus to restore a separatist state in Epirus and Thessaly. Only Matthew Cantacuzenus attacked the Serbs, who captured him and sent him to John V. When the Ottoman emir died of the plague in 1362, John also did nothing, even rejecting a generous Venetian offer for an alliance against the Turks. Instead John fought the Bulgarians, for some reason visited Hungary, then was surprised that the Bulgarian emperor refused to permit his return through Bulgaria.

John remained stranded in Hungary until his mother's nephew, Count Amadeo of Savoy, arrived with a small army of Crusaders to help. In 1366 Amadeo retook Callipolis from the Turks and forced the Bulgarians to let John pass. But the emperor missed his chance to clear Thrace of Turks, who soon seized Adrianople. Instead John went to Rome to renegotiate his debts and to join the western Church, as a purely personal act that made little impression on either Byzantines or westerners. The emperor agreed to cede the small but strategic island of Tenedos to the Venetians to cancel his debts, but back in Constantinople his son and temporary regent Andronicus refused to hand Tenedos over. The Venetians kept the insolvent emperor a virtual prisoner until his younger son Manuel brought the money to release him.

On his return to Constantinople John remained passive while the Turks spread over the Balkans and defeated the Serbs. In 1372 John actually consented to become a vassal of the Ottoman emir Murād, who had taken the title of sultan. At John's humiliating submission his son Andronicus rebelled, but was subdued, imprisoned, and blinded in one eye at the sultan's insistence. Yet in 1376 Andronicus escaped from prison and won Murād's support by promising to surrender Callipolis. Capturing Constantinople with Turkish and Genoese help, he proclaimed himself emperor as Andronicus IV. The new emperor imprisoned his father John and his brother Manuel, and surrendered Callipolis to the sultan.

Andronicus reigned only three years before John and Manuel escaped to Murād in their turn. They apparently bid for his help by promising him Philadelphia, the last Byzantine outpost in Anatolia. Backed by the sultan and the Venetians, they drove Andronicus from Constantinople, and eventually agreed to a settlement that gave him control over the nearby region of Selymbria. Manuel received authority over Thessalonica, while their younger brother Theodore took the Byzantine Peloponnesus after the death of its former ruler Manuel Cantacuzenus. The Ottomans overran still more of Serbia and Bulgaria.

At Thessalonica, Manuel recruited a small army and persuaded the petty princes of Epirus and Thessaly to make their submission to Byzantium. Fifteen or twenty years earlier, such a strategy might well have succeeded in pushing back the Turks. As it was, the sultan understood what Manuel was doing and had him besieged in Thessalonica. Manuel held out until 1387, when he fled and the Ottomans occupied the city. Two years later Murād died winning a victory over the Serbs, but his son Bāyezīd quickly took over his power.

In 1390 Bāyezīd backed a plot in favor of the emperor's grandson John, son of the recently deceased Andronicus IV, who had succeeded his father at Selymbria. John captured most of Constantinople and proclaimed himself emperor as John VII. But his grandfather John V held out in a fort inside the capital, and with the help of his son Manuel soon expelled the usurper. The sultan put young John back in Selymbria, but summoned Manuel to his court as a virtual hostage. Manuel had to help the Turks conquer nominally Byzantine Philadelphia, which until this time had held out in autonomous isolation.

John V died in 1391, fifty years after his accession. His reign was a time of almost unremitting disasters, which he did not cause but did scarcely anything to prevent. Evidently his misfortunes overwhelmed him, and he soon decided his empire was past saving. That judgement was probably wrong at the time of his victory in 1354, when the empire still held several important cities and some good farmland, the Serbs had only a weak hold on northern Greece, and the Turks occupied only one precarious base in Europe. By the end of John's reign, however, Byzantium was indeed a practically hopeless case, since the Ottomans surrounded it with overwhelmingly superior power as its recognized overlords. They might already have taken it if they had tried, and whenever they tried they could expect to take it in a few years at the most.

The End of Byzantium

The story of Byzantium's survival for six more decades is remarkable, but pathetic. By this time all that remained of the so-called empire was Constantinople itself, a few ports in Thrace, and about half the Peloponnesus. Of these, only Constantinople, with its still-mighty walls, could possibly be defended against a determined Turkish attack. The sultan Bāyezīd actually held John V's preferred successor Manuel at his court at Prusa, though Manuel managed to decamp so that he could be crowned at Constantinople. Aged forty, Manuel II was a man of ability, experience, and tact, but he had no illusions about his position. He humbly petitioned Bāyezīd for recognition, agreeing to help the sultan campaign against other Turks in Anatolia.

Bāyezīd had a strong hand, but overplayed it. In 1393 he annexed Bulgaria outright after its vassal emperor rebelled. Then the sultan individually summoned Manuel and all his other Byzantine and Serbian vassals to Serres near Thessalonica, where they arrived to find themselves together and wholly defenseless. After bullying them, Bāyezīd allowed most of them to depart unharmed, though he detained Manuel's brother Theodore. After what they considered a near escape from death, the Byzantine vassals became desperate. Theodore escaped to his domain in the Peloponnesus, while Manuel ignored the sultan's next demand for his attendance. Rather than trust Bāyezīd, the emperor gambled on holding Constantinople until some sort of help might arrive.

The sultan put the city under siege in 1394. The emperor had prepared as best he could, and could count on receiving supplies by sea from the Venetians. King Sigismund of Hungary, already disturbed that the Turks had reached his borders, was doubly alarmed at the siege of Constantinople, and many other westerners also awoke to the danger. In 1396 Sigismund marshaled a good-sized crusading army of French, Germans, Poles, and others, and advanced through Turkish-occupied Bulgaria to Nicopolis on the Danube. Bāyezīd had to turn from Constantinople to Nicopolis, but there his army crushed the crusaders. Sigismund was one of the few to escape, carried down the Danube and through the straits on a Venetian ship.

Even though the Crusade of Nicopolis failed, it bought some time for Constantinople, which continued to hold out with the help of the Venetians and Genoese. In 1399 the French king Charles VI sent a small relief force under his marshal Boucicault. The marshal convinced Manuel to return with him to France to ask for more reinforcements, leaving Manuel's nephew, the former emperor John VII, as regent in the besieged city. The emperor had little hope that his plea would succeed, and he trusted his nephew so little that he left his own wife and sons with his brother Theodore in the Peloponnesus. Yet Manuel decided that doing something was better than doing nothing.

The next year Manuel landed in Venice, traveled by land across northern Italy and southern France, and visited King Charles in Paris. Everywhere Manuel received a warm and courteous welcome. Renaissance Italy and France were already full of enthusiasm for Greek culture, and the dignified emperor made an excellent impression. He spent Christmas in England with King Henry IV before returning to Paris. Charles, Henry, Pope Boniface IX, and various other western notables promised to do what they could, but provided no actual aid. Unwilling to leave empty-handed, the emperor remained in France, while his nephew John held on despondently in Constantinople.

Then, in 1402, Timur the Lame, who had recently led a Mongol army to conquer Turkestan, northern India, Iran, and Iraq, attacked the Ottoman Sultanate. In a battle near Ancyra, Timur defeated and captured the sultan Bāyezīd. As Timur restored the petty Turkish emirates of Anatolia that the Ottomans had absorbed, Bāyezīd's sons began fighting over the remainder of the sultanate. The eldest son Sulaymān, who took over the European part, wanted to avoid the least trouble with Byzantines or Latins until he could secure his power.

Therefore, abandoning the Ottoman claim to suzerainty over Byzantium, Sulaymān ceded to John VII the whole coast of Thrace from the Bulgarian ports on the Black Sea almost to Callipolis, plus another coastal enclave around Thessalonica for John to rule when Manuel returned from the West. By the time Manuel arrived in 1404, he could only confirm his acceptance of these munificent terms. By this treaty, and other concessions to the Venetians, Genoese, and Serbs, Sulaymān forestalled any possible Christian alliance that might have driven the Ottomans from Europe. No such alliance formed even during the next ten years of Ottoman civil warfare. Meanwhile Manuel gained firmer control over his empire's three parts when his brother Theodore died in the Peloponnesus and John VII died in Thessalonica. The emperor had his possessions confirmed by the eventual winner of the Ottoman civil wars, Mehmed. But Byzantium remained far weaker than the reunited Ottoman Sultanate.

At Mehmed's death in 1421, Manuel's son John persuaded his reluctant father to back a pretender to the Ottoman throne, Mustafa. Mustafa promised to cede Callipolis to the Byzantines, which might have led to dividing the Ottoman holdings into separate Balkan and Anatolian parts. But the legitimate sultan Murād II made short work of Mustafa, and besieged Constantinople and Thessalonica in retaliation. Constantinople held out, but the Byzantines postponed the fall of Thessalonica only by giving it to the Venetians. In 1424 Manuel, in failing health, ceded most of his remaining Thracian ports to Murād in return for peace.

The next year Manuel died and was succeeded by his thirty-two-year-old son John VIII, like his father a competent ruler with scarcely anything to rule. John entrusted the Byzantine Peloponnesus to three of his brothers, who by a combination of warfare and dynastic marriage added most of the Latin Peloponnesus to their domains. Resisting the Ottomans, who had now conquered Thessalonica, Serbia, Albania, and northern Greece, was far beyond the Byzantines' power. But at least John had a strategy that offered some chance of success: church union with the West by means of an ecumenical council, to be followed by a Western Crusade against the Turks. The emperor took the utmost care in pursuing his plan.

After painstaking negotiations and preparations, in 1437 Pope Eugenius IV arranged passage to Italy for seven hundred Eastern delegates, including the emperor, the Patriarch of Constantinople, and representatives of nearly all the major Eastern churches as far off as Egypt, Syria,

Georgia, and Russia. During the next two years the Eastern delegation discussed every relevant issue with the Pope and Western bishops at the council, sitting first at Ferrara and then at Florence. The basic principle adopted was mutual toleration of all existing practices and doctrines, with the Westerners accepting Hesychasm and the Easterners accepting the right of the Pope to call ecumenical councils. Final acceptance of the council's decisions was almost unanimous, including the approval of the dying Patriarch of Constantinople. In 1440, when the emperor and his delegates left for home, the Pope began organizing as large a crusade as he could.

Although the Union of Florence aroused widespread and passionate resistance in the East, the emperor exercised his discretion in implementing it, appointing a unionist patriarch without officially proclaiming the union. Despite the obstacle of a serious civil war in Hungary, the Pope did everything possible to advance the crusade. With support from the major Western powers, a crusading army massed in Hungary, and a crusading fleet assembled at Venice. Serbs, Albanians, and Bulgarians rebelled against the Turks as the Byzantines advanced north from the Peloponnesus under John's brother Constantine in 1444. The worried sultan Murād offered a truce recognizing Serbian independence. The Crusaders first accepted it, but were released from their oath by a papal legate. While some 20,000 Crusaders advanced across Bulgaria to Varna on the Black Sea, their fleet sailed into the straits to stop Murād from bringing his army from Anatolia. The sultan however evaded the fleet, fell on the army at Varna with superior numbers, and destroyed it.

That the Crusade of Varna could in the best of circumstances have driven the Ottoman Turks out of Europe seems unlikely, but it posed a serious threat to their power, as the sultan realized. Its failure strengthened the Ottomans' already overwhelming domination over the Balkans. The Turks soon chased the emperor's brother Constantine back to the Peloponnesus and returned the Byzantines to vassalage. A makeshift crusade mounted in 1448 by the Hungarians and Albanians came to nothing. That year John VIII died, after a reign which can be counted an honorable failure. Since he was childless, his successor was his enterprising brother Constantine XI, aged forty-three.

The sultan Murād accepted the homage of Constantine as emperor and of his two younger brothers as subordinate rulers of the Peloponnesus. Unfortunately for Byzantium, in 1451 Murād died, and within a year his son and heir Mehmed II began preparations for an assault on

Constantinople. Though deeply discouraged by the failure of the Crusade of Varna, some of those to whom Constantine appealed sent a few troops, principally Venetians and Genoese. In 1453 the sultan put Constantinople under siege, offering only to spare the lives of those who would surrender. The city's walls were nearly as strong as ever, but Mehmed had cannons, which recent improvements had made much more effective against fortifications.

After two months of bombardment, the Ottomans opened a breach in the walls and broke into the city. The Byzantine garrison fought almost to the last man, and the emperor Constantine himself died fighting. Once all was lost, many of the Italians escaped by ship. The sultan sacked most of the city thoroughly, executing the Byzantine officials whom he captured. He then set about rebuilding and repopulating it as his capital. He appointed a new Patriarch of Constantinople, and for a time allowed Constantine's two brothers to go on ruling the Peloponnesus as his vassals. Tiring of this arrangement, in 1460 Mehmed simply annexed their domains. The next year the sultan seized the Empire of Trebizond, the last surviving splinter of Byzantium.

A Defensive Society

Byzantine history from 1204 to 1461 took an extraordinary course. The Byzantine Empire, apparently destroyed in 1204, gave rise to the three successor states of Nicaea, Trebizond, and Epirus, all of which soon claimed to be Byzantium reconstituted. By 1261 one of them, the Empire of Nicaea, made its claim reasonably good by recovering Constantinople and more than half the territory of the empire of 1204. This restored empire held its own for some forty years, until the Ottoman Turks and its own Catalan mercenaries reduced its size by about half, costing it the Anatolian base from which it had originally expanded. The empire halted its decline and carried on for another thirty years, until a ruinous civil war, capped by a devastating plague, reduced it to a rump. Even after the plague something might have been salvaged under an effective ruler, but none emerged until Byzantium was utterly wrecked. Even then, it eked out a miserable existence for sixty more years.

This strange tale becomes more intelligible when we realize that the small and unsettled Byzantine successor states represented a much more comprehensive and stable Byzantine society, surviving from the earlier empire. In the widest sense, this society included all the members of the Eastern Church. Yet the Serbs, Bulgarians, Russians, and Georgians, the subjects of the new Romanian principalities of Wallachia and Moldavia, and the remaining Christians of the eastern patriarchates under Muslim rule all had their own languages and their own church hierarchies, and only the Bulgarians had been under Byzantine rule recently. Where a truly Byzantine society survived was the southern Balkans, the Aegean islands, and northern and western Anatolia, roughly the territory of the empire as it had been around 1190, after the Bulgarian revolt.

The regions where society remained Byzantine were mostly though not exclusively Greek-speaking, and by the standards of the time urbanized and economically developed. Most of their people, and especially their leading citizens, still considered themselves Byzantines, resented Latin rule, and were ready to join any Greek-speaking potentate who seemed able to restore something like Byzantium. From such would-be Byzantines came the backers of the three Greek successor states that formed after 1204. The same attachment to the idea of Byzantium inspired the Bulgarian, Latin, and Epirote subjects who joined John Vatatzes of Nicaea after 1230, the other Latin and Epirote subjects who rallied to Michael VIII after 1261, and the Epirotes and Thessalians who favored the Byzantine Empire after their own dynasty died out in 1318. Recognizing the Balkan Mountains and the northeastern edge of the Anatolian plateau as the natural limits of Byzantine society, the Byzantine successor states confined their ambitions within those bounds.

The Empire of Trebizond was the least aggressive but the longest-lived of the successor states. Its land link with the others was tenuous even before the Seljuks severed it in 1214. Thereafter the emperors of Trebizond, who called themselves the Grand Comneni, held only the southeastern Black Sea coast and part of the Crimea, and were content to keep what they had. They were blessed with fine harbors on major trading routes, a sliver of fertile farmland, and the natural defenses of the high Pontic Alps on one side and the sea on the other. The Grand Comneni avoided warfare by accepting Seljuk, Mongol, Byzantine, and Ottoman suzerainty in turn, on occasion more than one at a time. Yet between 1340 and 1349 the Trapezuntines engaged in civil strife like that of the main Byzantine Empire, with rival emperors from rival factions. These struggles, and the arrival of the Black Death in 1347, led to the loss of the western part of the empire to the Turks and probably of the Crimea to the Genoese and Mongols. Though the tiny empire made a somewhat better recovery than Byzantium proper, it was always feeble, and if the Turks had wished they could probably have taken it long before 1461.

The Despotate of Epirus, which briefly became the Empire of Thessalonica, like Trebizond had a base that was well defended by mountains and sea but far from Constantinople. The Epirote capital of Arta was a fairly small town, and though Thessalonica was a large one its empire failed to prosper. That Epirus played as important a role as it did was mainly the doing of its rulers Michael I, Theodore, and Michael II Ducas, whose abilities almost matched their ambitions. They attacked or joined their neighbors with dizzying agility, made great gains, and lost most of them in the end. Often calling on the help of Latins, they were particularly treacherous to their fellow Byzantines of Nicaea, and then to the restored Byzantine Empire. Yet the members of the Ducas family kept Epirus itself, along with their early conquest of Thessaly, and retained the allegiance of their people as long as their dynasty lasted.

The Empire of Nicaea was the most successful of the three aspiring Byzantiums. One of its advantages was a base in the richest and most strategically located territory, in northwestern Anatolia, just across the straits from Constantinople. Another was the sagacity of its rulers from Theodore I Lascaris to Michael VIII Palaeologus, who often created opportunities for themselves. These included Theodore I's careful organization of his state and creation of a patriarchate in exile, John Vatatzes' minting of hyperpyra and expansion into Europe, and Michael VIII's acquisition of part of the Peloponnesus and tireless military and diplomatic offensives. After 1261 the possession of Constantinople, however damaged it had been by the Latins, gave the restored empire a defensible, revenue-rich, and incomparably prestigious capital. Once Michael VIII had established his suzerainty over Epirus, Thessaly, and Trebizond, little of the Byzantine world was wholly outside his authority except for some of the Greek islands and about a quarter of mainland Greece, all in Latin hands.

Western Anatolia had provided the resources that enabled the Empire of Nicaea to enlarge itself, and cannot have contributed much less than half of Michael VIII's revenues. Michael and his son Andronicus worked hard to defend Anatolia, though Andronicus' efforts failed disastrously, and the Byzantines seem to have given up on it only after Andronicus III's defeat in 1329. With a competent defense it could surely have been held, as it had been continuously for two centuries despite a lack of good natural frontiers. Yet the way the Ottoman Turks conquered it, by occupying the countryside and starving out the towns, made it difficult to recover. As many Turks settled there, and many Byzantines fled from Anatolia to Europe, the country became mainly Turkish and Muslim. The remaining Christian population despaired of a Byzantine reconquest, and some of it, especially in the villages, converted to Islam.

With the loss of Anatolia, the obvious eastern boundary for Byzantium was the straits. Andronicus III and John Cantacuzenus evidently wanted, and almost won, an empire consisting of all of Europe south of the Balkan range. Since 1261 the Byzantines had held the best part of this region: the farmlands of Thrace, Macedonia, and the Peloponnesus. The conquest of Epirus and Thessaly added more farmland and shortened the southern frontier, while the proposed submission of the Latins of the Peloponnesus would have added still more farmland and ports and completed Byzantine control of Greece.

The Ottomans' capture of Callipolis in 1354 soon frustrated plans for a secure Byzantium in Greece and Thrace. At first the Turks seem to have been more interested in raiding than in conquest, but when they sacked the towns they found that they could also hold them. Since the numbers of Turkish settlers were small, and the Christian population had no obviously safe places to flee to any longer, the lands taken by the Ottomans remained heavily Christian and Greek-speaking. After 1453 the Balkans stayed mostly Christian except for Constantinople itself, where the sultan did settle many Turks.

Michael VIII made a valuable and lasting addition to the empire when he extorted the southeastern Peloponnesus as the ransom of William of Villehardouin. The Byzantine province was only about a quarter of the peninsula, but it was the best part, the fertile valley from which Sparta had risen to be master of Classical Greece. The local capital, Mistra, was near Sparta but on a more defensible hilltop. From it the Byzantines slowly but steadily retook the rest of the Peloponnesus, until the province rivaled isolated Constantinople in importance. The empire was also a power in the Aegean Sea from the time of John Vatatzes of Nicaea, who conquered the large islands near Anatolia and supported persistent Greek rebels on Venetian Crete. Under Michael VIII the Venetian mercenary Licario took most of Euboea and some other Aegean islands for Byzantium, and though Andronicus II lost most of them again the empire held a few in the north to the end.

Despite the spread of regional revolts in the empire just before 1204, and the squabbling and weakness of the Byzantine successor states, after the Fourth Crusade Byzantine regionalism lost much of its appeal. Nicaea, Epirus, and Trebizond were dynastic states rather than regional ones, as appears from Epirus' collapse after the extinction of the Ducas family. In Nicaea, the only successor state to change dynasties, Michael Palaeologus' removal of John IV Lascaris aroused opposition that lasted half a century, until the end of the Arsenite Schism. The largely unsuccessful Palaeologus dynasty itself became Byzantium's most enduring, unless we count the Grand Comneni of Trebizond. Popular devotion to the Palaeologi kept the gifted John VI Cantacuzenus from ever becoming an effective ruler. Although the members of each dynasty repeatedly fought among themselves, they failed to shake their subjects' dynastic loyalties. Apparently after the Fourth Crusade most Byzantines felt an overriding need to stand by their inherited leaders against their foreign enemies.

The division between magnates and merchants however persisted, and was inflamed during the civil strife between Cantacuzenists and loyalists. Yet the mostly Cantacuzenist magnates, who still led the army and had always been richer than merchants or bureaucrats, found themselves at a disadvantage and ultimately lost the war. They might have expected to profit from anti-Latin sentiment, because they were generally more hostile to Latins than the loyalists were and John V's mother Anna of Savoy was Italian. Yet the Cantacuzenists were more favorable to the Turks, who had become a greater threat than the Latins. Above all, the loyalists had the legitimate emperor, and John Cantacuzenus' professions of fealty to John V never carried full conviction, even before he dropped them.

In the contemporary struggle at Trebizond, the party formed mostly of magnates also lost to a party formed mostly of bureaucrats and merchants, which supported emperors more widely considered legitimate. While the main feature of these civil troubles was the triumph of legitimacy, with the growth of cities and commerce the merchants do seem to have been gaining wealth and power, and territorial losses surely took a toll on the magnates' estates. One sign of this shifting balance of wealth is that later in the fourteenth century some magnates began to invest in trade.

After the Fourth Crusade destroyed the old Byzantine central government, some former officials made their way to Nicaea, Trebizond, and perhaps Arta, but the bureaucracies formed there were much smaller and weaker than the one formerly at Constantinople. The chief officials of the successor states were courtiers as much as bureaucrats, servants more of the emperors than of the state. The Empire of Nicaea and later the restored Byzantine Empire bestowed old Byzantine honorific titles like Caesar and Despot, the latter on the rulers of Epirus when they supposedly submitted to imperial authority. The Nicene and restored Byzantine empires had a bureaucracy headed by a Mesazon and a Grand Logothete, an army headed by a Grand Domestic, and a navy headed by a Grand Duke. The themes were mostly a thing of the past, and provinces were entrusted to regional civil and military governors, based in the main towns. John VI began the practice of dividing the empire into separate domains for members of the imperial family, which suited an empire that by then consisted of disconnected enclaves.

Although Michael VIII's army must have had at least 10,000 regular soldiers at its height, the Nicene army before him and the Byzantine army after him seem to have been smaller, except when Andronicus II briefly hired the Catalan Grand Company. Until Andronicus' reduc- - tions, the army and navy did a creditable job of defending the empire's far-flung frontiers against its many enemies, but they were stretched thin and hard to pay. Afterward the smaller army and navy apparently buckled, unable either to hold Anatolia or the islands by themselves or to keep control of the Catalans or other foreign mercenaries.

By 1320 Andronicus had brought the army and navy back to some 4000 soldiers and 3000 oarsmen. These could hold the Balkan part of the empire, but not the remaining scraps of Anatolia. Since they were not particularly hard to pay, Andronicus should have hired more of them and tried to keep more land, but he never fully learned the folly of cuts that cost more in revenue than they saved in expenditure. Andronicus III's army seems to have been somewhat stronger than his grandfather's, and after his reign the main cause of the empire's military disasters was civil warfare rather than low military spending.

By Andronicus II's reign a variety of tax exemptions and pronoia grants had considerably reduced state revenues. The government seems to have been collecting an average of only about half as much revenue per subject as it had in the eleventh century. Some of the shortfall was in pronoia grants that supported around 500 heavy cavalry, who performed services of some value in return for the taxes they collected. But most of the decline in revenue during these three centuries represented either outright corruption, or immunities granted over the years to courtiers, imperial relatives, and the Church.

What the loss evidently did not represent was any general reduction in prosperity. Up to the time of the Black Death, the Byzantine economy appears to have been in good condition, to judge from the large resources that the merchants and magnates were able to squander on civil wars, and the high profits being earned in Byzantium by the Venetians and Genoese. Recorded figures for trade duties at Constantinople indicate that trade increased significantly between the twelfth and fourteenth centuries. The rise of the Empire of Nicaea, Stephen Dushan's Serbia, and the Ottomans showed that Byzantine territory could still nurture powerful states. The decline of the Byzantine Empire occurred for other reasons than its subjects' poverty.

The overall population growth that had begun in the eighth century continued up to the time of the Black Death wherever it can be measured in Europe and the Mediterranean region. Nothing suggests that warfare on Byzantine soil caused more than temporary and local disruptions. As population density increased in Byzantium, more land came under cultivation, and peasant plots became smaller. The magnates with their superior resources continued to buy out peasants, and could charge their tenants higher rents, as long as land was in greater demand than labor. Yet no widespread economic distress occurred. Even when Catalan raiding caused a famine in Byzantine Thrace, just to the north Bulgaria could supply the surplus grain to make up the shortfall.

Byzantines as well as Venetians and Genoese benefited from an expansion of the Black Sea trade. Grain, furs, and slaves from the Mongol Khanate of the Golden Horde supplemented the Chinese goods that came along the old Silk Route. Most of this trade went through the ports of the Crimea or Trebizond, and nearly all of it passed through the harbors of Constantinople. Though Constantinople failed to regain its size of 1203, the less centralized economies of the various states that grew up after the Fourth Crusade fostered the growth of other cities like Thessalonica, Adrianople, Mistra, Trebizond, and Arta. Yet the volume of trade passing through Byzantine and Trapezuntine territory meant that the Black Death did Byzantium and Trebizond disproportionate damage. While most other powers soon recovered from the plague and resumed their growth, the Ottomans, who had suffered less, recovered better, and by their conquests forestalled a Byzantine recovery.

Although Byzantine defeats during this period were to a great extent caused by Byzantine mistakes, many Byzantines blamed foreigners for their plight, with some reason. Not only the Fourth Crusade itself but the seemingly mindless destruction wreaked by the Crusaders after their victory was difficult to excuse and almost impossible for the Byzantines to understand. The Venetians, Genoese, Serbs, Bulgarians, and Turks all repeatedly exploited Byzantine weakness during the thirteenth and fourteenth centuries, breaking their treaties with the empire far more often than the empire broke its treaties with them. Even if such exploitation was merely politics as usual, the Byzantines naturally resented it. While some Western Europeans tried to help by crusading, their crusades failed, unlike the Fourth Crusade that had defeated the Byzantines. Under the circumstances, some Byzantines could be forgiven for feeling that they could trust only their own kind.

A Lost Renaissance

The Byzantine society and culture that after 1204 covered the area of the former empire survived in much the same territory after 1453. The Greek language, like many Byzantine attitudes and customs, remained widespread throughout the formerly Byzantine lands. Somewhat altered by loan words from Italian and Turkish, and somewhat curtailed by the Turkicization of central Anatolia, Greek continued to be the predominant language in Greece, Thrace, the Aegean islands, Cyprus, and the Anatolian coastlands. The Byzantine Church, which preserved still more Byzantine traditions than the language did, survived with even less diminution and alteration. Through all the upheavals of the thirteenth through fifteenth centuries, the Patriarchate of Constantinople retained its leadership of the Greek-speaking Church and the allegiance of most Russian, Bulgarian, Serbian, Romanian, and Georgian Christians.

Although one of the main purposes of the Fourth Crusade had supposedly been to reunite Byzantium with the western Church, in this the Crusaders were even less successful than in maintaining their Latin Empire. In contrast with the Turkish conquests, which permanently expanded Islam at the expense of eastern Christianity, Latin occupation attracted few eastern Christians to lasting union with Rome. The patriarchate at Nicaea, though created in exile by a successor state of dubious legitimacy, easily won its competition with the Latin Patriarchate that actually held St Sophia in Constantinople. Within the Latin Empire and its dependencies, the Latin hierarchy gained only the most grudging acceptance from the native clergy and laity. The rulers and people of Epirus, Trebizond, Bulgaria, and Serbia, even when they were at war with Nicaea or the restored Byzantine Empire, generally recognized the Patriarchate of Constantinople reestablished at Nicaea.

Most of them however withheld that recognition when the patriarchate itself subscribed to Church union with the West. Hatred for Latins worked strongly against the Union of Lyons of 1274, but circumstances were also against it. The Latins did nothing to promote it but stop an anti-Byzantine crusade already in progress. Michael VIII, having already provoked the Arsenite Schism by blinding his predecessor, suffered from a moral taint that he passed on to any patriarch he chose and any cause he espoused. Before concluding the Union the emperor had consulted no one else of importance, not even his own Patriarch Joseph, whose opposition caused the Josephite Schism. The Union would probably have gained more acceptance at Byzantium, and had a chance of ultimate success, if it had kept the support of the Papacy and won that of Andronicus II, who had fewer enemies than his father. Condemnation of the Union of Lyons amid frantic denunciations of unionists made achieving Church unity even harder than it had been before.

With the end of the Josephite and Arsenite schisms, the Byzantine Church at least regained its own internal unity, and seemed ready for peaceful coexistence with the Western Church until Hesychasm became an issue. Though Hesychast practices in themselves marked no major departure from earlier forms of mysticism, the most extravagant claims made for them enraged some learned and pro-Western Byzantines. Soon identification with the Cantacuzenist side in the civil war made Hesychast doctrines even more contentious. Nevertheless, in the compromise of exhaustion that ended the war, they won official approval in spite of the Cantacuzenists' defeat. By then the Byzantines were so tired of controversy that John V could submit to the Western Church without objections from the Patriarch Philotheus, a fervent Hesychast and former Cantacuzenist who had no interest in unionism himself.

Although subsequent years saw a growth of mutual tolerance between the Eastern and Western churches, the failure of the carefully prepared Union of Florence is not difficult to explain. Whatever chance of success it had depended on the Crusade of Varna. If the Crusade had managed to restore Serbia, Bulgaria, and Byzantium as independent and viable states, which westerners continued to aid, unionist sentiment would probably have spread in the East, and in time the schism might even have faded away. Once the Crusade failed, however, a full Ottoman conquest of the Balkans became almost inevitable, and the Ottomans could only regard collaboration between their Christian subjects and western Christians as disloyal. Unionism was incompatible with the internal unity and accommodation with the Turks that the Byzantine Church needed, if it was to survive as an institution under Turkish rule.

While the Ottomans strongly encouraged conversion to Islam in Anatolia, and by confiscating church property severely weakened the church hierarchy there, in the Balkans they accepted that Christianity would last for the foreseeable future, and recognized the bishops as leaders of the Christian population. Although the Ottomans abolished the Serbian and Bulgarian patriarchates, Mehmed II reestablished the Patriarchate of Constantinople the year after he took the city. The sultan assumed the prerogative of a Byzantine emperor to select a patriarch, and named a strong antiunionist, Gennadius II Scholarius. In the absence of serious competitors for leadership of the Eastern Church, the Patriarchate won general acceptance among Eastern Christians even in independent Russia and Georgia.

Like the Church hierarchy, Byzantine monasteries survived or recovered from the Latin and Turkish conquests fairly well in the Balkans, though less well in Anatolia. With the destruction or decline of most Anatolian monastic centers, the monasteries and hermitages of Mount Athos became more important than ever, and attracted monks from Serbia, Bulgaria, Russia, and Georgia as well as the Byzantine successor states. The Athonite monasteries added to their already large landed property, and the triumphant approval of their practice and doctrine of Hesychasm enhanced their prestige. On their isolated peninsula, taking little part in politics, the monasteries were less affected than the rest of the Byzantine world by the Turkish conquest.

The most influential theologian of the period was the Hesychast Gregory Palamas, an Athonite monk of aristocratic family and good education whom John VI made Archbishop of Thessalonica. Palamas gained prominence by defending Hesychasm against the scholarly monk Barlaam of Calabria, who denounced it as anti-intellectual and unorthodox, only to be condemned himself as a heretic at John Cantacuzenus' council of 1341. Palamas' theology, which became known as Palamism, consisted of a traditional and reasoned argument that Hesychasm was a means of knowing God. Though later Hesychasm won acceptance from the Western Church at the Council of Ferrara-Florence, some Palamites unquestionably had anti-Western and anti-intellectual tendencies, and pursued their defeated opponents with rancor.

Yet Palamism was in its way part of a general flourishing of higher culture at Byzantium, which appeared to defy most political, social, and economic trends. Though Byzantium had never been smaller, weaker, poorer, or more xenophobic than it was at this time, its scholars and artists showed more knowledge, skill, and even openness to outside influences than ever before. From what seemed to be the ingredients for a dark age, Byzantium produced a renaissance envied and emulated by the scholars and artists of the contemporary Renaissance in Italy. Admittedly, most forms of scholarship and art are so cheap that even an impoverished society can afford them if it wishes, and Byzantine scholars and artists were among the least xenophobic Byzantines. Yet the cultural revival was still a remarkable development, and needs explaining.

To all appearances, the Fourth Crusade should have dealt a crippling blow to Byzantine culture. The fires and vandalism at Constantinople that accompanied the Crusade destroyed so many manuscripts that later Byzantine scholars could refer to only a few more Greek texts than those that survive today, though earlier scholars had consulted about twice as many. The Crusade put an end to the schools at Constantinople that had educated the empire's secular and ecclesiastical officials. The smaller and poorer government established at Nicaea, and the still smaller and poorer governments at Trebizond and Arta, could support far fewer officials, schools, teachers, scholars, or artists than those of the earlier Byzantine Empire. Officials and aristocrats also had less money to spend on artistic patronage. Since scholars and artists often train, encourage, and inspire each other, the shrinkage of the Byzantine scholarly and artistic communities should have done disproportionate harm to scholarship and art. In fact, the leading scholar of the generation born around 1200, Nicephorus Blemmydes, had to wander the Byzantine world in search of scattered books and teachers.

The most plausible explanation for the beginning of the cultural revival is that educated Byzantines took the catastrophe of the Fourth Crusade and the competition of the Italian Renaissance as a cultural challenge. With a sense of superiority to Westerners and a glorious past to recover, the Byzantines set about trying to undo the Fourth Crusade in cultural as well as political terms. Thus John Vatatzes sent his son Theodore II to study with Blemmydes, both John and Theodore tried to persuade Blemmydes to accept a state professorship, and after the recovery of Constantinople Michael VIII restored the public philosophical school and patriarchal academy closed in 1204. A variety of scholars set to work copying and studying whatever Greek manuscripts they could find. Once begun, the cultural revival assumed its own momentum, though a feeling that Byzantine ways were the only right ones still made many scholars oppose the toleration of Western practices required for Church unity.

After Nicetas Choniates took refuge at Nicaea to finish his work, no contemporary Byzantine wrote a history of the confusing and distressing events of the exile. Then Blemmydes' student George Acropolites, the first professor of philosophy under Michael VIII, continued Choniates' history down to the recovery of Constantinople, a glorious ending that gave the earlier story a suitable theme. Though short, Acropolites' history is of the classical type, and it sufficed to revive the old tradition. It found a continuer in Acropolites' student George Pachymeres, a professor at the restored patriarchal school, who reached the events of 1308 before he died, shortly thereafter. Unlike Acropolites, Pachymeres wrote in great detail, and like Nicetas Choniates tried to understand what he regarded, reasonably, as a period of catastrophe. Two even longer and similarly pessimistic histories came a half-century later. The polymath Nicephorus Gregoras, who as one of the few anti-Palamite Cantacuzenists took the losing side in both politics and theology, wrote a lively but partisan account of the years from the Fourth Crusade to 1359, just before his death. Then the retired emperor John VI himself wrote eloquent and intelligent memoirs spanning the whole period of the civil wars from 1320 to 1356.

Most scholars of this time were true renaissance men in their versatility. Among the historians, Acropolites was also a philosopher, unionist theologian, bureaucrat, and general; Pachymeres a philosopher, bureaucrat, rhetorician, and mathematician; Gregoras an anti-Palamite theologian, rhetorician, mathematician, and scientist; and Cantacuzenus a Palamite theologian, general, and emperor. Some others had equally diverse talents. Andronicus II's Mesazon Theodore Metochites was a philosopher, essayist, astronomer, hagiographer, and poet. Metochites' contemporary Maximus Planudes was a mathematician, rhetorician, geographer, scribe, and commentator on Greek texts. Demetrius Cydones, Mesazon of both John VI and John V, was an anti-Palamite and unionist theologian and an orator and philosopher known for his elegant letters. Well-educated Byzantines may not have been very numerous, but they labored tirelessly.

Although these writers had great respect for earlier Greek literature, they knew it well enough to make full use of it, to criticize it, and at times to go beyond it. Gregoras tried in his youth to persuade Andronicus II to reform the increasingly inaccurate Julian Calendar. Planudes' student Demetrius Triclinius puzzled out the long-forgotten rules of Classical Greek meter, and used them to correct the texts of the Greek tragedies. Planudes himself wrote a treatise to promote the use of Arabic numerals, and translated Cicero, Ovid, St Augustine, and other Latin authors into Greek. Cydones translated Thomas Aquinas.

The first Byzantine scholar to win fame in Western Europe was the early anti-Hesychast theologian Barlaam of Calabria, whose expertise extended to philosophy, mathematics, astronomy, and Italian. After his condemnation in 1341, Barlaam traveled to the Papal court at Avignon, joined the Western Church, and made such an impression with his knowledge that he received a bishopric in his native Calabria. After Barlaam, other Byzantine scholars made their way to Italy with Greek manuscripts, and taught Italian humanists both the Greek language and Greek literature. The Byzantine who probably made the most brilliant impression in Renaissance Italy was the Platonist philosopher George Gemistus Plethon, who attended the Council of Ferrara-Florence. After the council, Plethon's student Bessarion became a Cardinal of the Roman Church and one of the leading figures of the Renaissance in Italy.

Byzantine art also bore comparison with that of Renaissance Italy, and often resembled it. The resemblances can be explained by direct Byzantine influence on Italian art by way of Venice, and by the Classical models separately adopted by both Byzantine and Italian artists. The ravages of the Fourth Crusade caused no perceptible decline in the quality of Byzantine art, and if anything seem to have stimulated it to improve. The rulers of Nicaea, Epirus, and Trebizond all built small but opulent churches and palaces. The best work done in the years following the recovery of Constantinople ranks at the summit of Byzantine artistic achievement, adapting naturalistic and classicizing treatment to traditional Christian subjects. Examples include a splendid mosaic of the Virgin and Baptist Supplicating Christ in St Sophia, probably put up under Michael VIII, and the stunning frescoes of the Church of the Chora in Constantinople, rebuilt and decorated by Theodore Metochites. Though the resources of the time limited the size of monumental buildings, an elegant palace probably built by Michael VIII and the delightful Church of the Chora itself show that Byzantine architects had lost none of their skill. Architects and artists from Byzantium also

Figure 13 Apse fresco of the *Anastasis* (Christ's raising the dead from hell) in the Monastery Church of the Chora, Constantinople. This vigorously executed masterpiece is part of the decoration commissioned by Theodore Metochites, Mesazon (chief minister) of Andronicus II Palaeologus (reigned 1282–1328). (*Photo*: Dumbarton Oaks, Washington, D.C., © copyright 1999)

did excellent work for contemporary Bulgarian, Serbian, and Russian rulers.

Later in the fourteenth century, the Black Death and the Ottoman conquests finally had an impact on Byzantine art, and even on Byzantine literature. The Byzantines could no longer afford mosaics or much building of any sort, but the quality of their frescoes and manuscript illustrations remained as high as ever. The level of Byzantine scholarship also maintained itself, as appears from the profound, innovative, and virtually pagan philosophy of Plethon. Yet the quantity of writing decreased as Byzantine scholars departed for Italy, and after John VI's memoirs the misery and uncertainty of the last century of Byzantine history deterred potential historians from tackling it. Only after the fall of Constantinople had ended the suspense did four Greek authors produce moving accounts of the last years of the empire. Afterward the disappearance of secular schools soon brought Byzantine secular literature to an end. For some time, however, Greek scholars and artists continued to find refuge in the West, where they helped see Greek texts into print and kept Greek influence on European art alive.

Since before its fall Byzantium was already a participant in the Italian Renaissance, and was in most ways in advance of the Italians themselves, the Byzantines would surely have continued to participate in the Renaissance if they had remained independent. Yet after the middle of the fourteenth century their empire was very far gone. Though it was a better organized state than its Ottoman or Slavic rivals in the sense that it had a more professional administration, it was so poor and small that it could scarcely have continued without Ottoman forbearance or massive outside help. Byzantium's failure was political, not cultural. Although its higher culture failed to outlive its government by very long, its language, literacy, Church, and spiritual traditions were to outlast the Ottoman Empire.

8

CONCLUSION

The Problem of Measurement

That Byzantium saw many dramatic reversals of fortune is obvious. Yet modern and Byzantine observers alike have disagreed about the importance of those changes in Byzantine history. The Byzantines, aware of how long their empire had lasted and assuming it had always been much as it was in their own times, usually underestimated change. In this modern scholars have sometimes followed their Byzantine sources and sometimes reacted against them. Occasionally disagreement among modern historians has been sharp, as in the dispute between those who think Byzantium became poorer between the tenth and twelfth centuries and those who think it became richer. More often, however, the modern disputes are over matters of degree, such as whether the political and military decline of the empire in the seventh century was utterly devastating or merely grave. In some cases, both sides have defined their positions so vaguely that they seem to disagree not so much about what occurred as about how best to describe it. For example, the controversy about whether Byzantine cities disappeared or merely shrank in the seventh century may simply hinge upon the size that each side considers the minimum to call a settlement a city.

One way out of such semantic disputes is to use surviving statistics, or, failing those, educated estimates, for such things as the empire's population or its government budget. However, trying to speak in quantitative terms gives rise to other sorts of controversy, over how significant and reliable the Byzantine statistics and modern estimates are. Their significance in principle, which appears obvious to most historians of the ancient or modern worlds, often seems dubious to historians mainly

234

familiar with medieval Western Europe, for which such numbers are of
very limited use. For example, anyone trying to estimate the land area,
population, cash budget, or army size of France in 1200 should realize
that the French king had very little control over most of that area or
population, while his tiny cash budget understated his resources and his
feudal army cannot be assigned a number applicable to more than a
single campaign. By contrast, the Roman Empire, which Byzantium
continued in even more centralized form, had set frontiers, a regular
census, a formal cash budget, and numbered legions assigned identical
numbers of men. After the sixth century Byzantium certainly changed,
but how much it changed is a question about precisely such things as
cash budgets and army size.

How reliable the statistics and estimates may be is a different question,
though again one on which many medievalists have different instincts
from other historians. Apart from rogue writers whose fabrications are
usually easy to detect, most ancient, modern, and Byzantine sources are
fairly reliable for most basic information, especially when they cite
official statistics. If the *New York Times* reports that men have landed on
the moon, or Procopius reports that Anastasius I left 320,000 pounds of
gold in the treasury at his death, the reports should be believed, even if
they seem strange. Yet not only were the standards for historical
accuracy in medieval Western Europe generally lower than in Byzantium, but official statistics for such things as armies were rare, and wild
guesses often took their place. Many historians of the medieval West
therefore doubt all statistics, and their influence has led some Byzantin-
ists to reject their own much more reliable material. The most extreme
skeptics refuse to use any statistic that is less than fully precise and
entirely accurate, which would mean rejecting every modern census.
While certain statistics and estimates can be hopelessly wrong, these can
only be found out by forming some idea of what numbers would be
right.

We have a good idea of the extent of Byzantine territory at most
dates, because we know what regions Byzantium controlled and we
know their land surfaces today. Byzantine and Arab sources contribute
detailed information about the size of the Byzantine army at various
dates, most of which is so self-consistent as to demonstrate its accuracy.
Surviving Byzantine sources are less informative about the state budget,
giving only one overall figure (for 1320), several figures for surpluses,
and miscellaneous figures for expenditures and revenues; but since we
can usually calculate the military payroll and it seems to have been the

largest part of the budget, we can make reasonably good budgetary estimates for many dates. Estimating the Byzantine population is a much more speculative endeavor, but the overall trends and approximate figures can be roughly determined. The best estimates in these categories that I have been able to make or borrow, to which I have added two educated guesses indicated by question marks, appear in Table 1. Some of these numbers, especially the rounded ones for population, may have a margin for error as high as 25%; but since any overestimating or underestimating is likely to affect the whole series of figures, the estimates are more reliable for comparative purposes than they are in isolation.

Even accurate statistics can mislead if they are misunderstood, and the interpretations are often more problematic than the numbers themselves. Most numbers in this table require some qualification. The figures for territory exclude all uninhabitable deserts. The figures for revenues, usually estimated by calculating expenses and adding any surplus, represent cash revenues only. Though the Byzantine government always collected some taxes and services in kind, and these

Table 1 Byzantine territory, population, revenue, and army size

Date	Territory (millions of square kilometers)		Population (millions of people, to nearest half million)		Revenue (millions of nomismata of 1/72 pound pure gold)		Army size (thousands of soldiers and oarsmen)	
ca. 300	1.68	132%	21.0	131%	9.4	121%	343	102%
ca. 457	1.27	100%	16.0	100%	7.8	100%	335	100%
ca. 518	1.30	102%	19.5	122%	8.5	109%	301	90%
ca. 540	1.86	146%	26.0	162%	11.3	145%	374	112%
ca. 565	2.07	163%	19.5	122%	8.5	109%	379	113%
ca. 641	1.15	91%	10.5	66%	3.7	47%	129	39%
ca. 668	1.07	84%	10.0	62%	2.0	26%	129	39%
ca. 775	0.69	54%	7.0	44%	1.9	24%	118	35%
ca. 842	0.79	62%	8.0	50%	3.1	40%	155	46%
ca. 959	0.85	67%	9.0	56%	3.9	50%	179	53%
ca. 1025	1.20	94%	12.0	75%	5.9	76%	283	84%
ca. 1143	0.65	51%	10.0	62%	4.9?	63%?	50?	15%?
ca. 1320	0.12	9%	2.0	12%	0.5	6%	7	2%

Each figure is also expressed as a percentage of the figure for the same item ca. 457. The figures for ca. 300 apply to the territory ruled by Diocletian and Galerius at that date.

tended to be more important when cash revenue was lower, such non-monetary resources cannot easily be estimated in money, and in any case the cash revenue remains a good index of monetarization. Note also that all cash revenues are quoted in nomismata struck at 72 to the pound of gold, so that sums in the more valuable solidi of the year 300 and the less valuable hyperpyra of 1143 and 1320 are converted into standard nomismata according to their gold content. Finally, the figures for army size include all soldiers and oarsmen on the rolls. Though in some periods, particularly in 565 and 1025, many of these men saw little active service, all were in principle available to serve and all received some remuneration from the government.

Perhaps the most striking indication in the table is that the empire held or recovered most of its territory, population, cash revenue, and military strength until late in its history. The figures for around 300 are somewhat misleading for purposes of comparison, because the reason for the decrease in territory between then and 457 is that in 285 Diocletian drew the administrative boundary of the East farther west in Illyricum than Theodosius I did in 395. Note that during the years from 285 to 457 the population decreased by only about as much as the territory, so that overall population density remained about the same, and that the cash revenues and army decreased by less than the territory, so that proportionally they actually increased. The various figures in the table are therefore expressed as percentages of those for 457 rather than 300. Naturally the imprecisions of the original figures make most of the percentages approximate as well.

In comparison with 457, the estimates indicate that the empire at its later high point around 1025 had some 94% of its earlier territory, about 75% of its earlier population and cash revenue, and some 84% of its earlier army. Even at its previous low point around 775, the empire had some 54% of its territory of 457, 44% of its former population, 24% of its former cash revenue, and 35% of its former army. As late as 1143, the empire had about 51% of its territory of 457, some 62% of its old population, and about the same proportion of its old cash revenue, though perhaps just 15% of its old army. Only after 1204 did Byzantium become a mere shadow of its former self, by 1320 having a mere 9% of the territory, 12% of the population, 6% of the cash revenue, and 2% of the army. While many of these numbers and percentages are disputable in detail, enough of the data is sufficiently reliable to establish the overall picture beyond much doubt.

The statistics are almost as clear in their implications for the disputed developments of the tenth to twelfth centuries and the sixth to eighth centuries. From 1025 to 1143 Byzantium's land area fell by some 46%, reflecting the Turkish conquests in the east. The size of the army plummeted, by roughly 80%, and even if in 1025 the army had been much larger than necessary, by 1143 the empire's military strength had plainly deteriorated. Yet more significant for most political and economic purposes is that the population and cash revenue fell far less, perhaps by some 17%. Moreover, if these numbers are even approximately correct, the empire was in proportion to its land area far wealthier and more populous in 1143 than in 1025, so that the weakness of its army shows a reluctance rather than an inability to increase military spending. Particularly interesting is that in both 1143 and 1025 Byzantium seems to have raised roughly the same amount of cash revenue from each of its subjects as it had in 457, about half a nomisma, and that at every other date the amount of cash revenue per subject seems to have been lower, at the lowest a mere fifth of a nomisma in 668. In other words, in both the eleventh and twelfth centuries the state raised as much cash from its subjects as it ever had, a sign that the Byzantine economy was as monetarized, and its government as centralized, as it had ever been.

As for the catastrophe of the seventh century, from the zenith in 565 to the nadir in 775 Byzantium lost about 67% of its territory, 64% of its population, 78% of its cash revenue, and 69% of its army. Though the losses of territory and population occurred more or less in tandem, the decrease in cash revenue shows a different pattern. After corresponding roughly to the territorial and population losses up to 641, between that date and 668 the revenue fell by about 46%, while territorial and population losses were only some 7% and 5% and the army remained about the same size. The reason was not that suddenly the Byzantines became poorer or their government less efficient, but that the introduction of the system of military lands, while eliminating cash revenues from whatever imperial estates were distributed among the soldiers, cut cash expenditures on military pay by even more. This deliberate and prudent reform caused decreases in monetarization and centralization at the date of the change, but not afterward. On the contrary, between 668 and 775, while the empire lost about another 36% of its land and 30% of its population, cash revenues scarcely fell at all, and in proportion to territory and population actually increased. The recovery of monetarization and centralization had already begun.

Further study of the sources can almost certainly lead to improving on some of these figures, though probably not so drastically as to change their implications for Byzantine history. What is discouraging about some recent discussions of the subject (though none of the longer ones) is a tendency to reject Byzantine sources on the basis of mistaken and undefended analogies with the medieval West, ignoring recent scholarship on the earlier Roman Empire, which was the direct predecessor of Byzantium. Throughout its history, the Byzantine Empire was comparable in its level of governmental organization to the Roman Empire. It was also comparable to several of the states of early modern Western Europe, after political centralization, monetarization, and standing armies began to reappear in the later Middle Ages. Yet only during the fourteenth century, when Byzantium was falling into ruin, did those European states surpass it in their degree of organization or even in their revenues. Byzantium was a modern state before its time.

The Legacy of Byzantium

By 1461 the Ottoman Turks occupied most of the same territory as the Byzantine Empire of 1025, minus some islands and parts of Armenia and Syria. Although Mehmed II's army and revenues were a good deal smaller than those of Basil II, the Ottoman Empire was formidable and expanding, and unlike Basil's Byzantium was unambiguously expansionist. Like Byzantium, the Ottoman Empire was not a national state, though its government gave preference to the Turkish language and Islam, as Byzantium had long preferred the Greek language and Christianity. Like the Byzantines, the Ottomans indiscriminately settled and mixed peoples of different languages and races all over their empire.

By the nineteenth century, after four centuries or so of Ottoman rule, the linguistic map of Anatolia and the Balkans still showed traces of the states that had existed before the Ottoman conquest. Many Greeks lived in what had been Byzantium, with many Serbs in what had been Serbia, many Bulgarians in what had been Bulgaria, and many Armenians in what had been the various Armenian states. Yet these groups were also scattered outside their former states, and within their original lands were mixed with Turks, Albanians, Vlachs, Jews, and others. Some Christians spoke Turkish, and some speakers of Greek, Serbian, Bulgarian, and Armenian were Muslims. In the context of the Ottoman

Empire, such diversity caused no problems, any more than the mixture of ethnic groups in America today leads Irish to fight Germans or Swedes to hate Italians.

In the nineteenth century, however, when the Greeks, Serbs, and Bulgarians began to regain their independence, they found themselves even more different from Western Europeans than they had been before the Ottoman conquest. In Western Europe education, commerce, democratic government, and the formation of nation states were well advanced, but not in the Ottoman Empire. The Ottomans, who had little interest in secular education for themselves, did nothing to foster it among their Christian subjects. The Ottomans were also not much interested in commerce, though they allowed their Greek and Armenian subjects to pursue it. The sultans had no interest at all in representative government for any of their subjects. Because of the mixed patterns of settlement in the empire, the question of where nation states could be formed was a vexed one. Though some Greeks, Serbs, and Bulgarians had answers, they claimed boundaries that overlapped with each other and included many people who spoke different languages. The most ambitious version of Greece favored by Greeks included Constantinople and was almost as big as the Byzantine Empire of 1190.

The first Greek, Serbian, and Bulgarian kingdoms created by the wars of independence left large numbers of Greeks, Serbs, and Bulgarians under Ottoman rule in between the kingdoms. But in 1913 the victory of Greece, Serbia, and Bulgaria in the First Balkan War drove the Ottomans out of most of the Balkans and raised the issue of boundaries. Border disputes led almost at once to the Second Balkan War, in which Serbia, Greece, and the Ottomans defeated Bulgaria and set most of today's boundaries in the southern Balkans, including those of an almost accidentally independent Albania. As a result of the First World War, Greece won southwestern Thrace from Bulgaria, and gained from the Turks part of western Anatolia and southeastern Thrace except for Constantinople. Yet when the Greeks tried to expand their holdings in Anatolia the Turks defeated them sharply in 1922. The Greeks gave up everything they had taken from the Turks in Anatolia and Thrace. Through a population exchange, almost all the Christians in Turkey left for Greece and the much less numerous Muslims in Greece left for Turkey. The Greeks had to abandon the idea of restoring something like Byzantium.

Many Eastern Christians have been disappointed by events since the First World War. The only Eastern Christians to do well out of that war were the Romanians, who expanded in every direction, and the Serbs, who became with the Catholic Croats the dominant group in the new state of Yugoslavia. The defeated Russian Empire turned into the strongly anti-Christian Soviet Union. Besides exchanging their Greeks, the Turks expelled their remaining Armenians, who were left with the Georgians under Soviet rule. After the Second World War, the Soviets imposed Communist and anti-Christian governments on Romania, Bulgaria, Yugoslavia, and Albania. Later, when Greece tried to take over the mostly Greek-speaking state of Cyprus, troops from Turkey seized part of the island. In the largely Christian Arab state of Lebanon a civil war ended by curtailing Christian power, and elsewhere in the Arab world Christian minorities were on the defensive. Since the fall of Communism, the ex-Communist Catholic and Protestant states have enjoyed more political stability and economic prosperity than the Eastern Christian states of Russia, Ukraine, Belarus, Georgia, Armenia, Moldova, Romania, Bulgaria, Macedonia, and Yugoslavia.

Yet the legacy of Byzantium seems to have little to do with these disappointments. The Byzantine Empire was admittedly not a nation state, but neither is the generally successful United States of America. While Byzantium lacked such modern features as democratic institutions or a capitalistic economy, it had a more advanced economy and a better-organized government than the Western states of its time. While its rulers were sometimes ruthless or incompetent, it overthrew the worst of them; no Byzantine emperor ever abused unbridled power like a Nero, Stalin, or Hitler. Before 1945 democracy was the exception rather than the rule in most of Europe, and such Western European states as Germany, Italy, and Spain were not notable for it. Greece, the only Eastern Christian country to be free of Ottoman or Communist rule since the early nineteenth century, has as good a record for democracy and economic enterprise as most Western European countries during that time, and is now a member of both the European Union and the Atlantic Alliance. Whatever obstacles are hampering democracy, capitalism, or nation building in Eastern Christian countries today are more plausibly attributed to Ottoman or Communist rule than to Byzantium. Certainly this is true of authoritarianism, corruption, and hostility to private enterprise.

Many of the twentieth-century failures of the Eastern Christian states have resulted from unsustainable ambitions, even though the states in question have claimed only to be defending their historic rights. Thus Bulgaria in the First Balkan War and Russia in the First World War both overreached themselves and suffered large territorial losses. After the First World War Greece tried to take more Turkish territory than it could hold, and as a result lost its chance to take Constantinople, which it probably could have held. At the same time a short-lived Armenian republic claimed unrealistic boundaries and ended up losing almost everything. In the widest sense, Soviet Communism was a colossal case of utopian ambitions leading to ignominious collapse. Recently Armenia in Azerbaijan and Serbia in Bosnia and Kosovo have taken unreasonable risks by refusing to compromise with their neighbors. Yet Germany, Italy, Japan, and some other countries that are not Eastern Christian have also overreached themselves badly during this century, and have recovered better from their defeats.

One handicap of Eastern Christian countries that does seem to date from Byzantine times, however strongly reinforced by later experience, is a sense of grievance. Such a feeling is explicable and partly justifiable. Byzantium used to be more powerful, prosperous, and cultured than the countries of medieval Western Europe, and today Western Europe is more powerful, prosperous, and technologically developed than the Eastern Christian countries. This relative decline of the East can partly be blamed on the Fourth Crusade, the Ottoman conquest, and that most disastrous of Western European exports, Communism. In modern times Western European countries have tended to band together, and to care more for their own interests than for those of Eastern Europeans. Although Eastern Europeans also care much more about their own affairs than about those of Western Europeans, they remain at a disadvantage, because as a group they are weaker and poorer. Finally, as Byzantine history shows, Eastern Christians have long been less aggressive and expansionist than Western Europeans or Muslims. The Byzantines had nothing directly comparable to the idea of Crusade or Holy War, and their main purpose in fighting was usually defensive. Yet, however understandable, Eastern Christian resentment of Western Christians or Muslims becomes self-destructive when it inspires hostility to Western investment or to Muslim minorities.

Given the effects of decades of Communist rule, the remarkable fact about the recent history of Eastern Europe is how much progress it has made rather than how little. At present, every Eastern Christian state but Belarus has held reasonably free multiparty elections and has a fairly free press. Several Eastern Christian countries are actively seeking membership in the Atlantic Alliance and the European Union. In almost all of Eastern Europe, the old Communist command economies have been dismantled, the largest share of economic activity has passed into private hands, and at least a shaky economic equilibrium seems to have been established. Whatever their defects, the Eastern European countries still have democracies and economies well in advance of most African and Muslim countries except Turkey, whose politics and economy are avowedly influenced by Western Europe and indirectly owe something to Byzantium.

If Eastern Europe is the heir of Byzantium, both Eastern and Western Europe are the joint heirs of the Christian Roman Empire. Their inheritance includes not just Christianity, with its whole system of ethics and theology, but the rule of law, the elements of a classical education, and ancient philosophy, mathematics, science, and art. Most of this inheritance is only partly shared by the non-Christian world. Although the schism between Eastern Orthodox and Roman Catholic Christians remains, their real doctrinal differences are far less than those between Roman Catholics and Protestants. The Pope and the Patriarch of Constantinople have already lifted the excommunications of 1054. As in the later years of Byzantine history, for the present Eastern Orthodoxy and Roman Catholicism may find that mutual tolerance is a more practical goal than full union, which would require some difficult compromises and the consent of a number of different Orthodox churches. Yet in the coming decades all sides will benefit if, following the example of Greece, the other countries of Byzantine heritage enter the European and Atlantic communities. While the borders drawn between East and West in 285 and 395 had some lasting significance, they did no more than distinguish two parts of a single civilization.

SELECT BIBLIOGRAPHY

This list, limited to books in English and except for a few hardy classics to fairly recent work, is mostly selected from the much more extensive references in my *History of the Byzantine State and Society*, pp. 873–970, which also include articles, older works, works in foreign languages, and my comments. The selection here is particularly comprehensive for books that appeared after 1992, when my earlier survey ended, even including some books about which I have serious reservations, marked by references to critical reviews of them, mostly my own. The list is divided into general works and those on different periods, ending with some translations of works by Byzantine authors.

Books on All or Most of the Byzantine Period

Browning, Robert, *The Byzantine Empire*, rev. edn (Washington, DC, 1992).
The Cambridge Medieval History, 2nd edn, vol. IV, *The Byzantine Empire*, ed. Joan Hussey, 2 parts (Cambridge, 1966–7).
Grierson, Philip, *Byzantine Coins* (London, 1982).
Hendy, Michael, *Studies in the Byzantine Monetary Economy* (Cambridge, 1985).
Hussey, Joan, *The Orthodox Church in the Byzantine Empire* (Oxford, 1986).
Lemerle, Paul, *The Agrarian History of Byzantium* (Galway, 1979).
——, *Byzantine Humanism* (Canberra, 1986).
Mango, Cyril, *Byzantine Architecture* (New York, 1975).
——, *Byzantium: The Empire of New Rome* (London, 1980).
——, and Gilbert Dagron (eds), *Constantinople and its Hinterland* (Aldershot, 1995).
Nicol, Donald, *Byzantium and Venice* (Cambridge, 1988).
Obolensky, Dimitri, *The Byzantine Commonwealth: Eastern Europe, 500–1453* (London, 1971).
Ostrogorsky, George, *History of the Byzantine State*, trans. Joan Hussey, 2nd edn (Oxford, 1968).
The Oxford Dictionary of Byzantium, ed. Alexander Kazhdan, 3 vols (New York, 1991).
Rodley, Lyn, *Byzantine Art and Architecture* (Cambridge, 1994).
Shepard, Jonathan, and Simon Franklin (eds), *Byzantine Diplomacy* (Aldershot, 1992).

Treadgold, Warren, *A History of the Byzantine State and Society* (Stanford, Cal., 1997).
——, *Byzantium and its Army, 284–1081* (Stanford, Cal., 1995).
Vasiliev, A. A., *History of the Byzantine Empire*, rev. edn, 2 vols (Madison, 1952).
Wilson, Nigel, *Scholars of Byzantium* (London, 1983).

Books on the Period from 285 to 602

Bagnall, Roger, *Egypt in Late Antiquity* (Princeton, 1993).
Barnes, Timothy, *Constantine and Eusebius* (Cambridge, Mass., 1981).
Brown, Peter, *Power and Persuasion in Late Antiquity* (Madison, 1992); but see Treadgold, *International History Review*, 15 (1993), pp. 535–45.
——, *The World of Late Antiquity* (London, 1971).
Bury, J. B., *A History of the Later Roman Empire from the Death of Theodosius I to the Death of Justinian I*, 2 vols (London, 1923).
The Cambridge Ancient History, 2nd edn, vol. XIII, *The Late Empire: A.D. 337–425*, ed. Averil Cameron and Peter Garnsey (Cambridge, 1998).
Cameron, Averil, *The Later Roman Empire, A.D. 284–430* (Cambridge, Mass., 1993), and *The Mediterranean World in Late Antiquity, A.D. 395–600* (London, 1993); but see Treadgold, *International History Review*, 17 (1995), pp. 350–3.
Clark, Gillian, *Women in Late Antiquity* (Oxford, 1993).
Corcoran, Simon, *The Empire of the Tetrarchs: Imperial Pronouncements and Government, AD 284–324* (Oxford, 1996).
Evans, J. A. S., *The Age of Justinian: The Circumstances of Imperial Power* (London, 1996).
Greatrex, Geoffrey, *Rome and Persia at War, 502–532* (Leeds, 1998).
Grubbs, Judith Evans, *Law and Family in Late Antiquity* (Oxford, 1995).
Jones, A. H. M., *The Later Roman Empire: A Social, Economic and Administrative Survey*, 3 vols (Oxford, 1964).
Haas, Christopher, *Alexandria in Late Antiquity* (Baltimore, 1997).
MacMullen, Ramsay, *Christianity and Paganism in the Fourth to Eighth Centuries* (New Haven, 1997).
——, *Corruption and the Decline of Rome* (New Haven, 1988).
Matthews, John, *The Roman Empire of Ammianus* (Baltimore, 1989).
Mitchell, Stephen, *Anatolia: Land, Men, and Gods in Asia Minor*, 2 vols (Oxford, 1993).
Southern, Pat, and Karen Dixon, *The Late Roman Army* (London, 1996); but see T. D. Barnes, *American Historical Review*, 102 (1997), pp. 1139–40.
Whitby, Michael, *The Emperor Maurice and His Historian* (Oxford, 1988).
Williams, Stephen, *Diocletian and the Roman Recovery* (London, 1985).
——, and Gerard Friell, *The Rome That Did Not Fall: The Survival of the East in the Fifth Century* (London, 1999).
——, *Theodosius: The Empire at Bay* (London, 1994).

Books on the Period from 602 to 1025

Bryer, Anthony, and Judith Herrin (eds), *Iconoclasm* (Birmingham, 1977).

Bury, J. B., *A History of the Eastern Roman Empire from the Fall of Irene to the Accession of Basil I* (London, 1912).

Haldon, J. F., *Byzantium in the Seventh Century* (Cambridge, 1990); but see Treadgold, *American Historical Review*, 97 (1992), pp. 829–30.

Harvey, Alan, *Economic Expansion in the Byzantine Empire, 900–1200* (Cambridge, 1989).

Jenkins, Romilly, *Byzantium: The Imperial Centuries, A.D. 610–1071* (London, 1966).

Morris, Rosemary, *Monks and Laymen in Byzantium, 843–1118* (Cambridge, 1995).

Runciman, Steven, *The Emperor Romanus Lecapenus and His Reign* (Cambridge, 1929).

Toynbee, Arnold, *Constantine Porphyrogenitus and His World* (Oxford, 1973).

Treadgold, Warren, *The Byzantine Revival, 780–842* (Stanford, Cal., 1988).

Whittow, Mark, *The Making of Orthodox Byzantium* (Basingstoke, 1996); but see Treadgold, *International History Review*, 19 (1997), pp. 889–91.

Books on the Period from 1025 to 1461

Angold, Michael, *The Byzantine Empire, 1025–1204: A Political History*, 2nd edn (Harlow, 1997).

——, *Church and Society in Byzantium under the Comneni, 1081–1261* (Cambridge, 1995).

Brand, Charles, *Byzantium Confronts the West, 1180–1204* (Cambridge, Mass., 1968).

Geanakoplos, Deno, *Emperor Michael Palaeologus and the West* (Cambridge, Mass., 1959).

Kazhdan, A. P., and A. W. Epstein, *Change in Byzantine Culture in the Eleventh and Twelfth Centuries* (Berkeley, Cal. 1985).

——, and S. Franklin, *Studies on Byzantine Literature of the Eleventh and Twelfth Centuries* (Cambridge, 1984).

Laiou, Angeliki, *Constantinople and the Latins: The Foreign Policy of Andronicus II* (Cambridge, Mass., 1972).

Lilie, R.-J., *Byzantium and the Crusader States* (Oxford, 1993).

Lock, Peter, *The Franks in the Aegean, 1204–1500* (London, 1995).

Magdalino, Paul, *The Empire of Manuel I Komnenos* (Cambridge, 1993).

Nicol, Donald, *The Despotate of Epiros, 1267–1479* (Cambridge, 1984).

——, *The Immortal Emperor: The Life and Legend of Constantine Palaiologos, Last Emperor of the Romans* (Cambridge, 1992).

——, *The Last Centuries of Byzantium, 1261–1453*, 2nd edn (Cambridge, 1993).

——, *The Reluctant Emperor: A Biography of John Cantacuzene, Byzantine Emperor and Monk* (Cambridge, 1996).

Runciman, Steven, *The Eastern Schism* (Oxford, 1955).

——, *The Fall of Constantinople, 1453* (Cambridge, 1965).
——, *The Last Byzantine Renaissance* (Cambridge, 1970).

Byzantine Works in Translation

Ammianus Marcellinus, selected and trans. Walter Hamilton as *The Later Roman Empire* (London, 1986).

Anna Comnena, *Alexiad*, trans. E. R. A. Sewter (Harmondsworth, 1969).

Digenes Acrites, ed. and trans. Elizabeth Jeffreys (Cambridge, 1998).

Ducas, trans. Harry Magoulias as *Decline and Fall of Byzantium to the Ottoman Turks* (Detroit, 1975).

Lives of St. Daniel the Stylite, St. Theodore of Syceon, and St. John the Almsgiver, trans. Elizabeth Dawes and Norman H. Baynes as *Three Byzantine Saints* (Crestwood, 1977).

Michael Psellus, trans. E. R. A. Sewter as *Fourteen Byzantine Rulers* (Harmondsworth, 1966).

Nicetas Choniates, trans. Harry Magoulias as *O City of Byzantium* (Detroit, 1984).

Photius, *Bibliotheca*, selected and trans. N. G. Wilson (London, 1994).

Procopius of Caesarea, ed. and trans. H. B. Dewing and G. Downey, 7 vols (Cambridge, Mass., 1914–40).

Theophanes Confessor, trans. Cyril Mango and Roger Scott with Geoffrey Greatrex (Oxford, 1997).

Timarion, trans. Barry Baldwin (Detroit, 1984).

LIST OF BYZANTINE EMPERORS

Eastern Roman (Byzantine) Emperors (284–1453)

The principal Eastern Roman emperor is listed in capitals, with other rulers (if any) listed under him.

DIOCLETIAN 284–305
Galerius, Caesar in Egypt and Syria 293–99
Caesar in Balkans 299–305

GALERIUS 305–11
Maximin, Caesar in Egypt and Syria 305–10
Augustus in Egypt and Syria 310–11
Licinius, Augustus in Balkans 308–11

LICINIUS 311–24
Maximin, Augustus in Egypt, Syria, and Anatolia 311–13
Constantine I, Augustus in Balkans except Thrace 317–24

CONSTANTINE I 324–37
Constantius II, Caesar in Egypt and Syria 335–37
Dalmatius, Caesar in Balkans 335–37

CONSTANTIUS II 337–61
Constans I, Augustus in Balkans except Thrace 337–50
Gallus, Caesar in Egypt and Syria 351–54

JULIAN the Apostate 361–3

JOVIAN 363–64

VALENS 364–78
Valentinian I, Augustus in Balkans except Thrace 364–75
Gratian, Augustus in Balkans except Thrace 375–79

THEODOSIUS I 379–95
Valentinian II, Augustus in Balkans except Thrace 382–92

ARCADIUS 395–408

THEODOSIUS II 408–50

248

MARCIAN 450–57

LEO I 457–74

LEO II 474
Zeno Tarasius, Augustus and regent

ZENO Tarasius 474–91
Basiliscus, rival Augustus in most of East except Isauria 475–76

ANASTASIUS I 491–518

JUSTIN I 518–27

JUSTINIAN I 527–65

JUSTIN II 565–78
Tiberius, Caesar and regent 574–78

TIBERIUS II Constantine 578–82

MAURICE Tiberius 582–602

PHOCAS the Tyrant 602–10

HERACLIUS 610–41

CONSTANTINE III Heraclius 641

HERACLONAS (Heraclius) Constantine 641
Martina, regent

CONSTANS II (Constantine) Heraclius the Bearded 641–68

CONSTANTINE IV 668–85

JUSTINIAN II the Slit-Nosed 685–95

LEONTIUS (Leo) 695–98

TIBERIUS III Apsimar 698–705

JUSTINIAN II the Slit-Nosed (again) 705–11

PHILIPPICUS BARDANES 711–13

ANASTASIUS II Artemius 713–15

THEODOSIUS III 715–17

LEO III the Syrian ("Isaurian") 717–41

CONSTANTINE V Name of Dung 741–75
Artavasdus, rival emperor at Constantinople 741–43

LEO IV the Khazar 775–80

CONSTANTINE VI the Blinded 780–97
Irene the Athenian, regent

IRENE the Athenian 797–802

JOHN II Comnenus   1118–43

MANUEL I Comnenus   1143–80

ALEXIUS II Comnenus   1180–83
Andronicus Comnenus, regent 1182–83

ANDRONICUS I Comnenus   1183–85

ISAAC II Angelus   1185–95

ALEXIUS III Angelus   1195–1203

ISAAC II Angelus (again)   1203–4
Alexius IV Angelus, co-emperor
Alexius III Angelus, rival emperor in Thrace

ALEXIUS V Ducas Murtzuphlus   1204
Alexius III Angelus, rival emperor in Thrace

ALEXIUS III Angelus (in Thrace)   1204
hereafter see also Emperors at Trebizond *and* Latin Emperors, *below*

THEODORE I Lascaris (at Nicaea)   1205–21

JOHN III Ducas Vatatzes (at Nicaea)   1221–54
Theodore Ducas, emperor at Thessalonica   1224–54
John Ducas, emperor at Thessalonica 1237–42

THEODORE II Lascaris (at Nicaea)   1254–58

JOHN IV Lascaris (at Nicaea)   1258–61
Michael VIII Palaeologus, co-emperor at Nicaea 1259–61

MICHAEL VIII Palaeologus (at Constantinople)   1261–82

ANDRONICUS II Palaeologus   1282–1328
Andronicus III Palaeologus, co-emperor 1321–28

ANDRONICUS III Palaeologus   1328–41

JOHN V Palaeologus   1341–76
Anna of Savoy, regent 1341–47
John VI Cantacuzenus, co-emperior 1347–54

ANDRONICUS IV Palaeologus   1376–79

JOHN V Palaeologus (again)   1379–91
John VII Palaeologus, rival emperor at Constantinople 1390

MANUEL II Palaeologus   1391–1425

JOHN VIII Palaeologus   1425–48

CONSTANTINE XI Palaeologus   1449–53

Emperors at Trebizond (1204–1461)

ALEXIUS I Comnenus   1204–22

ANDRONICUS I Gidus Comnenus   1222–35

JOHN I Axuch Comnenus   1235–38

MANUEL I Comnenus   1238–63

ANDRONICUS II Comnenus   1263–66

GEORGE Comnenus   1266–80

JOHN II Comnenus   1280–97
  Theodora Comnena, rival empress ca. 1284

ALEXIUS II Comnenus   1297–1330

ANDRONICUS III Comnenus   1330–32

MANUEL II Comnenus   1332

BASIL Comnenus   1332–40

IRENE Palaeologina   1340–41

ANNA Comnena   1341

MICHAEL Comnenus   1341

ANNA Comnena (again)   1341–42

JOHN III Comnenus   1342–44

MICHAEL Comnenus (again)   1344–49

ALEXIUS III Comnenus   1349–90

MANUEL III Comnenus   1390–1416

ALEXIUS IV Comnenus   1416–29

JOHN IV Comnenus   1429–59

DAVID Comnenus   1459–61

Latin Emperors (1204–61)

BALDWIN I of Flanders   1204–5

HENRY of Flanders   1206–16

PETER of Courtenay   1217

YOLANDA   1217–19

ROBERT of Courtenay   1221–28

JOHN of Brienne   1228–37

BALDWIN II of Courtenay   1237–61

INDEX

under Lombards, 68–70, 73, 76,
   78, 100
under Odoacer, 54–5
under Ostrogoths, 55, 60–7
under Western Roman Empire,
   14, 24, 30, 53–5
see also Papacy, Sicily

Jacob Baradaeus, 63, 65, 69
Jacobite Church, 63, 65
Jerusalem, 89, 90, 92, 144, 173,
   174
   Kingdom of, 174, 178
   Patriarchate of, 35, 38, 93, 118,
      192
Jews, 17, 44, 47, 80, 89, 90, 105,
   153, 239
Joasaph (monastic name of John
   VI), 213
John I Chrysostom, St (patriarch of
   Constantinople), 32, 47, 48
John I Tzimisces (emperor,
   969–76), 139, 140, 142–5, 149,
   152–4, 157, 162, 187
John II Comnenus (emperor,
   1118–43), 175–6, 178, 186, 192,
   195
John II Comnenus (emperor of
   Trebizond), 205
John (III) Ducas Vatatzes (emperor
   of Nicaea, 1221–54), 200–3,
   220–2, 229–30
John (IV) Lascaris (emperor of
   Nicaea, 1258–61), 202–4, 223
John V Palaeologus (emperor,
   1341–76 and 1379–91),
   209–15, 223, 227, 230
John VI Cantacuzenus (emperor,
   1347–54), 209–13, 222–4, 228,
   230, 232
John VII Palaeologus (emperor,
   1390), 214, 216, 217
John VII the Grammarian
   (patriarch of Constantinople),
   129, 130, 131, 159
John VIII Palaeologus (emperor,
   1425–48), 217–18

John VIII Xiphilinus (patriarch of
   Constantinople), 190, 191
John XIV Calecas (patriarch of
   Constantinople), 210, 211
John Italus, 191–2, 193
John Malalas, 84
John Moschus, 117
John of Damascus, St, 118, 119,
   120
John the Almsgiver, St (patriarch of
   Alexandria), 117
John the Cappadocian, 59, 61, 63,
   77
John the Orphanotrophus, 167, 187
John Vladislav (Bulgarian
   emperor), 149, 150
Joseph I (patriarch of
   Constantinople), 204–6, 227
Josephites, 205, 206, 227
Jovian (emperor, 363–4), 28
Jovius (title), 14
jugum, 15
Julian (emperor, 361–3), 26, 27–8,
   29, 30, 37, 40, 44, 47, 48, 57, 83
Julian Calendar, 231
Jupiter (god), 44
Justin I (emperor, 518–27), 58, 76
Justin II (emperor, 565–78), 68–70,
   73, 81, 2
Justinian I (emperor, 527–65),
   58–68, 69, 74–9, 82–6, 100,
   151, 152, 163
Justinian II (emperor, 685–95 and
   705–11), 100–4, 102–3, 104,
   106, 118, 119, 121
Justinian Code, 59, 61, 67, 135, 160

Kaloyan (Bulgarian emperor), 199
Kars, 150
Kavād II (Persian king), 91
Khazars, 91, 99, 102
Khurramites, 129, 130, 155
Khusrau II (Persian king), 71, 73,
   87, 89–91
Kosovo (modern), 242
Kotrigurs, 66
Krum (Bulgar khan), 127–8

measles, 7
medicine, 48
Mehmed I (Ottoman sultan), 217
Mehmed II the Conqueror
  (Ottoman sultan), 218–19, 228,
  239
Melitene (modern Malatya), 138,
  145, 152
  Emirate of, 131, 132, 134, 137,
  138
Melkites, 119, 126, 192
mercenaries, see army
Mesazon, 187, 224
Mesopotamia, 14, 28, 34, 37, 38, 49,
  61, 91, 138, 152
  Ducate of, 143
Methodius, St (missionary to
  Moravia), 132
Methodius I, St (patriarch of
  Constantinople), 131
Metochites, Theodore, 230, 231
metropolitan bishops, 81
Michael I Cerularius (patriarch of
  Constantinople), 169, 190–1
Michael I Ducas (ruler of Epirus),
  181, 199–200, 221
Michael I Rhangabe (emperor,
  811–13), 127–8, 154, 164
Michael II Ducas (despot of Epirus),
  200–2, 204–5, 221
Michael II the Amorian (emperor,
  820–9), 128–9
Michael III the Drunkard (emperor,
  842–67), 130–3, 135, 163–4
Michael IV the Paphlagonian
  (emperor, 1034–41), 167, 185
Michael V the Caulker (emperor,
  1041–2), 167, 185
Michael VI Bringas (emperor,
  1056–7), 169, 187, 190, 191
Michael VII Ducas (emperor,
  1067–78), 169–71, 190, 191,
  193
Michael VIII Palaeologus (emperor,
  1261–82), 202–5, 220–4, 227,
  229–31
Milan, 19, 60, 61

military lands, 96, 107, 111, 115,
  185, 186, 238
Military Logothete, 97, 156
minuscule hand, 159
Mistra, 222, 225
Mohammed (prophet), 92
Moldavia, 220
Moldova (modern), 241
monasticism, 45, 46, 80, 81, 109,
  117, 159, 160, 184, 191, 228
  see also nuns
monetarization, 56, 77, 188, 212,
  236–9
  see also coinage
Mongols, 201, 216, 220, 225
Monoenergism, 92, 93, 116, 117
Monophysitism, 34–6, 46–7, 80, 81,
  84, 99, 108, 118
  in Egypt and Syria, 36, 49, 75, 90,
  117–19, 192
  under Anastasius I, 56–7
  under Heraclius, 92, 93
  under Justin II, 69, 81
  under Justinian I, 58, 61–3, 65–8,
  82
  under Maurice, 71
  under Zeno, 54–5
Monotheletism, 93, 95, 99, 103, 116,
  117
Moors, 60, 63, 64, 69, 73, 76, 86
morality, 44, 45, 119
Moravia, 132–4, 159
mosaics, 86, 121, 163, 194–6, 231–2
Mosul, Emirate of, 143, 145
Murād I (Ottoman sultan), 214
Murād II (Ottoman sultan), 217–18
Mustafa (Ottoman pretender), 217
mutilation (as punishment), 105,
  119
Myriocephalum, 178

Naples, 60, 152
  Kingdom of, 206, 207
Narses (general under Justinian I),
  60, 65–6, 68
Narses (general under Maurice), 71,
  73, 87

Yolanda-Irene (wife of Andronicus
     II), 206–7
Yugoslavia, 240–1

Zaützes, Stylianus, 135
Zaützina, Zoë, 135
Zealots, 210, 211, 212

Zeno (emperor, 474–91), 51, 53–5,
     56, 57, 73, 76, 81, 84
Zeus (god), 9, 12, 14, 44
Zoë (empress, 1042), 165, 167–9
Zoë Carbonopsina, 136, 137
Zoroastrianism, 116
Zosimus (historian), 83